LITERARY CRITICISM AND CULTURAL THEORY

Edited by

William E. Cain
Professor of English
Wellesley College

A ROUTLEDGE SERIES

LITERARY CRITICISM AND CULTURAL THEORY

WILLIAM E. CAIN, *General Editor*

Transatlantic Engagements with the British Eighteenth Century

Pamela J. Albert

Routledge
Taylor & Francis Group

LONDON AND NEW YORK

First published 2008
by Routledge

2 Park Square, Milton Park, Abingdon, Oxon OX14 4RN
711 Third Avenue, New York, NY 10017, USA

Routledge is an imprint of the Taylor & Francis Group, an informa business

First issued in paperback 2016

Typeset in Adobe Garamond by IBT Global

Library of Congress Cataloging in Publication Data
A catalog record has been requested for this book

ISBN13: 978-0-415-95743-4 (hbk)
ISBN13: 978-1-138-99377-8 (pbk)

Kelly Hillgrove,
who died on December 26, 2004 during the tsunamis in Sri Lanka.
Linda Albert, my sister I never knew,
who is always watching over me.
My daughter, who is about to be born.

Contents

Acknowledgments

I am deeply indebted to the many scholars and colleagues at the University of Colorado, Boulder, who generously contributed to the production of this project. I am particularly grateful for the unwavering support and critical eye of Charlotte Sussman, who stood by me as a mentor and friend from the inception of this project to submission. My admiration for Adéléké Adéèkó, who introduced me to so many different worlds and never ceased to act as my guide, knows no bounds. A heartfelt thanks to Jeffrey Cox, Frederick Aldama, and John Stevenson for graciously agreeing to participate in this project, and for challenging me each step of the way with their provocative questions and constructive feedback. The Graduate School George F. Reynolds Dissertation Fellowship and the College of Arts and Sciences Emerson and Lowe Dissertation Fellowship, both of which Katherine Eggert helped me to win with her meticulous editing, and the Arts and Humanities Award for Dissertation Excellence, supported different phases of this project.

I am also grateful for funding provided by the University of Colorado's Centre for British Studies J.D.A. Ogilvy Fellowship for Research in Great Britain and the University of Kent Overseas Scholarship. While in England, I had the opportunity to do preliminary research under the guidance of C. L. Innes and Abdulrazak Gurnah at the University of Kent, Canterbury. I am thankful for their invaluable tutelage during the early stages of this project. Renée Dickinson and Robin Calland, my comrades-in-pens, bravely served as midwives for the first draft, and kept me on track throughout the writing process with their intellectual curiosity and steadfast encouragement. My dear friend and colleague, Pamela Rader, read sections of this project and shared her always thought-provoking insight.

I would also like to acknowledge the numerous people outside of academia whose loving care kept me going when my body threatened to break down: Angelo Cicero, Nancy Foss, Kevin Shepard, Barb Beard, Gina Tajchman and David Boynton. I am deeply beholden to Suzanne Pope, my soul sister and surrogate mother, without whom I could never have completed this project, and without whom I might not be here today. I am profoundly grateful to my father, William Albert, who never stopped reminding me to be true to myself, and my mother, Nina Albert, who took this ride filled with smiles, sweat, and tears right alongside me in ways that we have both yet to comprehend. I would like to thank my brother Jimmy and sister Dini for being my cheerleading squad over the years. My husband and guardian angel, Michael Monahan, deserves an honorary degree for preventing me from spontaneously combusting on more than one occasion. No words can fully express my gratitude for keeping the laughter and music alive in our lives, for never losing faith in me, and for teaching me more than I could ever teach him: how to love.

Introduction

Transatlantic Retrospections

Caleb Deschanel's 1989 film *Crusoe* is a visually stunning revision of Daniel Defoe's *Robinson Crusoe* (1719). Set in the nineteenth century, Deschanel's Crusoe is a southern aristocrat who sets off from America on a venture to bring slaves from Africa. He is caught in a storm, shipwrecked on an uncharted island and, after some time, he too encounters natives performing a ritual of human sacrifice. Crusoe rescues an intended victim, and nicknames him Lucky because there is no one to sell him to. In an intriguing twist to the classic plot, Lucky is slain during the night and Crusoe finds himself wrestling with the native warrior who evidently did the deed. However, rather than kill Crusoe, the warrior saves him from drowning when they roll into quicksand. From this moment onward the two men struggle to coexist on the island despite their individual prejudices and the language barrier, and a relationship of mutual respect eventually develops between them. When natural scientists on a specimen-collecting mission arrive from "civilization," they capture the warrior and lock him in a cage on their ship anchored offshore. Now, Crusoe must make a choice.

Deschanel's film exemplifies what postcolonial theorists and critics refer to as "writing back" to the empire. The figure of Crusoe is, at least initially, entirely comparable to Defoe's protagonist in that he is a colonist and slave-trader. Moreover, he rationalizes enslaving the natives whom he considers wild "cannibals." Through the filmmaker's vision, the warrior's humanity and the richness of his culture and language are highlighted, and Crusoe's decision in the final moments of the film to help the warrior escape suggests symbolic reparation. Defoe's imperialist narrative is thus seemingly inverted as Deschanel's "white master" returns to "civilization" with a wholly transformed attitude toward race and cultural relations. This kind of analysis implies that all's well that ends well, so to speak, as long as the ending is rewritten.

But assuming that eighteenth-century cultural artifacts and twentieth-century revisions sit neatly on opposite sides of the same political, cultural and social issues overlooks the ways that revisions and sources engage with each other. In this study, I revisit eighteenth-century culture through the lens of what I call *transatlantic retrospections*: creative works by contemporary African and Caribbean writers that engage with, rather than solely contest, the storytelling practices and fictional figures that emerged in eighteenth-century England. While these engagements take different forms, they reveal that writers from once-colonized regions of the globe, despite their political differences, detect similarities between their own aesthetic struggle to represent a "new" world and the aesthetic struggles of eighteenth-century British writers, artists and dramatists, who were similarly confronted, literally and figuratively, with a New World.

Transatlantic retrospections operate on two distinct levels. By adapting textual elements, themes, and fictional figures from historical narratives to represent or allegorize a modern situation, transatlantic retrospections invite awareness that the past is comparable to the present. The preservation of the source work's design and story can be understood as what Lorna Hardwick refers to in *Translating Words, Translating Cultures* as an "enactment of equivalence" between historical and current debates and crises. In this way, transatlantic retrospections draw attention to trans-historical, cross-cultural, and inter-textual correspondences and continuities, and thus they serve to destabilize formulaic and rigid assessments of the distinctions between historical moments and cultures. At the same time, by transforming the generic forms in which eighteenth-century representations of colonialism and the Atlantic Slave Trade were disseminated, the postcolonization writers whose works I examine assert their difference and distance themselves from their cultural forbears.[1] The genre shift is particularly crucial, as it enables a detached analysis of how the source work is being both adapted and transformed to represent the present, and also functions to expose ambiguities and contradictions in eighteenth-century political thought. Subsequently, transatlantic retrospections provide unique insights into the legacies of western cultural history for the colonized and descendents of the enslaved, and invite reinterpretations of the eighteenth-century cultural artifacts they revise.

I use the term "transatlantic" alongside "retrospections" with caution, as the term "transatlantic" has been associated with a multitude of diverse histories and institutionalized disciplines. As David Armitage explains, the Atlantic and Atlantic world are subjects of study among historians of North and South America, the Caribbean, Africa and western

Europe, and encompass economics, politics, sociology, race relations and the early history of globalization. However, in the last decade or so the study of Atlantic history has emerged as a "subfield, or even subdiscipline, within the historical profession" (13). While the study of the Atlantic was at one time an analysis of the relations between North American societies (especially the United States) and Europe, "by means of a common set of pluralistic, democratic, liberal values," today the study of the Atlantic world includes the histories of the slave trade and slavery, the African continent and its diverse peoples, slave rebellions, abolition, and race relations.[2] Armitage subsequently proposes a "threefold typology" of Atlantic history: *Circum*-Atlantic history, the transnational history of the Atlantic world; *Trans*-Atlantic history, the international history of the Atlantic world; and *Cis*-Atlantic history, national or regional history within an Atlantic context.[3] I have opted to use the term "transatlantic" because, as Armitage suggests, "*trans*-Atlantic indicates the history of the Atlantic world told through comparisons." Moreover, it is especially suited to seventeenth- and eighteenth-century histories of the Atlantic world, when state formation went hand-in-hand with empire-state building, and it has most frequently been undertaken "within an imperial framework, often explicitly divided between centers and peripheries" (20).[4] While this study seeks to complicate, rather than reinforce, such paradigms as center and periphery, I nevertheless use "transatlantic" because the term resonates with the histories of the Atlantic Triangle.

While analyses of transatlantic retrospections can be grounded in the historical, social and political realities that inform cultural production, these engagements with eighteenth-century cultural artifacts are "retrospections" because they look back on and contemplate eighteenth-century culture, specifically the period's generic innovations and aesthetic experimentation. By transforming the generic forms of the works they revise, and thus by doing something *literary*, the postcolonization writers who produce transatlantic retrospections remind us that, as much as the eighteenth-century works they engage with contributed to and continue to reflect political agendas, those who produced them were first and foremost involved in the act of literary production. While transatlantic retrospections do reflect knowledge and belief systems inherited via colonial educations and ongoing relations with a metropolitan "center," they are literary creations. Thus even writings that are seemingly invested in or dependent upon "western" history, and even those works that represent the writer's own histories and experiences as well as their socio-political critique, are above all else products of the writer's imagination and creative ingenuity.

***

Postcolonial theorists and critics have typically viewed rewrites of classic or canonical works as counter-discourse and embraced them for their politically transformative potential. The origins of this so-called "revisionist project" can be located in the 1950s, when the founders of colonialist discourse, Aimé Césaire, Frantz Fanon, Albert Memmi, Dominique O. Mannoni, and Tunisian Jew Albert Memmi published their works in French.[5] These early analyses of the profound psychological effects of the colonial situation on both the colonizer and the colonized spawned such groundbreaking studies as Edward Said and Abdul JanMohamed's inquiries into the processes by which colonizers enforce domination, and the means with which the colonized respond to and resist colonial ideologies.[6] In their influential but controversial study of the literature of the former colonies, *The Empire Writes Back: Theory and Practice in Post-Colonial Literatures* (1989), Bill Ashcroft, Gareth Griffiths and Helen Tiffin took Said and JanMohamed one step further by insisting that the term "postcolonial" can be used "to cover all the cultures affected by the imperial process from the moment of colonization to the present day" (2), and that "subversive maneuvers . . . are the characteristic features of the post-colonial text" (196).[7]

However, as Patrick Colm Hogan argues in *Empire and Poetic Voice*, the emphasis on resistance does not "adequately represent the multiple and complex relations" of postcolonization authors to either metropolitan or indigenous traditions. For example, "discussions of writing back tend to assume that the indigenous author has a critical intention and this intention actually produces resistance." In actuality, "things do not operate in such a straightforward manner." According to Hogan, "critical and theoretical writing on colonialism and literary tradition tends to suffer from two limitations: first, an overly narrow understanding of the postcolonization author's relation to metropolitan tradition; second, the virtual absence of reference to the postcolonization author's relation to indigenous tradition." While there are "individual exceptions at the level of textual criticism, and occasionally at the level of theory," the "general trend seems indisputable" (19). Hogan responds to this situation by examining—in addition to texts that exemplify resistance—texts that are (perhaps unintentionally) even "more complicit with colonial ideology than the metropolitan works" they write back to, texts that "outdo the paradigms of one's chosen genre," and the ways in which an author "might neither compete with nor simply imitate his/her precursors, but rather continue the trajectory of a generic tradition, extending it along paths suggested, but not followed out, by precursors." Significantly, Hogan's study is founded upon a conviction that "postcolonization authors are, after all, authors with literary interests, ambitions, and sensibilities much the same as those of authors anywhere" and, I would add, anytime (20).

By revisiting the British eighteenth century through the lens of transatlantic retrospections, I endeavor to expose what may seem for scholars who subscribe to such politically motivated theoretical approaches as "writing back" to be a paradox: writers from once-colonized regions of the globe and descendents of slaves are identifying with the same British cultural producers they reintroduce and the same British cultural artifacts they revise. More specifically, transatlantic retrospections reflect their authors' interests in eighteenth century generic developments and aesthetic innovations. Thus transatlantic retrospections can be understood on one level as trans-historical, cross-cultural dialogues enabling the authors to better understand and represent their distinct colonial histories and current encounters with neocolonialism and racism. At the same time they reflect the fact that, like those who produced the works they confront, contemporary writers are experimenting with different modes of representation to articulate and portray their experiences in a world that continues to be traumatized by political conflict and violence.

To identify with eighteenth-century writers and artists, and the cultural artifacts produced in Britain during the heyday of colonialism and slavery, seems like a paradox because it implies that the colonized, oppressed and exploited are aligning themselves with the western culture and vessels of imperial ideologies that served to impose and maintain European hegemony, and therefore to subjugate the colonized. This is not to suggest, however, that transatlantic retrospections are devoid of resistance tactics, such as exposing how the works they confront operate(d) to promote an identity of "Englishness." As Stuart Hall explains in "The Local and the Global," in the eighteenth century there emerged a "strongly centered, highly exclusive and exclusivist form of cultural identity," which placed everybody else in their "otherness," in their "marginality," by the nature of the "all encompassing 'English eye'" (20). Not only were the colonized, enslaved and *everybody else* prohibited from inhabiting this supposedly fixed and stable identity, but those who imagined they inhabited this identity of "Englishness" authorized the transportation, exploitation, enslavement and murder of Africans and native peoples, and the deliberate obliteration of local cultures.

In the mid-twentieth century, there began throughout the world a mass attempt to recover, reconstruct, and promote the local, non-European histories, languages, traditions and identities that had been lost, displaced and destroyed. In "Old and New Identities," Hall proposes that this "enormous act" of "imaginary political re-identification, re-territorialization and re-identification, without which counter-politics could not have been constructed," is how the margins began to speak and how those who had been excluded and marginalized came to represent themselves. Hence the critical approach to writings that emerged from the "margins" or "periphery" as counter-discursive resistance, the analytical focus on how these writings represent silenced or absent histories, and the institutional debates regarding whether these works constitute *authentic* representations of ethnic, national, and racial identities.

But just as categorizing all postcolonization writings under the rubric of "writing back" is a highly misleading act of containment, the implicit assumption in the "writing back" framework—that there is a static British identity or culture that is being *written back to*—is likewise deceptive. As Hall explains in the "The Local and the Global," Englishness "never was and never possibly could be" some stable point of reference "in relation to those societies with which [Britain] was deeply connected, both as a commercial and global political power overseas" (22).[8] Moreover, just as the notion of Englishness as a fixed identity emerged as a consequence of, or in reaction to, what Hall refers to as the "unfolding of global processes" (21), so too did the supposedly stable identities "African" or "black." But the words "African," "black," and "British" all meant different things to different people in different times, and *what it meant to be* African or black or British was something that changed over time and depended on the context. In addition, identities do not exist in isolation. Identities are products of encounters and formulated under gazes, and therefore always subject to negotiation, always unstable and fluid. In their introduction to *Black Experience and the Empire*, Philip D. Morgan and Sean Hawkins similarly contend that "all identities are constructed and therefore highly variable over space and time," and the problem with calling them "identities" is that they are "assumed to be inherently true or authentic, rather than strategic and political." To examine how, in the history of the British empire, particular terms were used by individual subjects and by imperial and metropolitan authorities is to "see that they were never stable, certainly not static in their meanings, and *not necessarily mutually exclusive*" [my emphasis] (3–4).

Transatlantic retrospections expose that cultural production is a space in which the ongoing processes of multiple yet oftentimes contradictory "identifications"—which constitute the *discursive* formation of identities—are played out. In *Questions of Cultural Identity*, Hall claims that "identification" is actually an "articulation," which is "constructed on the back of a recognition of some common origin or shared characteristics with another person or group, or with an ideal." Identifications can never lead to a "total merging" because there is always "'too much' or 'too little,'" "an over-determination or a lack" (4), and therefore any identification with a person, group, idea or ideal does not eliminate the "difference" between the identifier and who or what they articulate an identification. For example, a postcolonization writer can concurrently identify with local histories and cultures and the western culture that is likewise their inheritance. Moreover, a postcolonization writer can simultaneously identify with and distance themselves from historical and/or fictional figures and texts.

Subsequently, as Carl Plasa asserts in *Textual Politics from Slavery to Postcolonialism*, "identification—whether white or black—emerges as a complex, highly charged and multi-faceted phenomenon, linking a number of major texts and the violent histories of slavery, colonialism and racial oppression by which they are traversed." But as much as these identifications are "sites of political struggle and friction," they also "constitute spaces" where "psychic and historical realities, the subjective and the ideological, dramatically collide" (8). Identifications ultimately constitute spaces in which notions of corporeal and discursive identities, global and local traditions, aesthetic practices and cultural artifacts, and various forms of representation mingle—harmoniously as well as antagonistically—but never fuse or merge.

***

Transatlantic retrospections also illustrate that *as a consequence of global exploration, conquest and trade, the early modern era witnessed the emergence and transformation of many literary genres.* Just as identities are not self-enclosed, the literary genres that we typically associate with eighteenth-century England, and that allegedly came into being as a means to understand distinctly "western" experiences in a rapidly expanding world, do not represent a closed, national culture. In fact, according to Andrew Smith, the "idea of a self-contained national literary tradition seems anomalous, time-bound, and hopelessly nostalgic. Increasingly, cultural products are exposed as hybrid, as tying together influences from many traditions, as existing not so much in a specific place and time but *between* different places at once." Smith further argues that, although the project of postcolonial literary studies begins "with the sense that 'other' places and stories are suddenly visible and vocal in the heart of the metropolis . . . it has also led to the recognition that those 'other' places have been there from the very beginning of the modern Western literary tradition" (245).[9]

In addition to correcting and contesting Eurocentric narratives and misrepresentations of the New World and its peoples, and in addition to using historical (cultural) artifacts to represent local and current conditions and concerns, transatlantic retrospections exemplify the varied and distinct ways African and Caribbean writers engage with and revise eighteenth-century works to reveal that certain genres of British literature cannot be considered hermetically British. In other words, just as imperial, transanational and cross-cultural forces influence *local* cultures and contribute to the production and transformation of cultural forms around the globe, so, too, encounters, exchanges and acts of resistance taking place around the globe during the eighteenth century influenced—even shaped—what we have come to think of as "western" cultural forms. Thus transatlantic retrospections reiterate or serve to illustrate that the circulation of culture has, as Paul Jay points out, "always been multidirectional." In "Beyond Discipline? Globalization and the Future of English," Jay argues that literary texts have always been "caught up in the transnational flow of commodities and cultures at least since the rise of [global] trade and colonial expansion," and therefore the "history of global expansion, trade, and intercultural exchange" can—and should—be given "precedence" over nationalist paradigms (43). This is not to suggest that critics should ignore how "literary writings have been theorized and politicized in efforts to define and empower nation-states," nor forgo investigating the asymmetry and inequality of global relations, exchanges and "multidirectional flows."[10] Rather, such an approach calls for a greater appreciation of the historical role literature has had in the "global network of forces—aesthetic, social cultural, economic—that transcend the borders of nation states" (42–43).

Interestingly, the push to globalize English literary histories is a relatively new academic endeavor, but the postcolonization writers who produce transatlantic retrospections have been recognizing and encouraging a global framework for literary history since the mid-twentieth century. Of course, such an approach can only be undertaken by acknowledging that globalization, rather than a contemporary (or postmodern) phenomenon, has been a long historical process. As Jan Nederveen Pieterse explains, because such definitions of globalization as the "*intensification* of worldwide social relations" (Giddens 64) necessarily presume the prior existence of "worldwide social relations," globalization can be thought of as a long-term process that began with the "first migration of peoples and long-distance trade connections, and subsequently accelerates under particular conditions (the spread of technologies, religions, literacy, empires capitalism)" (63). Felicity Nussbaum determines in *The Global Eighteenth Century* that the prehistory of globalization can be located in the eighteenth century, an era when the "increased mobility of commodities and ideas, the unprecedented expansion of global trade, improved navigational techniques, and cultural and racial mixing are of course very germane" (8). Moreover, as Kathleen Wilson points out, in England the "mesmerizing spectacle of Britain's global expansions" fueled British imaginations in ways that "gave it particular salience within domestic politics and culture" (24). Transatlantic retrospections, which likewise recognize a "global" eighteenth century, invite us to chart intersections between global activities and cultural developments in England by exposing correlations between global trade, intercultural contact and exchanges, the rapid commercialization of culture, and an upsurge of aesthetic experimentation in London.

For example when (often inaccurate) images of the New World and its inhabitants initially appeared in early explorers' and merchants' reports, writers and artists in England adopted these images to either represent or conceal relations with those the British were subjugating. By disseminating through their works depictions of "noble savagery," or rather, images against which British readers and audiences could compare themselves, writers and artists perpetuated the maintenance of such stereotypes as "primitive" or "savage." Aphra Behn reportedly visited Surinam in the early 1660s, and her *Oroonoko* (1688) was one of the first extended portrayals of a "noble savage" in print and also, significantly, the first realist prose narrative in English literature. With the publication of Behn's "true history" of a "royal slave," a blurring of fictional and historical "eye-witness" accounts was established as the genre for representing colonialism, slavery and non-European peoples, and a new mode of storytelling came into being. Behn's narrator insists that her story has "enough of Reality to support it . . . without the Addition of Invention. I was myself an Eyewitness to a great part . . . and what I cou'd not be Witness of, I received from the Mouth of the chief Actor in this History, the *Hero* himself" (8). Despite such claims, Behn's portrait of Oroonoko conforms more to the Renaissance conventions of romance and tragedy than the realities of life in the colonies and the slave trade. Nonetheless, the inclusion of such realist narrative tactics enables the brutal treatment of African slaves in Surinam to be both represented *and* suppressed, embellished *as well as* masked.

Transatlantic retrospections recognize that this pioneering combination of "noble savage" imagery and so-called realism enabled the British to convincingly project fantasies of domination over the Africans, Amerindians, and Caribs whose presence around the globe (and in England) posed a challenge to their sense of sovereignty and cultural supremacy.

A combination of realist narrative tactics, claims to historicity, and "noble savage" imagery similarly allowed Defoe to create the illusion that he was disseminating factual information in *Robinson Crusoe* (1719), which played an instrumental role in shaping the British public's global vision. The introductory assertion, that the "editor believes the thing to be a just History of Fact; neither is there any Appearance of Fiction in it," serves as an invitation to readers to embrace the text as an authentic depiction of reality (3). Early eighteenth-century English readers would have identified with Crusoe because he represented their middle-class dreams of upward mobility and economic progress, and the story of Crusoe's island would have accommodated their desires to see and possess the New World. Consequently, they would not have questioned Defoe's depiction of a shipwrecked English merchant as "master" or his portrayal of Friday as a cannibal-turned-docile servant. Defoe defended himself against charges that the false "claims to historicity" brands his text a "Romance" by claiming that this "sort of lying" is offset by the novel's moral lessons.[11] But these "lies" paved the way for linguistically- or discursively-created worlds (Crusoe's island) and identities (the subservient Friday) to usurp global realities in the minds of the British reading public. Defoe's portrayal of the New World is fundamentally *un*real because it idealizes British dominance and deflects attention away from, or enables disengagement from, the actual atrocities accompanying global trade, colonialism and slavery. While Defoe's account of one man's colonial, economic and spiritual progress is indeed an allegory of the empire's desire for power, mastery and wealth, it is the so-called realist *form* of *Robinson Crusoe* that made it a vessel of ideology.

Thus while such popular genres as the periodical essay, captivity narrative, travelogue and realist novel seem to testify to the long eighteenth-century's reverence for objectivity and accurate information, and arguably emerged in conjunction with the European Enlightenment, they can be implicated in the early processes of globalization. Yet it is the confrontation and transformation of the generic forms that emerged during the eighteenth century as a consequence of, or in tandem with, global expansion, colonialism, and slavery that enable us to *reinterpret* the cultural artifacts that are being revised. As Hardwick explains, writers experiment in using genres different from that of the original to "transform the perspective of the reader or audience" (113). The translation or transformation of historical sources serves "either as a means of 'distancing' debate about current issues by using a remote mythological setting or as a means of inducing cultural shock by suggesting more overt correspondences and equivalences between ancient and modern crises and debates in a way which destabilizes modern certainties" (67–68). More simply, the translation or transformation of historical material may produce an allegory of a modern situation, or result in a play on the differences as well as correspondences between the past and present, or be both at once. As Michael Valdez Moses proposes in *The Novel and the Globalization of Culture*, the historical work "takes on new meaning in the context" of the postcolonization text it anticipates, and the postcolonization text "emerges as a telling critique of the Western literary history and cultural tradition it self-consciously evokes" (xii). In the case of transatlantic retrospections, the genre shift serves to liberate and make readily visible what had previously been either peripheral to the historical text or suppressed from our social memory of the long eighteenth century.

***

In chapter one, "Reading Periodically," I argue that by transforming Richard Steele's *The Spectator No. 11* (1711) into a captivity narrative, *Inkle and Yarico* (1996), Guyanese-born Beryl Gilroy highlights Steele's subtle anti-colonial and abolitionist rhetoric while concurrently calling attention to how the generic form with which he depicted the story Inkle and Yarico operated as a vehicle for identity constructions and reiterated colonial ideologies. Throughout the eighteenth century over sixty versions of this romantic encounter between a shipwrecked Englishman and an Amerindian, Carib, or African girl, who rescues and loves him, appeared in English. Yet the story never appeared in the form of a novel until Gilroy produced her adaptation of the tale. Gilroy's version is certainly a commentary on Steele's essay, as she includes an excerpt from *The Spectator No. 11* as an appendix to the narrative she constructs for Inkle. Gilroy thereby reminds her readers that, although Richard Ligon provided the historical source with his *A True and Exact History of the Island of Barbados* (1657), it was Steele who gave the English traveler his name, and it was with the appearance of Steele's essay in *The Spectator* that both Inkle and Yarico were inscribed with their allegorical meanings: Inkle as the British empire and Yarico as the colony/slave.

However, despite her African heritage, Guyanese upbringing, background in ethno-psychology, and femininity, Gilroy works against the tradition of "writing back" by conveying identification with Steele himself and not rewriting the story from Yarico's perspective. Instead, the narrative she constructs for Inkle is a first-person record of his supposed subjugation by a supposedly inferior culture. According to Joe Snader, in the seventeenth and eighteenth centuries such narratives served to restore the captive's "sense of cultural imbalance" and represented their "cultural victory" (63). While the experience of captivity in the Americas occasionally transformed a European's notions of racial hierarchy and personal identity, more frequently narrators drew on such cultural stereotypes as "savage" and "barbarian" to depict their captors. Thus the captivity genre "leant itself to national agendas" and served as propaganda for such imperial enterprises as colonialism and slavery. At the conclusion of his narrative, Gilroy's Inkle accordingly declares, "I am a man who believes that our civilization is superior and permanent. I hold all others to be ephemeral—and at times grotesque. That is our way as a nation." He then informs the reader that he is now a "leading anti-abolitionist," and the fact that he is crippled has "proved a boon, for it is blamed . . . upon the barbarity of the savages, who should be kept chained and set to work" (157). Gilroy exposes through the narrative she constructs for Inkle that he is—to borrow from Linda Colley—"held captive by the dream of global supremacy."[12]

Gilroy's Inkle's cultural arrogance reflects the sense of British moral, intellectual and cultural superiority that periodical essays such as Steele's promoted and, by transforming Steele's essay into a novel, Gilroy illustrates Kathleen Wilson's argument in "The good, the bad, and the important" that the periodical press "produced forms of ethnocentric knowledge . . . that supported British superiority and power, fed the growing enthusiasm for the exotic and primitive, and legitimated British domination" (242). Gilroy's novel can therefore be understood as a critique of the generic form that, despite its best intentions, ultimately contributed to the exclusive sense of Englishness or Britishness that, in turn, fueled ethnocentrism and enabled colonial brutality. Gilroy's Inkle exemplifies her determination that racism is the "ethnocentric mind which matures in a gnarled and distorted way," and that racists are those who are "unmindful of experience and bondaged by power needs and ethnic falsehoods" (*Leaves in the Wind*, 5). Thus with her portrayal of Inkle, Gilroy illustrates the continuities between eighteenth-century ethnocentrism and the racism that West Indian migrants encountered in post-World War II Britain.[13]

While Gilroy transforms Steele's essay into a novel to comment on the eighteenth-century periodical essay, Derek Walcott's transformations of what postcolonial scholars have come to consider the quintessential colonialist novel, Defoe's *Robinson Crusoe*, into verse and drama serve as unique commentaries on eighteenth-century realist prose narratives and pantomimes. In chapter two, "Novel Poetics and Pantomimes" I consider how Walcott portrays his personal identification with Crusoe's aesthetic struggle to represent the New World by adopting the figure of the castaway as a symbol of the West Indian condition and metaphor for artistic isolation in his Crusoe poems: "The Castaway," "Crusoe's Island" and "Crusoe's Journal" (1965).[14] By conveying identification with the figure of Crusoe as a castaway and artist in isolation, Walcott pays homage to Defoe's aesthetic experimentation and illustrates Roy Porter's observation that, in the early eighteenth-century, "fiction emerged as the choice of medium for 'rethinking the self.' Novels were precisely that: novel—constituting one of the literary genres born since the invention of printing." The influential histories or narratives, which only later became known as novels, "invited identification with the protagonist as outsider or loner" (283). Yet by transforming a novel, which according to Firdous Azim is the generic form that colonized subjects generally view as the "discourse of the master"(10), into verse, Walcott distances himself from Defoe's imperialist vision, endorsement of colonialism, and apparent tolerance of slavery.

With his play *Pantomime*, first performed in 1979, Walcott endeavors to transform Defoe's imperialist narrative into a liberating narrative by depicting the Crusoe-Friday relationship as one that goes beyond subjugation and alienation. *Pantomime* is to a certain extent a counter-discursive text in that Walcott's English "castaway," Harry Trewe, seems at first to symbolize British imperialism, white economic power and domination, but he is ultimately much weaker than his native employee, Jackson. As the emotional bond develops between Harry and Jackson, who forces Harry to confront his demons—memories of his divorce and the death of his son—the roles of colonizer/colonized and master/slave are seemingly neutralized. In addition, the fact that Harry and Jackson are rehearsing a Christmas pantomime of *Robinson Crusoe*, which turns into a lively debate about European and Caribbean culture and behavior, serves as an invitation to readers/audiences to reinterpret the relationship between Crusoe and Friday as one that holds the potential for mutual respect and equality. At the same time, because Harry and Jackson are rehearsing a pantomime of *Robinson Crusoe*, Walcott's play invites readers/viewers to revisit eighteenth-century dramatic productions based on the same story. While English pantomimes are typically filled with racial epithets and depictions of stereotypical "cannibals" or "savages" that viewers would have considered humorous, at the conclusion of the spectacular 1781 production at Drury Lane, Friday is invested with the magical powers of the Harlequin and rewarded for his heroism with the hand of Columbine. Of course, the fact that this production appeared toward the end of the eighteenth century may explain its apparent abolitionist slant. Nonetheless, by transforming the genre and alluding to the eighteenth-century pantomimes that always included "transformation" scenes, Walcott implies that race relations in the Caribbean can be transformed if Friday is liberated from his seemingly "fixed" identity as an inferior "other" and whites recognize that Britishness is, likewise, an identity construction.

Whereas Walcott identifies with the figure of Crusoe in his Crusoe poems as an artist in isolation, Nigerian Wole Soyinka identifies with the figure of Gulliver in Lilliput as a lone seeker after social justice. In chapter three, "Satire's Spectacles," I argue that, by transforming Jonathan Swift's *Gulliver's Travels* (1726) into a prison narrative in verse, "Gulliver" (1972), and dislodging the humor from Swift's satire, Soyinka reintroduces Swift's protagonist as a prisoner of conscience. Soyinka produced his retrospection of *Gulliver's Travels* while imprisoned by the Federal Military Government of Nigeria for supporting a cease-fire in the war against Biafra and his narrator, like Swift's Gulliver, is charged with treason for refusing to partake in the state's demand for another country's total annihilation. Yet unlike Swift's Gulliver, who escapes when the Lilliputians threaten to blind him, Soyinka's narrator is sentenced to "lose his sight" (l. 102), which reflects the actual punishment inflicted upon the writer himself: for nearly two years between 1967 and 1969 Soyinka was placed in solitary confinement, deprived of books, writing materials and human companionship, and forced to endure attempts by the Nigerian authorities to destroy his mind.

But Soyinka's identification with Gulliver in Lilliput extends only as far as his victimization, and throughout his poem he maintains that Gulliver in Lilliput is an object of satire because he is trapped in blindness to the realities of government corruption and oppression, and because his potential for heightened consciousness remains unrealized and turns instead to overblown pride. Soyinka's Gulliver, unlike Swift's, is anything but gullible, as he sees his captors' corruption and lust for power with clarity. By portraying his Gulliver as a witness, Soyinka communicates his identification with Gulliver in Laputa and Lagado, whose observations provide an alternative perspective on tyranny. However, while Swift's Gulliver observes the political structures of Laputa and scientific experiments in Lagado with detached neutrality, Soyinka's Gulliver is neither a detached nor neutral witness, and thus the writer's identification with Gulliver in Part III of *Gulliver's Travels* only extends as far as his role as an observer of tyranny.

Rather than "write back" to Swift, whose writings are already deeply subversive, Soyinka exposes that Gulliver's encounters with, and observations of, tyranny are strikingly prophetic and have come to pass in Nigeria during the Nigerian Civil War. Soyinka thereby draws attention to Swift's prophetic vision, as well as his crusade against war, government corruption, tyranny and crimes against humanity. Swift's other "best sellers" include *The Conduct of Allies*, which was designed to influence public opinion toward ending the War of Spanish Succession, and *The Drapier's Letters*, which mobilized Irish resistance to English economic oppression. Moreover, like Swift, Soyinka utilizes a fictional persona to call for the kind of heightened consciousness in the twentieth-century that, according to Said, was Swift's "greatest contribution to political thought" (3). Yet by transforming Swift's prose into verse, Soyinka also exposes the contradictions and ambiguities in Swift's political thought, and even distances himself from this eighteenth-century writer who, according to Frederick V. Bogel, "feared" (along with Dryden, Pope, and Johnson) "revolutionary change" (16).

In chapter four, "Visual and Textual Narratives" I consider how David Dabydeen draws on and transforms visual as well as literary genres to convey that behind the images and off stage are stories and experiences that the period's art and drama displaced. Dabydeen's retrospection of Hogarth's satirical series, *A Harlot's Progress* (1732) is perhaps most comparable to Gilroy's retrospection of Steele's *Spectator No. 11*, as his *A Harlot's Progress* (1999) is likewise an inquiry into how eighteenth-century culture contributed to identity constructions that served political agendas. Also like Gilroy's *Inkle and Yarico*, Dabydeen's novel could be viewed as a text that exemplifies the postcolonial "writing back" tradition, although in this case it is because he gives voice to one of "Hogarth's blacks" to expose the distinctions between how Africans were represented visually and how they represented themselves textually. However, while Dabydeen (as a migrant from the West Indies) identifies with the black figure in Plate 2 of Hogarth's satirical series, he too works against the "writing back" paradigm by identifying with the artist himself, whose engravings and prints comprise a critique of British society. Moreover, while Dabydeen identifies with the Africans in eighteenth-century Britain whose literary texts served to refute the pro-slavery arguments that Africans were incapable of attaining European levels of literacy, Dabydeen also suggests that the circumstances surrounding the production of eighteenth-century Afro-British texts (inadvertently) reiterated racial stereotypes. Thus with his version of *A Harlot's Progress*, Dabydeen challenges the very concept of "writing back" by demonstrating that no historical figure or cultural artifact represents a fixed socio-political position.

In addition to Hogarth's *A Harlot's Progress*, Dabydeen also engages with or alludes to Ignatius Sancho's *Letters*, *The History of Mary Prince*, Olaudah Equiano's *Interesting Narrative*, Isaac Bickerstaff's play *The Padlock*, and possibly a pantomime entitled *Harlequin Mungo*, to comment on the complex relations between identity constructions and generic forms. Dabydeen ultimately exposes that, just as the harlot was "at once the object of desire and disgust, of power and subjugation, a creature of evil ambition or heart" (Uglow 193), the figure of the African symbolized conflicting myths, which is perhaps why white artists and writers exploited the image and, subsequently, why images of Africans figure so frequently in the period's art and drama. However, Dabydeen's protagonist, Mungo, is thoroughly aware of the disparate ways he has been represented, and that white society views him as a composite of stories rather than as an individual in his own right. Instead of giving the abolitionist who is taking his testimony a "beginning, middle and end," Mungo weaves together half-truths and wild tales, recounts conflicting accounts of the same event, and rejects the abolitionist altogether when he confides in the reader. Given that Mungo's story is neither a linear narrative nor a straightforward tale of evil British slavers versus oppressed Africans slaves, it reflects Elizabeth Kowaleski Wallace's claim that the story of the Atlantic Slave Trade is "not simply a story to be told, but a series of overlapping narratives in which competing voices still struggle for dominance" (237). Mungo's narrative also reflects twentieth-century concerns, particularly the West Indian migrant's encounter with persistent, pervasive, and oftentimes violent racism, and serves as a reminder that identities are always being re-invented and remade in the face of what David Richardson refers to as "spatial dislocation and personal trauma" (79).

In chapter five, "Literary Impersonations," I return to Beryl Gilroy, whose novel *Stedman and Joanna: A Love in Bondage* (1991) is an engagement with both *The Journal of John Gabriel Stedman: 1744–1797* (unpublished until 1962) and John Gabriel Stedman's *Narrative of a Five Years Expedition Against the Revolted Negroes of Surinam* (first published in 1796 with William Blake's engravings). As with her *Inkle and Yarico*, with *Stedman and Joanna* Gilroy works against the tradition of "writing back" by conveying her identification with the white, European Stedman, who she believes should be remembered for sympathizing with the oppressed and documenting the abuses inflicted upon slaves in Surinam. While Gilroy acknowledges that Stedman's behavior—particularly with regard to women—was contemptible, she views him in a much more sympathetic light than literary critics and cultural historians, claiming in *Leaves in the Wind* that when he went to Surinam his "conscience was so stirred he was able to confront the condemned and record their terrible deaths for posterity" (86). By transforming Stedman's diaries of his early life and his more stylized (as well as extensively edited) *Narrative* into a novel, Gilroy invites her readers to reread his *Narrative* as an anti-slavery treatise that played a crucial role in the abolitionist movement.

At the same time, Gilroy draws attention to the fact that Stedman's *Narrative* is an amalgamation of cultural forms. As Tassie Gwilliam observes, the *Narrative* is at once the description of a "suicidal military expedition" against the maroons (rebel slaves) of Surinam, a travel book detailing the natural history of South America, a narrative of a "man of sensibility encountering a brutal and corrupt plantation society founded on the spectacular torment of slave bodies," a picaresque masculine adventure modeled on *Roderick Random*, *Tom Jones*, and *Joseph Andrews*, and an overly sentimentalized tale of the romance between Stedman and the mulatto slave Joanna, "hopefully redefined by Stedman as a reversal of *Inkle and Yarico*" (653). Stedman's portrayal of Joanna, like Steele's portrayal of Yarico, is not only informed by images of "noble savagery" and sentimental conventions, it is also reminiscent of English domestic fiction, particularly Samuel Richardson's *Pamela*. By rereading Stedman's *Narrative* through the lens of Gilroy's novel it becomes particularly apparent that Stedman draws on literary conventions and imitates literary characters to sanitize his encounters with Africans in Surinam for British consumption, and consequently he re-inscribes imperialist, colonialist and racist ideologies. By recycling cultural forms and images that his readers would have been familiar with, and which had been serving nationalist and empire-building agendas for over a century, Stedman assures the British reading public of the empire's political and cultural dominance at a moment in history when slave rebellions in the colonies were threatening "western" hegemony and global order.

However, Gilroy also reveals that the historical Stedman, like Inkle, did not return home from Surinam unscathed. Gilroy's text is filled with such lines as, "'Joanna,' I often whispered, 'you will be forever locked in my soul'" (114), implying that his encounter with Joanna permanently marked him. When their son Johnny arrives in Europe he learns that Joanna, too, had kept their love alive in "song, dance, story, and ritual." He tells his new and racist Dutch wife: "'My need of him is in his presence—within him, his form, his face, He reminds me of people and places I once truly loved'" (171). For Gilroy, the historical Stedman is indeed the opposite of Inkle; he represents her hope that racism throughout the world can be overcome.

***

In *Hogarth's Blacks*, Dabydeen declares that *A Harlot's Progress* "amounts to Hogarth's most bitter representation of the squalid and dehumanizing commercialism of the times." Moreover, the title of the series is "ironic: 'Progress' is in reality degradation, physical and moral, eventual death, the experience of the harlot being symbolic of that process" (101). Transatlantic retrospections reveal that such symbols abound in eighteenth-century culture and, significantly, these figures are all interconnected with how they represent, explicitly or implicitly, "progress" as degradation. Hogarth's engravings point to Steele's essay via the pregnant black woman in Plate 4, who can be viewed as a reference to the colonial and sexual exploitation depicted in the story of Inkle and Yarico. Yarico signifies the enhanced economic value of pregnant black slave women in the colonies and she is, like Hogarth's Moll and black servants, Defoe's Friday, Swift's Gulliver and Stedman's Joanna, a prisoner of a viciously materialist and racist British society. It is no wonder, then, that the postcolonization writers whose works I examine in this study do not wholly contest, or "write back" to, the British cultural artifacts that are part of their colonial legacy. Moreover, the transatlantic retrospections produced by Gilroy, Walcott, Soyinka, and Dabydeen reflect twentieth-century encounters with neocolonial oppression and racism, and thus their engagements with British cultural artifacts double as inquiries into whether the modern world has progressed since the eighteenth century.

Chapter One

Reading Periodically

Beryl Gilroy's *Inkle and Yarico* and
Richard Steele's *The Spectator No. 11*

In *Colonial Encounters*, Peter Hulme writes: "Yarico begins her career embedded as an anecdote in a biographical/historical memoir and is transferred by means of an 'essay' to the whole gamut of 'literary' genres" (9), including prose sketches, poems, epistles, plays, operas, ballets and pantomimes. Indeed, Richard Ligon provided the historical source for *The Spectator No. 11* (Tuesday 13 March 1711) with his *A True and Exact History of the Island of Barbados* (1657), and it was via Steele's essay that the story of a native girl, who rescues and loves a shipwrecked English merchant, was propelled into British cultural production and the imaginations of English readers. Critics generally attribute the widespread and enduring popularity of this story to George Colman the Younger's musical extravaganza (1787), which appeared at the onset of the abolitionist movement and was one of the most popular comic operas of the late eighteenth century. But according to Hulme, "from the standpoint of literary history" Steele's version of Inkle and Yarico is surely the most influential.

In her *Inkle and Yarico*, Gilroy includes the same basic plot elements that appear in almost every other version of the tale: Inkle's shipwreck; his love affair with Yarico, who protects him from her tribe; their rescue and transportation to Barbados, his original destination; the betrayal of an exploited and pregnant Indian/African woman. However, Gilroy retells the story from Inkle's perspective by imagining how he would construct a narrative of his seven-year "captivity" amongst a tribe of Black Caribs and his experiences (after he is rescued) on a slave-holding plantation in Barbados. When the reader turns the last page of the narrative Gilroy constructs for Inkle, he or she discovers that Gilroy has included an excerpt from Steele's periodical essay as an "afterword." Gilroy thereby instructs her readers to read these two different versions of the tale in that order. In doing so, she takes on a role that is comparable to that of Mr. Spectator, through whom Steele endeavored to reform the behavior, morals and manners of English society. Although Gilroy's instructions consist merely of placing the source text *after* her revision, the implication is clear: the reader will understand *The Spectator No. 11* better, or rather, see it through her eyes, if he or she reads it after or through her revision. To read Steele after Gilroy is to look past the gender debate within which Steele contextualized this romantic colonial encounter and more readily see Steele's subtle anti-colonial rhetoric and sentimental plea for human rights.[1] Gilroy's novel therefore invites attentiveness to how Steele condemns, if not the Atlantic Slave Trade itself, its inhumanity and cruelty.

However, whereas Steele's critique of Inkle's lack of virtue is dependent upon the reader sympathizing with Yarico as a victim of colonial brutality and sexual exploitation, Gilroy directly attacks Inkle by laying bear for public viewing the psychological operations of a literary figure who had previously only been represented via generic forms that masked or suppressed his interiority. By turning Steele's essay into a first-person captivity narrative with the subtitle "Being the narrative of Thomas Inkle . . . ," Gilroy exposes that Inkle is a narcissistic hand of the British empire and, significantly, plays with the notion that the realist form of early eighteenth-century prose narratives, which later became known as novels, enabled writers to portray an individual's inner life and emphasize his or her psychological depth.[2] Moreover, by transforming the genre Gilroy reveals that Inkle's utterly dishonorable treatment of Yarico in *The Spectator No. 11*— seducing, enslaving and abandoning her—renders absurd the moral lesson regarding individual virtue that frames Steele's version of the story. This is likely the reason Gilroy removes the introductory frame narrative in which Mr. Spectator visits Arietta's salon and is privy to a debate on the "old Topick, of Constancy in Love."

Thus Gilroy ultimately distances herself from Steele and critiques the form of the early eighteenth-century periodical essay established by Defoe's *Review* and further developed by Addison and Steele with *The Tatler* and *The Spectator*. While these periodicals were designed to construct a moral and virtuous British reading public, the essays themselves contributed to the national solidarity that bound Englishmen together and made them feel superior to foreigners, thereby justifying their tyranny over indigenous peoples and African slaves. Similarly, by having her Inkle produce a captivity narrative that serves a nationalist agenda by insisting on European superiority, and which could be considered a novel, Gilroy illustrates Azim's claim that the English novel is an "imperialist project."[3] Yet by using the novel to illustrate how colonial encounters and exchanges influenced eighteenth-century print culture in England, Gilroy challenges the notion that the novel belongs exclusively to the West. [4]

***

At the beginning of his narrative, Gilroy's Inkle portrays himself as the epitome of western privilege, cultural superiority and progress. He even compares himself to a mythic god, or a neoclassical god-like figure: "My youth streamed ahead of me into the future. Of the three sons, I was the tallest, the strongest, the Adonis of the family, greatly petted by my mother and spoilt by my father" (7). In addition, he informs his readers that his social position and economic security are guaranteed by the arrangement of his forthcoming marriage to Alice, who not only "possessed a substantial fortune" but "was beautiful too" (7). According to Adele Newson, with her beauty, breeding and fortune, Alice represents imperial or "mother" England. She is the "symbol of yearning, the ideal for whom the *explorer* labors" (436). While preparing to depart on a commercial venture to the West Indies to labor for his betrothed and imperial England, Inkle reads a farewell letter from his father reminding him that he is of "the first class," and thinks: "How irksome! I knew only too well where I belonged" (11). As Newson points out, his "father's words reinforce and firmly ground Inkle's cultural arrogance" (436). In Steele's essay, Arietta introduces Inkle as "our youth," and "our adventurer," as he is likewise embarking on a journey that will "improve his fortune by trade and merchandize." In the early eighteenth century, when the increase of capital in the metropolitan regions of the world was dependent upon global commerce and colonial conquest, Steele's readers—as Gilroy's Inkle expects of his readers—might have embraced Inkle as a national hero.

But by having her Inkle offer a detailed account of his family's history, Gilroy highlights the fact that this literary figure symbolizes the brutality of imperial expansion. Inkle explains that, during the Commonwealth period, when Cromwell ruled the kingdom, his "great-grandfather had bought lands on the British islands of Barbados, and upon it had settled indentured Irish malefactors and English miscreants who had fallen foul of the law" (9). These lands had passed to his grandfather and then his father. During his rule, Cromwell conquered Ireland and Scotland, made England a feared military power in Europe, and expanded its overseas empire. Although Cromwell was hailed by his supporters as England's religious and martial defender, and praised for quelling Irish rebellion and Scottish threats, his critics considered him a tyrant because his military methods were particularly bloody. The fact that Inkle's family bought land in Barbados during the Cromwellian era, and settled indentured Irish malefactors and English miscreants there, implies not only that they were supporters of Cromwell but that they were influenced by the propaganda that stirred up passions in England and invoked calls for a rapid suppression of "barbarous" rebels.[5] By boasting that his inheritance dates back to Cromwell, Inkle aligns himself with both Cromwell and the practice of distributing nationalist propaganda to gain the support of the masses.

Gilroy's Inkle's references to his inheritance also point to what historians have argued is the symbiotic relationship between the growth of trade, empire-building, and the emergence of a British identity. By the end of the seventeenth century, overseas commerce was conducted within the mercantilist framework of the Navigation Acts, which stipulated that all commodity trade should take place in British ships, manned by British seamen, trading between British ports and those within the empire. Despite these developments, in 1688 Britain was still a vulnerable competitor for stakes in overseas colonies and trade, and her rivals included the trading empires of France and the Netherlands (the inspiration for and focus of Defoe's *Review*), as well as Spain and Portugal. But after the Royal African Company's monopoly was rescinded in 1698, the British became the largest and most efficient carriers of slaves to the New World. The growth in imperial commerce went hand in hand with British hegemony in empire. As Linda Colley determines in *Britons: Forging the Nation 1707–1837*, after the Act of Union joining Scotland to England and Wales a sense of British identity was forged. This "invention of Britishness" was directly tied to the belief that "commerce, especially foreign commerce, was the engine that drove a state's power and wealth" (62). For the next one-hundred-and-thirty years there was a "widespread conviction that trade was the foundation of Britain's greatness and identity" (61). When Steele's Inkle sets off for Barbados he is not only participating in the global commerce that was an indispensable part of the British economy and empire-building agenda but also contributing to the invention, and upholding the notion, of Britishness.

However, rather than setting out on his own accord to pursue his fortune, as in Steele's essay, Gilroy's Inkle is going to Barbados to assess the situation on his family's plantation and acquaint himself with the reasons why their slaves, "although housed and fed, had failed to work conscientiously" (9). Despite the plentiful addition of African slaves, the plantation had been "badly managed by overseers and attorneys" and the "lands had not prospered," which "greatly aggrieved" Inkle's father (9). Gilroy thereby draws attention to the fact that in the early eighteenth century the English were becoming anxious about their overseas investments, and absentee plantation owners were beginning to experience financial difficulties. Gilroy also brings to the forefront of her text the global reality that Steele directs his readers away from by focusing on the gender debate, which is that Englishmen like Inkle were brutally exploiting Africans for England's financial gain. According to Mary Louise Pratt, although the "allegory of romantic love mystifies exploitation out of the picture" (87), the story of Inkle and Yarico "articulates about as clearly as one might wish the business-to-business of underwriting slavery" (100). The "trade that is the blood of this country"(9) that Gilroy's Inkle is so eager to participate in, and that is behind the scenes of Steele's essay, is the trade in humans. With her depiction of Inkle, Gilroy draws attention to the irony of referring to Inkle as "our hero," although in her vision it is not simply because of his heartlessness in the arena of love.

Moreover, by constructing a narrative for Inkle that is essentially a narrative of captivity, Gilroy draws attention to another behind-the-scenes aspect of Steele's essay, which is that the same non-European peoples whom the British were exploiting and colonizing were resisting European hegemony by turning Europeans into captive bodies. According to Colley, "two parables exist about the making and meanings of the British empire." In one, which is the narrative Britons embraced, a man sets out on a trading voyage and is shipwrecked on a desert island. The "despair" of this lone survivor "soon gives way to resolution." Empire-making in this parable "involves being a warrior and taking charge. It means seizing land, planting it, and changing it. It means employing guns, technology, trade and the Bible to devastating effect, imposing rule, and subordinating those of a different skin pigmentation or religion." This is Defoe's *Robinson Crusoe*, which I discuss in Chapter Two. The other parable is a man who "sets sail from Bristol, centre of transatlantic commerce and slaving, bound for successive zones of European imperialism: Spanish America, the West Indies, coastal India. He never reaches them. Instead, his voyages are aborted, time and time again, by events and beings beyond his control." For this man, "overseas venturing brings no conquests, or riches, or easy complacencies: only terror, vulnerability, repeated captivities, and in the process an alteration of self and a telling of stories" (1–2). This is Swift's *Gulliver's Travels,* which I discuss in Chapter Three. Although Steele's Inkle participates in empire-building by imposing rule, trading/owning slaves and subordinating a native, Gilroy's Inkle thinks of himself as Crusoe but is actually more like Gulliver. He sets out to participate in British maritime and imperial projects, but his arrival in Barbados is delayed when he is shipwrecked and held captive by a tribe of Black Caribs. Upon his return to England, he produces a narrative in which he describes his captivity and how he dealt with the "challenges and sufferings that ensued" (13). According to Colley, for captives who escaped, were released or rescued, and returned to England, it might have seemed "essential" to "seize control of" and tell their own tales. "Translating any experience of trauma into one's own words is cathartic. It gives victims back a measure of control. They can tell their side of the story, put themselves at the centre of the plot, and make clear that they still matter" (*Captives* 84).

Significantly, narrators of captivity narratives insist on the authenticity of their narrative but rely on cultural stereotypes to depict their "unjust" subjugation at the hands of a supposedly inferior culture. Gilroy's Inkle likewise claims that his narrative is factual, but his depictions of the Black Caribs are evidently drawn from the stereotypical imagery of allegedly primitive and barbaric non-Europeans that circulated throughout England and Europe. For example, Gilroy's Inkle tells his readers that when he met Yarico's tribe for the first time the women wore hibiscus flowers in their hair and stood behind the men. When the "headman" stepped forward, two men pushed him to his knees before him. The priest "rattled his gourd," muttered "an incantation," and broke into a "feeble song and a lumbering dance." He then hurled pebbles from his pouch onto the ground in "an act of divination," and drew a circle around the pebbles, "as if he needed more power to interpret the message." It is only when the Chief, who is an African and (thus of course) wears a feathered headdress, a necklace of animal teeth and a piece of puma hide over his shoulders, touches him, that "he is purified and made acceptable to the tribe" (22–23).

Gilroy's Inkle reports that he maintained his conviction that his "civilization" is superior to Yarico's "uncivilized" world and that by teaching "these savages the beautiful cadences" of the English language and its songs" he could "improve the nature of the Carib race to a prodigious extent." But Paiuda, the priest, thought his songs were "warlike chants for calling up spirits to haunt them" and commanded him to stop. As if to further illustrate for his western readership that he is "in the midst of savages," Inkle tells his readers that the men "sat in groups, plucking the hair from their bodies, picking their teeth, grooming the thick, oily thatch on their box-like heads, and exchanging information that would be of no earthly use to civilized men." Although Gilroy's Inkle's attempts to colonize the Caribs are thwarted at every turn, he repeatedly insists that he failed only because the Caribs were "profligate with time and ideas" (27). While Inkle claims he eventually decided that the Caribs were undeserving of his instruction, his demeaning and derogatory descriptions of his captors suggest that he experienced what Joe Snader refers to as the "crisis of identity" that occurs as a consequence of a captive's transformation from the "status of free Briton to the degraded position of slave, commodity, or object" (80). Gilroy's readers can see through Inkle's narrative and, although Inkle claims that the Black Caribs are a "backward tribe of children," it is apparent to the reader that they view him merely as an object Yarico had found and treat him accordingly as a "child or idiot" (28).

Inkle attempts to deal with his confinement by reveling in the freedom of his sexual relations with Yarico and his conviction that she "delighted in my person, my height, my hairy body, which fascinated her, and my manhood" (19). But in actuality Inkle is utterly and completely dependent upon Yarico for his survival. Only as long as she values him will he "be safe" (30). He is constantly "scolded" by Paiuda, whom he refers to as the "irascible" priest, "for violating some rule," and when he asks Chief Tomo to intervene he is informed, "'Paiuda keeps the tribe and sings its songs. You are not yet a man or a warrior. You must obey Paiuda'" (30). Inkle's resentment regarding his subjugation fuels his longing to escape from what he calls "this accursed place" (31). Although Inkle thinks it is Yarico's "duty" to protect him from the "malice" of the Priest, he concurrently realizes that he had "nowhere to go and no other woman could bear [his] hairy body, colourless legs" (39).

In order to deal with the aftershocks of the "identity crisis" he experienced while amongst the Black Caribs, Gilroy's Inkle portrays himself in his captivity narrative as a hero who learned to "play their game" in order to survive (42). One game that he boasts he learned is the Carib ritual of dream interpretation. In celebration of surviving his tribal initiation, Inkle inhales from the smoking pot that the male members of the tribe pass to him. He observes that everyone else seemed fine, but with regard to his own experience he reports: "I was overcome by feelings of the most unspeakable horror. I had truly descended into hell, where grotesque creatures danced and performed mysterious gestures before my eyes." When he awoke, "snakes that became dancing women" sat on his knees. Then Yarico, "wielding a spiked club, slew them all and turned me into a toucan so large, she had to tether me to a tree in the jungle." Inkle tells his readers that he "had seen nothing except the images" but, since it would not have been in his best interest to reveal this, he lied and told the chief, "'I saw you lying dead, old man . . . and then I made you well again'" (58–59).

Inkle's assertion that the hallucinations lack validity indicates his desperate attempt to preserve his sense of himself as culturally superior and suppress his awareness that Yarico and her tribe rule over him. But Inkle is evidently experiencing severe insecurity and anxiety, otherwise he would not have eliminated Yarico altogether from the story he tells the chief. Despite the fantasy of seduction represented by the dancing women on his knees, a mysterious, grotesque, and threatening Yarico demonstrates her power over Inkle in this vision by drawing a weapon and slaying the other women. While Inkle has indeed been "tethered" and emasculated by his Amerindian wife, he makes up a story that prevents his new status as an initiated male from being compromised, and which is utterly self-serving in that it impresses Yarico and makes Chief Tomo beholden to him. He even believes that, consequently, he elevates his status within the tribe. By presenting himself to his readers as a man who successfully manipulated his captors, Inkle attempts to prove that he was not a *willing* participant in Carib culture during his captivity but, rather, an Englishman who maintained his sovereignty throughout the ordeal.

Another game that Inkle claims he learned to play in order to manipulate his captors is the Carib ritual of storytelling:

> Of all the curiosities open to me, I was keen to see the 'House of the Sea Ghosts.' First, I had to let them know of my intention, through a story; and in the best tradition of the folkteller I told them the 'Priest's Tale' from Chaucer and, not caring what they thought of it, I inserted bits of the 'Good Samaritan' and the story of Jonah in the belly of the whale. The silence which followed showed that the sense of magic had won through. I again told my story and agreed with the men that we should move our settlement after they tattooed me with the mark of the condor on the upper arm. It was a painful process, but my English blood sustained me and I did not cry out like a child who is hurt. (59–60)

Rather than make up a story to suit the situation, as members of the tribe would do, Inkle recycles stories from "western" literary history and the Christian Bible. Inkle experiences great pleasure in the production and performance of this hodge-podge of stories simply for the effect he imagines it has on his audience, and he is unaware of the irony (given his lack of morality) that the stories he draws from are all morality tales. Moreover, Inkle interprets the silence that follows his recitation as evidence that a "sense of magic had won through." Thus the event is mediated for eighteenth-century readers by the narrator's cultural arrogance. However, it is evident to Gilroy's readers that the Caribs respond to Inkle's "western" stories by imprinting their culture indelibly upon his skin with a tattoo of the condor, which could mean that they have finally accepted Inkle as a man in the tribe, thus neutralizing cultural hierarchies, or that they have branded him just as European slave traders/owners branded their African slaves. Inkle cannot or will not acknowledge either of these scenarios and simply presents himself to his readers at home as a British hero whose "English blood" enabled him to endure such travails of captivity as corporeal mutilation.

But whether he admits it or not, Gilroy's Inkle eventually becomes a willing participant in Carib culture, although he rationalizes his participation in tribal warfare by explaining that the difference between the Caribs and white men who also seize people is that the Caribs raid for their daily food. Here, Inkle unknowingly criticizes the brutality of European slave traders/ owners. According to Chief Tomo, "We lay no whips upon our people. We don't brand them, nor do we torture them. Death is noble when it comes to war" (62–63). Chief Tomo is clearly referring to what he personally witnessed and experienced as a slave when he was kidnapped and forced to endure the Middle Passage, although he was liberated when pirates attacked the slave ship. But when the Black Caribs invade an Arawak tribe, they find that white men had already been there and taken their men into slavery. Now, Inkle suggests that the Caribs are more, rather than less, brutal than white men when he recounts how the women pleaded to be taken but the Black Caribs refused: "Women must be fought for and won with dried blood on the club and the head of the enemy for a trophy." The failure of the raid resulted in much disharmony in the tribe. The men were angry and disappointed. They blamed Paiuda for misreading his pebbles. Paiuda blamed the length of time he had exposed his pebbles to the Devil. The women—who needed more women to help them with their work—refused to entertain their husbands' attentions. There had to be another, "and this time successful, raid" (63).

So, according to Inkle, the tribe invited the "trusting" Iaruma people to attend a feast and tricked them. The men were either clubbed to death or managed to escape, and the women were all taken captive. Yarico took two women for their household, one of whom was a "sweet and fragile, fawn-like and shy" girl named Zeze. Inkle is so "bewitched" by Zeze that he no longer has any "qualms" about being one of them. He confesses: "At that moment I rejected myself, my body, my heritage . . . I would have her, I reasoned. In my old world she was merely a child. In their world, she was a woman. I would have her" (65). Inkle is well aware that, although polygamy was part of the Black Carib culture, he belonged to Yarico and was prohibited from having another partner. But he cannot control his desire for this girl, who could not have been more than fourteen years of age. He commands her to follow him into the bush, and "took her, gently relishing her virtue, savour- ing her virginity" (67). He tells his readers that, when he took a second wife, the men treated him more as an equal and Chief Tomo told him that he is now "a man." In order to make his pedophilia more palatable for a western readership, he claims that he "courted [Zeze] as I would have done an Eng- lish girl" (68), and that, because of his love for her, she "set me free of my captivity" (69). However, it is only because Inkle has taken a captive of his own and thinks of Zeze as "completely mine" that he feels liberated, and his feelings of utter bliss do not last for long. The tribe brands Zeze a witch and she is soon poisoned. His first son with Yarico, Waiyo, accidentally drinks the poisoned water that Inkle set out for the dog to prove his theory that Zeze was murdered. Then Chief Tomo, with whom Inkle spoke about "enlightened matters," dies.

Although the tribe began to disintegrate after Chief Tomo's death, Inkle and Yarico rekindle their relationship and she becomes pregnant with their second child. Inkle reports that, despite his betrayal, Yarico "followed me faithfully for there was no more faithful creature than a Carib woman" (78). When Inkle is finally rescued, Yarico swims behind the boat and risks drowning in order to accompany him. She rows herself to land in order to give birth and returns to Inkle on her own accord with their newborn child, who with his blond hair and blue eyes is obviously Inkle's son. While Inkle insists that he had never thought of parting with Yarico, when the captain tells him—looking at Yarico and the child—that he will need money to get started and "fate had provided it," he realizes that he "must henceforward look to my advantage" (82). Gilroy's Inkle immediately reverts back to his pre-captivity, imperialist and capitalist mindset and sells Yarico and their child into slavery. He then lies to Yarico by telling her that she will be taken back to the island and her people.

But Gilroy's Yarico is "no fool." According to Inkle, she peered at him "accusingly." Inkle finds himself the object of a gaze that seemed to challenge him "to toy with her soul," and he tells his readers that with "true Carib intuition she knew the truth before Dunbar's slave chained her." Gilroy's Yarico reacts to being sold by constructing her own narrative, which includes not letting anyone enslave her child, whom she tosses into the sea: " . . . she rushed to the full extent of the chain and wrenched the child from her breast . . . she tossed him with a piercing scream into the sea. I watched the surf close over him and knew he was no more" (94). This is one body—and one story of the Atlantic Slave Trade—that neither Inkle, nor any writer or artist in England, will ever put into the service of the empire for the purpose of instructing moral and virtuous British subjects.

In Steele's essay, when the lovers are rescued and the ship carries them into *"English* territories," Inkle "began to seriously reflect upon his loss of time, and to weigh with himself how many days interest of his money had been lost during his stay with *Yarico.* The thought made him pensive, and careful what account he should be able to give his friends of his voyage." Thus in addition to his loss of income, it is concern for how to construct a narrative, an "account," of his encounter with Yarico that compels Inkle to sell her to a Barbadian merchant. The story of recouping his financial losses by selling the pregnant Yarico into slavery is a story he can tell in England and that serves the British empire.

But just as Gilroy's readers can see through her Inkle's attempt to portray himself as a hero and establish an opposition between "civil" and "savage," the British reading public can see that Steele's Inkle is hardly "our hero." Readers of *The Spectator* are instructed via the sentimental language of Steele's essay to recognize that Inkle's behavior with regard to Yarico is utterly reprehensible: the "poor girl, to incline [Inkle] to commiserate her condition, told him that she was with child by him," but Inkle "only made use of that information, to rise in his demands upon the purchaser." When Mr. Spectator claims that he "was so touch'd with this story" that he "left the room with tears" in his eyes, he condemns—and instructs his readers to condemn—Inkle's betrayal of his loyal Amerindian lover.

According to Erin Mackie, Mr. Spectator's "outpouring of compassionate tears" serves to "enlist the reader's sympathy for the virtuous and victimized woman" and "affirm the moral superiority of women" (173). At the same time, this tale sentimentalizes slavery and "disown[s] the brutality and greed of merchants like Inkle" (174). By *de*-sentimentalizing the story and linking Inkle's commercial activities directly to colonialism and slavery, Gilroy reveals that Steele's essay, as Mackie argues, "does not lay a blanket condemnation on commerce per se, as much as it selectively acknowledges and disowns this instance of exploitation as an egregious abuse of commercial and imperial power." Steele's readers joined with Mr. Spectator and Arietta" in their "sentimental censure of Inkle and empathy for Yarico," and were subsequently "reassured that a humane ethical standard is still in place" (174). To read Steele after Gilroy is to acknowledge that the essay's call for a "kinder, gentler approach" to colonialism and slavery does not do justice to the actual atrocities that Britons were committing throughout the empire.

Gilroy's novel thus ultimately serves as a critique of the way periodical essayists in England appropriated stories originating in the New World to reform the sensibilities—even if they are the callous romantic and commercial sensibilities—of English readers. Literatures purporting to be transcriptions of fact, and those such as Steele's in which the narrator claims to be drawing on an eyewitness account, gave individuals a distorted sense of their rights and privileges and malformed their visions of the New World and its peoples. Gilroy's Inkle takes for granted—as if he is reading the world through the lens of such essays as Steele's—that Yarico, the Black Caribs, and his African slaves in Barbados are all racially and culturally inferior, and that he is entitled to exercise what he conceives of as his colonial and racial superiority. Gilroy's Inkle arrived on Yarico's island with a sense of himself as a "master" to be honored and obeyed. Initially, he attempts to "civilize" the Black Caribs by imposing his culture upon them, but to no avail. Although his book of poetry is his most prized possession, they are simply not interested in his "sentiment well expressed" or his songs (27). During the seven years he spends on Yarico's island, Inkle's sense of his cultural superiority is repeatedly undermined. He is physically tortured, such as when the tribe throws him into a pit of red ants and casts him out alone in the forest as part of his initiation ceremony, publicly embarrassed when he fails to understand a tribal ritual or superstition, treated (even by the children) as a child, and emasculated by Yarico. But Inkle never relinquishes his conviction that a "gulf of civilization" (39) exists between Yarico and himself. Inkle suffers severe anxiety and emotional pain as a consequence of his subjugation, alienation and disorientation, but he clings to his cultural arrogance as if his survival depends upon it.

Over time, as Gilroy explains in *Leaves in the Wind*, the "psychosocial baggage of his class" mutates into "resentment, hatred and raging xenophobia." Gilroy's Inkle begins to see himself as a "man robbed of his destiny; a man foiled by the passage of time and opportunity. When he should have become a successful merchant, loving husband and father of children, he had been thrown into a world where time stood still and where natives spurned him" (83). After Inkle sells Yarico into slavery, he attempts to reenter English society on Barbados. Dunbar, the merchant to whom he sold Yarico, takes him to the men's club, where they sit in a paneled room that closely resembles the place where his father had sat with his friends "making bargains and hatching plots to empty other traders' purses" (96). Inkle's reaction to the men at the club seems to suggest that he has undergone considerable transformation: "They seemed a breed of men found wherever others bought, sold or bartered goods or traded in men, women and children as though they were the beasts of the earth . . . They were all kith and kin, white and English with the power of life and death over those they owned and branded on their own" (96). These men are all masters of ships and plantation owners and, having heard of his ordeal, they immediately donate money to help ease the expense of rehabilitating to a "life of ease and comfort" (98). Inkle's rehabilitation is further aided by "the motherly care" of British women who lost their sons to "war or adventure in foreign parts" (98). He eventually settles on his family's plantation and launches a thriving furniture business.

During a trip to St. Lucia to acquire antiques, Inkle reunites with his betrothed Alice, who is now married to Dr. John Clarkson. After recovering from the shock that Inkle is still alive, Alice confesses: "'We are abolitionists. John's Uncle Thomas is, in England, a founder of the cause and under the physician's cloak we gather information attesting to the cruelties endured by slaves'"(126). Inkle, however, is guilty of such atrocities. When he detected unrest on his plantation, he ordered all the troublemakers to be caged, which "meant inserting them in a wooden slatted cage and starving them until they repented or died." One of the first he ordered to be caged was the son of his "most faithful slave, who kept his distance from all trouble" and kept Inkle "informed about affairs in the slave quarters" (139). Even more ruthless, he had ordered the boy to be removed from the cage and "hanged for his father's temerity" (140). Inkle's cruel abuse of his slaves implies that he does not distinguish them from the Caribs, whom he believes stole his life from him, and memories of his captivity fuel his drive for revenge. Although thoughts of Alice were once a lifeline for him, reminding him of the superiority of his nation as well as his upper-class breeding and social status as a wealthy gentleman, as an abolitionist she is a threat to his sense of cultural dominance and British identity as he understands it; Alice is now his enemy.

By introducing Alice and the Clarksons as abolitionists, and by incorporating a direct historical reference to Thomas Clarkson, one of the foremost campaigners against slavery, Gilroy alerts her readers that it is no longer the mid-seventeenth century of Ligon's travelogue, or even the early eighteenth-century publication date of Steele's essay. When Steele wrote his version of Inkle and Yarico, the abolition of the slave trade had not really entered into political debates, although it is evident from *The Spectator No. 11* that Britons were beginning to experience some ambivalence regarding slavery. By the end of the eighteenth century, which is the time period of the latter part of Gilroy's Inkle's narrative, abolitionists had appropriated the tale to exemplify the evils of slavery and Yarico had become a symbol of colonial and sexual exploitation.[6] In 1787, Clarkson was one of the twelve men who formed the Committee for Abolition of the African Slave Trade. Clarkson gathered extensive evidence against the trade, which he passed to William Wilberforce, who used it in parliament as part of his campaign for abolition. Clarkson also made his evidence available to the wider public by writing books and pamphlets. Even after the abolition of the slave trade, Clarkson remained committed to the abolition of slavery around the world and the complete emancipation of the slaves in British colonies. By moving the time period ahead by more than seventy-five years, Gilroy reinforces that her Inkle really did experience the "uncivilized" Carib world as a place where time stood still.

Once Inkle is back in the supposedly "civilized" world, he repeatedly insists that he had never been a "powerless hostage," and had "sought at every turn" to show the Caribs the "superiority" of his nation (143). But with Alice he attempts to solicit sympathy for having been held "captive" by the Caribs. This claim, although purely manipulative on his part, is probably the closest Inkle comes to speaking facts about his life amongst the Caribs, which included subjugation and torture. According to Gilroy, Inkle's position among the Caribs is like that of the slaves on a plantation, and for her "this is the whole point of the book . . . he is a slave" (Bradshaw 393). Inkle is so blinded by his cultural arrogance he cannot see the irony in using his "captivity" as a means to gain Alice's sympathy and convince her of the futility of abolition. He proclaims: "'Oh, Alice! Alice! What is right is what keeps us in our separate places. We are a superior race. We need others lower than ourselves. Irish, Jews, slaves . . . Put such ideas of abolition out to shrivel in the sun'" (126). As the abolitionist movement gains momentum in the West Indies, Inkle's sense of his British identity is further threatened, and he becomes even more emphatic about keeping intact what Morgan refers to in "Encounters between British and indigenous peoples, c. 1500—c. 1800," as the "imagined communities," "constructed associations," "invented traditions" and "manufactured myths" that his sense of Britishness depends upon (45).

When Alice and her husband come to Barbados and visit his plantation, Inkle realizes that he would be nowhere, no one, without slavery. His identity as a white, male, European colonizer and slave trader/owner is dependent upon the abolitionist movement failing, and he views Alice's claim that "all men are brethren" as a betrayal (126). Inkle tells his readers: "My hatred of her sanctimonious airs had turned into a fierce desire for her," and he tries to prove he still holds a position of power by attempting to rape her:

> I dragged her along the path . . . I concentrated on Alice—prim, proper, dressed in clothes as if in armor. What was she hiding? I had roamed around the forest dressed in paint for seven years. I plunged my hand into the neck of her dress and ripped it away from her. I was conscious only of the angry rip and tear of the fabric. I was shredding her clothes as we ripped the leaves off the forest trees. She screamed . . . Then, he snarled at her: 'I will teach you piety . . . I wanted you, waited for you, dreamt of you and now what are you doing? Loving savages as I was forced to do.' (149)

Inkle does not realize that, by attempting to taint Alice, to steal her virtue, he actually compromises his pro-slavery agenda. As Charlotte Sussman explains, "white women living in the Caribbean were supposed to be defined by the same moral engagement with and physical disengagement from economic production as were women in England." Moreover, in order for the hierarchies of plantation society to remain in place, women of African descent and women of European had to remain polar opposites. If Afro-Caribbean women, slaves and free coloured women deserved their oppressed status because of their sexual promiscuity and lack of domestic virtue, as advocates of slavery claimed, then white women had to prove the existence of another kind of femininity, and were represented as passive, asexual and pious. (161)

By stripping Alice of her clothing, Inkle removes the cultural marker that in the eighteenth century distinguished white and black women's physical bodies. In fact, one of the continuities in depictions of sexual encounters between Europeans and natives is that indigenous peoples are often described or represented as naked to signify their lack of civility and cultural inferiority. European colonizers and slave traders/owners subsequently felt justified in sexually exploiting native women and African slaves.[7]

Interestingly, while attacking Alice, Inkle screams, "'You want to be a martyr? To die defending your virtue! You will not succeed! I am the devil.'" (149). The term "the devil" is a term that was used all too frequently and colloquially during the eighteenth century by Europeans in reference to all non-Europeans.[8] By announcing, "I am the devil," Inkle refers to himself with a racial epithet reserved for black males. Gilroy thereby suggests that Inkle is the embodiment of racial myths regarding black men, which include possessing sexual prowess and being predators of white women. In *Black Skin, White Masks*, Fanon writes: "*In Europe, the black man is the symbol of Evil* . . . The torturer is the black man, Satan is black . . . the black man stands for the bad side of the character . . . the Negro is the symbol of sin" (188–189). In addition, by having Inkle refer to himself as a "devil," Gilroy exposes yet another crucial blind spot in Inkle's self-awareness and reiterates that he has been emasculated. Earlier in the narrative, Inkle tells his readers that on the day that his tribal initiation was to begin he took "courage in both hands . . . [and] walked into the forest and carefully hid some rations as well as a hammock in case [he] needed to flee from torturers" (53). When he returns to the compound on the morning of the seventh day, the shaman welcomes him back and tells him, "'They found your bundle. Men do not do such things.'" Inkle tells his readers, "By men, he meant Caribs. I shrugged and said jocularly, 'Inkle is Yawahoo.' (That is, I am a devil.)."[9] Inkle seems to take the shaman's claim that he is not a man lightly, but the point is that he is *not* a man in Carib culture. He has been emasculated in his relationship with Yarico, upon whom he was dependent for his safety and survival, and his cultural practices have been rendered powerless in the presence of theirs.

In the presence of Alice, and by extension the abolitionist movement, Inkle is yet again—and perhaps even more so—emasculated. The attack on Alice, like his violent treatment of his slaves, is evidently a desperate attempt to regain what he imagines is his role as British explorer, conqueror and merchant, whose character and activities were essential aspects of the empire and components of Britishness. Alice had always been for Inkle a "female figure of Britannia" for which he labored. However, according to Kathleen Wilson, "despite the persistence of iconography which symbolized the British imperial presence as the female figure of Britannia, colonial conquest was described and glorified as a *manly* occupation, the proving ground for national, as well as individual, potency, strength, and effectiveness, and vehicle of paternalistic largesse and duty." Moreover, the "basic categories through which the imperial project was valorized (or later in the century denigrated) . . . both reinforced and exaggerated dominant cultural categories of sexual difference. Empire cultivated and bolstered 'manly' characteristics—strength, fortitude, courage, aggression." For Inkle to maintain his identity as an Englishman as he understands it, he must cultivate and demonstrate these "manly" characteristics. If these characteristics are no longer valorized, Inkle becomes a symbol of the "effeminate nation," which is characterized by "cowardice," and "destined for international ignominy and derision." By exhibiting aggressive masculinity in his attack on Alice, Inkle endeavors to counter his effeminacy and be the embodiment of this new "imperial saga," yet another story of the British nation that continued through the nineteenth and into the twentieth centuries (255–256).

But before Gilroy's Inkle can rape Alice, a Carib boy shoots him with a poison arrow. If not for the efforts of the "Spirit Woman," whom the reader recognizes as Yarico and who knew the antidote to the poison, he would have died. But, he will never walk unaided again. The wound is disfiguring and crippling and, like the tattoo, indelible. Yarico, however, is no longer the same either. In fact, Alice had told Inkle during their initial reunion that many years ago they had saved a Carib woman's life and returned her to her island. She never spoke, except to Tim, the Carib boy. "'He said there were stories of sadness in her heart. We never learned her name or whence she had come. She was a beautiful woman, the colour of sapodillas. In the red material she wore around her shoulders she carried a piece of wood carved like a child. Sometimes she whispered a name but no one could decipher it'"(127). How has the Spirit Woman, or Yarico, come to Inkle's plantation? She was saved from the sea, "'but was so famished and distracted she lost her mind—exchanged it with the sea spirits for her life, so she puts it'" (151). To Inkle, she seems familiar but "too old and broken" to be Yarico (148).

Nonetheless, this woman (who *is* Yarico) saves his life and Gilroy once again dramatizes the lesson of Steele's moral prose essay, which is that Yarico exemplifies loyalty, constancy, and above all else, virtue. The Carib boy who shoots Inkle with the poison arrow is from the same tribe as the Spirit Woman, and is certain "that in another life [Inkle] poisoned his friend called Waiyo," Inkle's first son with Yarico. But Inkle lies, and "muttered, as if calling up a ghost, 'Waiyo . . . I did not know him. Tim is mistaken'" (150). But Tim has already recognized the tattoo, the condor of the forest Caribs, on Inkle's body. Although Inkle lies to his white, European friends and to the western readers of his captivity narrative, his body speaks the truth, which is that he participated in Carib culture and they wielded power over him, just like the scars on the bodies of the slaves serve as evidence of the torture inflicted upon them by white masters. Through the narrative she constructs for Inkle, Gilroy exposes that, as a consequence of his encounter with the Caribs, his psyche (like his body) is permanently damaged.

At the same time, Inkle's captivity narrative reflects Snader's assertion that captivity authors "assumed that the Christian cultures of northwestern Europe shared common bonds of civility that separated them fundamentally from non-European cultures" (66). Because former captives "reconstructed their experiences in alien cultures for homeland audiences," they often represented their captivity as a "national struggle, with the captive acting as a representative of the homeland, and his or her captors acting as representatives, not only of particular alien culture, but also of alien cultures in general" (63). Inkle likewise produces his narrative to rectify what he, and what he imagines his western readers, would consider a violation of the imagined hierarchy that placed western above non-western cultures.

***

By transforming Steele's essay into a captivity narrative, and by *de*-sentimentalizing this now mythic, trans-cultural, romantic encounter, Gilroy reminds her readers that it was the place of this story "in the literature of false love and sentiment" that "enhanced its popularity and psychological implications for the nations of Europe" (*Leaves in the Wind* 77). According to John Mullan, in the early eighteenth century the word "sentimental" became a word for a type of text that "promised an *occasion* for fine feeling. This fine feeling could be experienced by both the characters in a narrative and the reader of that narrative" (238). Literature of sentiment is fundamentally moral and rational *and* it encourages moral and rational behavior in the reader. As I discuss above, Steele utilizes such sentimental tropes as Mr. Spectator's tears to solicit compassion for Inkle's brutal betrayal of Yarico in the arena of love, which in turn invites readers to critique Inkle's callous commercialism and betrayal of Yarico. Devoted readers of *The Spectator* would already be familiar with Mr. Spectator's stance on violations of the heart, which he had previously articulated in *The Spectator No. 6*:[10]

> . . . love, during the time of my speculations, shall be carried on with the same sincerity as any other affair of less consideration. As this is the greatest concern, men shall be from henceforth liable to the greatest reproach for misbehavior in it. Falsehood in love shall hereafter bear a blacker aspect than infidelity in friendship, or villany in business. For this great and good end, all breaches against that noble passion, the cement of society, shall be severely examined.

In *The Spectator No. 11*, Steele (via Mr. Spectator) serves up Inkle as an example of "[f]alsehood in love" to English society for examination and judgment, and to teach his readers about virtue.

Similarly, as Markman Ellis explains, the sentimental novel was a "recognized agent for the dissemination of argument and advice," and reading sentimental fiction was to be an "improving exercise, refining the manners by exercising the ability to feel for others" (16–17). Yet as Nancy Armstrong argues, English domestic fiction "adapted the colonial paradigm of captivity narratives for its national purposes." She prefaces her discussion of the inherent relation between captivity narratives and the sentimental novel by pointing out that, during the same period when Samuel Richardson's *Clarissa* and *Pamela* were "enthralling" European readers, accounts of Europeans held captive in America "flooded" into England from the colonies. "English readers consumed these captivity narratives almost as avidly as they did sentimental fiction, and they consequently knew exactly what kind of story would ensue once they recognized it as the testimony of a captive woman."[11] Just as Armstrong contends that the captivity narrative genre "provided the principle of continuity consolidating Richardson, Jane Austen, and Charlotte Bronte as a single literary tradition" (373), Michelle Burnham determines that captivity narratives and eighteenth-century sentimental novels operate within a "system of imaginative exchange" and "develop within a context of other exchanges across cultural, national, and continental boundaries." In fact, the "exchanges and transgressions within and between these two genres are fundamental." Significantly, both novelistic discourse and nationalist discourse rely on the "profoundly affective experience of sympathy" (49). By having her Inkle produce a captivity narrative that endeavors to invoke the sympathies of an imagined community of *English* readers and contains some of the fundamental elements of a sentimental novel, Gilroy illustrates the recent critical analyses regarding the interconnectedness of these superficially distinct genres, both of which portray and thereby disseminate the fantasy of a homogenous Christian and English community by insisting on their captors' difference.

However, as Burnham concludes, "what the novel and the nation most deeply share" are "ambivalent relations between subjects who are, in fact, not alike" (70). By using the novel herself to critique the ways in which the novel served nationalist and imperialist agendas, Gilroy reinforces Burnham's claim that the heteroglossia which, for Mikhail Bakhtin, characterizes novelistic discourse is both an "internal characteristic of the genre" and an "external condition for its production: novels appear out of the exchanges that take place across the zones of contact where cultures and nations chaotically cross" (63). Deidre Lynch and William B. Warner comparably propose in their introduction to *Cultural Institutions of the Novel* that it is precisely because the novel is "neither a Western invention nor a Western franchise" that novels "serve as a nexus of transnational exchange." In fact, the essays in this collection challenge literary histories that view the novel as a "new type of narrative" invented in seventeenth-century Spain or France, or eighteenth-century Britain, and such sequels as those that "recount how the novel then disseminates its form and idea outward to the peripheries of the European empires, producing new inflections of the original paradigm." Rather than an Enlightenment narrative of the novel's vertical "rise," the essays in this collection develop "narratives of novels' horizontal displacements," and revise accounts of the "rise of the novel" by tracking the novel "within and between nations, and backwards in time" (4–5).

Gilroy takes a similar approach to the early eighteenth-century periodical essays produced by Addison and Steele, which can be considered precursors to the novel, were often adaptations and transformations of stories originating abroad or in the New World and, like sentimental novels, were designed to instruct and shape a moral and virtuous British reading public. However, in order to fully comprehend how Gilroy's *Inkle and Yarico* functions as a commentary on the periodical press, it is necessary to trace developments in the form from its introduction by Defoe, whose *The Review* (1704–1713) reflects the encounter between global and local forces that epitomizes the early eighteenth-century periodical press. Defoe infused a personality (Mr. Review) into his essays, and in doing so he created the prototype for the periodical essay that would be adopted and further developed by Addison and Steele.

Stylistically, the *Review* differed from newspapers because Defoe chose not to imitate their supposedly factual approach, but rather, to offer a running commentary on important foreign and local affairs. According to Arthur

Wellesley Secord, the *Review* was a "journal of opinion—a commentary, which taught the masses of Queen's Anne's reign *what to think* upon important political and social questions" (xv). The initial title of Defoe's *Review* advertises that the publication is a compilation of the global and the local:

> A Review of the Affairs of France: And of all Europe, as Influenc'd by that Nation; Being, Historical Observations, on the Public Transactions of the WORLD; Purg'd from the Errors and Partiality of *News-Writers*, and *Petty-Statesmen* of all Sides. With an Entertaining Part in every Sheet, Being, Advice from the Scandal Club, to the Curious Enquirers; in Answer to letters sent them for that Purpose.

Defoe's *Review* was not only the first long-running editorial on foreign affairs, but with it Defoe brought the "WORLD" to London. Anglo-French warfare (1689–1815), the *Review*'s primary concern, was a global affair. Both France and England had overseas possessions in North America, the Caribbean and India, and the European power struggle over these possessions evolved into a series of world wars as each tried to extend its empire at the expense of the other. At stake were extremely valuable trades: West Indian sugar, African slaves, Indian silks and spices, American furs and fish. These were maritime wars, in which the exercise of sea power played an ever-increasing part in deciding the eventual outcome.

Throughout its publication, the *Review* consisted of a principal essay on such global activities as Marlborough's battles against the French, the English-Scottish Union, trade in China, the War of Spanish Succession, African trade, the slave trade and the Treaty of Utrecht. Defoe distinguished his publication from newspapers by acting on his awareness that readers needed more than accounts of the news; they needed to be told what, and how, to think of them. Perhaps more significant, English readers needed to be told how to understand themselves—their individual, national and cultural identities—in relation to world events. Although Defoe situated himself as an interpreter of foreign affairs, the tradesmen in him must have known that this in and of itself would not be enough to keep the paper afloat. Defoe seduced readers into purchasing the paper and reading his editorials on foreign affairs by appealing to their local, social concerns. In his "Advice from the Scandal Club" column, Defoe answered letters from readers, both real and fiction, and provided social commentary.[12] In the Preface to Volume 1, Defoe explains that the subjects he chose for his column served to "exalt Virtue, expose Vice, promote Truth, and help men to serious Reflection," and thus one might argue that he is as much the father of the didactic periodical essay as he is the father of the English novel.

When *The Tatler* appeared on 12 April 1709, Defoe declared it "a continuation of his efforts at social instruction" (Secord, xx). Addison and Steele's motive for starting *The Tatler*, according to their Dedication, similarly stemmed from the "desire to improve his fellow-creatures" and "enlighten, as well as entertain," his "fellow-talkers."[13] The thrice-weekly *Tatler* was dedicated to the reformation of manners and morals, and the "general Purpose of this Paper, is to expose the false Arts of life, to pull off the Disguises of Cunning, Vanity and Affectation, and to recommend a general simplicity in our Dress, our Discourse, and our Behavior." Like Defoe, Addison and Steele set out to give the "most trustworthy foreign news" and to tell those who participated in coffeehouse discussions what to think about matters "which occupied this discursive and critical generation." Yet with the publication of *The Tatler* the form of the periodical essay experienced a metamorphosis. Whereas Defoe established himself as an advisor or guide for the reading public by injecting his own personality, Addison and Steele set out to instruct the public through, or behind the mask of, their fictional persona Isaac Bickerstaff.

Moreover, whereas Defoe's *Review* consisted of an essay on foreign affairs and a separate column relating to social observation and moral instruction, Addison and Steele's periodical consisted of a single-essay format. What is particularly notable is the way in which they adopted, with a twist, Defoe's foreign correspondence format. In *The Tatler No. 1*, Bickerstaff introduces himself as a foreign correspondent who will report from different "regions," or rather, different London coffeehouses.[14] While Defoe reigns in the world by reporting on global news, Addison and Steele collapse the discourse of the global and the local. The essays in *The Tatler* can be divided, and dated, according to their subjects from particular coffeehouses. One subject, "Accounts of Gallantry, Pleasure, and Entertainment," would be from White's Chocolate House, a locale popular with men of fashion. Another subject, poetry, would be from Will's Coffeehouse, the gathering place of literary gentlemen. All "Foreign and Domestic News" would be from St. James Coffeehouse. The first bit of news from St. James to be included in *The Tatler* was about The Hague, which was at the time a major arena in England's war with France. According to Bickerstaff, "any other subject" would be from "my own Apartment." In other words, he pretends to be traveling the world, but in fact Bickerstaff never leaves London or, for some stories, even his own home.

The Tatler thus followed the traditions first established by Defoe, such as an editorializing spokesperson and the convergence of news and miscellany. But by intertwining the foreign and the domestic in one essay, Addison and Steele entirely collapse Defoe's categorizations and set in motion the second generation of the English periodical essay. Also unlike Defoe's *Review*, for *The Tatler* (and later *The Spectator*), "social improvement was central from the start." According to Roy Porter, both publications "brought enlightened views and values to the pubic at large, polishing manners, popularizing the new philosophy and refining tastes. By splicing dramatized scenes with moral chats and readers' correspondence, genuine and fictitious, a collusive sense of shared superiority was forged through the medium of the daily essay" (80). In the process of collapsing the global and the local, and intermingling such diverse generic forms as news, fiction, dialogues and gossip, Addison and Steele created a medium that bridged the gap between public and private realms, and dissolved factual distinctions between home and abroad. Moreover, Addison and Steele's essays operated as tools for promoting a collective sense of British moral, intellectual and cultural superiority. It no longer mattered whether instruction was disseminated through foreign or domestic news, or via reports of actual events or fictions, as long as the essay served the didactic purpose of shaping and constructing British subjects, or Britishness. With their second periodical, *The Spectator*, Addison and Steele took the development of the periodical essay as a didactic tool even further by dropping, as Mackie points out, "those reports of current political, military, and financial" news and producing mostly "self-contained, thematically, unified essays," which allowed *The Spectator* more scope for "sociocultural and ethical criticism" (2). But according J. A. Downie and Thomas N. Corns, although Addison and Steele pretended that they were excluding politics from the pages of their papers, what "they were actually involved with was the evolution of a more sophisticated method of influencing their readers' political preconceptions" (3): one that was much more covert.

In *The Spectator No. 6*, Mr. Spectator addresses the lack of morality he has observed in England by stating that the "most polite Age is in danger of being the most vicious," and the "affectation of being gay and in fashion has very near eaten up our good sense and religion." In *The Spectator No. 10*, Mr. Spectator establishes himself as a divinely-sanctioned, sociocultural critic by claiming that there may be "about Three-Score thousand Disciples in *London and Westminster*, who I hope will take care to distinguish themselves from the thoughtless Herd of their ignorant and unattentive Brethren."[15] More simply, those who read *The Spectator* are his disciples, and those who do not are part of the "thoughtless herd." Mr. Spectator implicitly positions himself as an omniscient figure whose moral tales and instructions regarding virtue will lead English readers to salvation. Perhaps even more significant is Mr. Spectator's assertion that his observations and instructions are for "every one that considers the World as a Theatre, and desires to form a right Judgment of those are the Actors in it." No reader is left unsolicited, not even those whom Mr. Spectator refers to as the "Blanks of Society," or those who are "altogether unfurnished with Ideas . . . until they have been given them." He entreats these readers in particular not to "stir out of the Chambers till they have read this paper."

However, while it seems that no member of society is left unsolicited and that all are welcome in this community of readers, a hierarchy of readers is certainly implied here. Jürgen Habermas has argued that the early periodical press in general, and *The Tatler* and *The Spectator* in particular, were vital participants in the creation of a "public sphere," a place for public debate and a counter-force to absolutism. In *The Structural Transformation of the Public Sphere*, Habermas explains that in *The Tatler*, *The Spectator*, and the *Guardian* "the public held up a mirror to itself . . . The public that read and debated this sort of thing read and debated about its self" (43). While the bourgeois public sphere was, in a sense, brought into being by publication or print culture, Michael Warner points out that "*persons* read and debated this sort of thing," and "in reading and debating it *as* a public, they adopted a very special rhetoric about their own personhood." Significantly, the "subject who could master this rhetoric in the bourgeois public sphere was, implicitly, even explicitly, white, male, literate and propertied" (382). Although the public sphere encodes itself "through the themes of universality, openness, meritocracy, and access," and supposes, "all particularities have the same status," it "has been structured from the outset by a logic of abstraction" that privileges whiteness and maleness (383–384). In the early eighteenth century, the Inkle of Steele's *Spectator No. 11*—white, male, literate and propertied—was literally a mirror of this (exclusive) public sphere.

At the same time, Inkle exemplifies Mr. Spectator's observation in *Spectator No. 6* that the "most polite Age is in danger of being the most vicious." With her revision of Steele's essay, Gilroy illustrates John Brewer's assertion that such essays

> reflect the tension between efforts to create a culture that was polite, moderate, reasonable, morally instructive, decorous and restrained . . . and the palpable intrusion of impulses—notably sexual passion and pecuniary greed—which were Rabelaisian and commercial and which undercut the claim that culture could and should be impartial, disinterested, dispassionate, and virtuous. (342)

Steele's Inkle's father "had taken particular care to instill in him at an early age a love of gain by making him a perfect master of numbers, consequently giving him a quick view of loss and advantage, and *preventing the natural impulses of his passions* [my emphasis], by prepossession towards his interests." But Inkle, like the public sphere he represents or mirrors, cannot control his sexual passions and material greed. While Steele's readers were seemingly assured that an ethical standard is maintained by joining with Arietta and Mr. Spectator in their indirect reproach of Inkle via sympathy for Yarico, for Gilroy's readers the question remains regarding the efficacy of sentimentalism and fictitious abstractions—Mr. Spectator, a community of readers, etc.—as modes of social critique. In fact, with her depiction of Inkle, Gilroy exposes that, despite Addison and Steele's best intentions, their attempt to reform society via commercialized sentimentalism failed.

In the process of commenting on the efficacy of sentimentalism and fictional abstractions as a means to enlighten the reading public, Gilroy also critiques the practice of utilizing and transforming stories that originated in the New World as a means of educating those at home. In Steele's essay, Arietta's claims to historicity lend credibility to the tale, bolster Steele's authority, and set the stage for what the reader would presume is a presentation of "factual" information about Barbados, one of England's most popular and wealthiest colonies. Arietta begins her rebuttal to the story of the *Ephesian Matron* by saying: "I was the other day amusing myself with *Ligon's* Account of *Barbadoes*; and, in Answer to your well-wrought Tale, I will give you (as it dwells upon Memory) out of that honest Traveller, in his fifty-fifth page, the History of *Inkle and Yarico*."[16] According to Arietta, she is merely repeating what Ligon, a first-hand witness, already reported. But as Kathleen Brown observes in "Native Americans and early modern concepts of race," Ligon's text is *already* an embellishment of the facts because his depictions of African and Amerindian women are subjective. Brown observes that Ligon's allegedly *True and Exact History of the Island of Barbados* contains several candid accounts of the author's erotic interest in three African women on the island of St. Jago, part of the Cape Verde island.[17] Ligon's depiction of the Indian maiden Yarico is also sexualized: "We had an *Indian* woman, a slave in the house, who was of excellent shape and color, for it was a pure bright bay; small breasts, with the nipples of a porphyry colour; this woman could not be woo'd by any means to wear clothes."[18]

With her revision of Inkle and Yarico, Gilroy exposes that Steele was not only reliant on such travelers as Ligon for images and stories of the New World but he also adapted these subjective, and therefore contaminated, images and stories for his periodical essays.[19] For example, Gilroy's Inkle sees Yarico as "voluptuous" and "tantalizing" (17), but determines that she had an "unfamiliarity with modesty as I knew it. It was *that* most of all which set her apart in my mind as being of a civilization inferior to my own" (18). Moreover, Inkle views her as "pure instinct, for to survive in her world, to be at one with Nature's rhythms and to heed its customs, there was no place for thought and reason" (20). Gilroy's Inkle's thoughts and observations are evidently informed by such representations of indigenous peoples as Steele's, in which Yarico is the native "Other" against which the European compares himself: "If the *European* was highly charmed with the limbs, features, and wild graces of the naked *American*; the *American* was no less taken with the dress, complexion and shape of a *European*, covered from head to foot." According, to Pratt, this "eroticized vocabulary of nakedness, embellishment, dress and undress introduced the desires of readers into the discussion" (87). Yarico is for Inkle, and readers of *The Spectator*, an Eve in Eden and an object of sexual desire. Frank Felsenstein proposes that Inkle's "intrusion into her 'lost' world is at once an apt metaphor for European conquest of the primordial native and also a temporary release for him from the social taboos and inhibitions that belong to his own culture" (7). Moreover, Yarico embodies the eighteenth-century myth of the "noble savage." She visits Inkle every day in a different dress of beautiful shells and glass beads and decorates his cave with luxurious animal skins and richly colored feathers.[20] By saturating her Inkle's description of Yarico with sexual desire and having her Inkle think of Yarico as "Nature's child," Gilroy draws attention to how Steele's essay (like Ligon's *History*) served to perpetuate such prevailing myths about New World peoples as rampant nakedness, promiscuity and noble savagery, all of which contributed to legitimizing colonialism, slavery and sexual exploitation. [21]

Despite the fantasies of uninhibited sexuality that Inkle's sexual liaison with Yarico may have evoked in readers, and despite the compassion that the betrayed Yarico's "noble" status invokes, Steele conveys through his descriptions of Yarico's appearance and actions that she is to be considered inferior, and viewed as a servant, domestic, or even a subservient English wife. Yarico protects Inkle from her "countrymen," feeds him, quenches his thirst, brings him "a great many spoils," and is wholly devoted to attending to his every need. As Gilroy reiterates in her novel, whether or not Inkle acknowledges it he is reliant upon Yarico for his livelihood and safety. However, Steele's Inkle rules over Yarico nonetheless by instructing her to watch for ships and signal to the one she spots off the coast. Moreover, Steele's Inkle's use of language is a marker (for eighteenth-century readers) of his cultural superiority. For example, Inkle tells Yarico he would be happy to take her to his country, "where she should be clothed in such silks as his waistcoat was made of, and be carried in houses drawn by horses without being exposed to wind and weather." According to Felsenstein, Inkle's amusing description of carriages as "houses drawn by horses" suggests that Inkle "deliberately talks down or pidginizes language to make himself understood by Yarico." Inkle may be the object of Steele's criticism because of his heartless commercialism, but through Steele's mode of storytelling his English readers are instructed to identify with Inkle's subject position and understand their culture and national identity as superior *in relation to* the primitive and illiterate Yarico (3).

By portraying Inkle as an Englishman who can only understand his identity in relation to Yarico and her tribe, Gilroy draws attention to the fact that Steele's Inkle and his English readers defined themselves in relation or opposition to the "Other." As Colley argues in *Britons*, after 1707 the British came to define themselves as a single people not because of any political or cultural consensus at home, but rather in reaction to the Other beyond their shores."[22] This sense of "common identity" did not come into being because of "an integration and homogenization of disparate cultures. Instead, British-ness was superimposed over an array of internal differences in response to contact with the Other, and above all in response to conflict with the Other" (6). In addition, as Morgan discusses in "Encounters between British and 'indigenous' peoples, c. 1500-c. 1800," because the Briton's "sense of self" was "rooted in a collective consciousness of 'us' versus 'them,'" and because neither "'we'" nor "'they'" are ever fixed, there could "never be a single, uni-tary, or monolithic British encounter with indigenous people" (44–45). Moreover, by the eighteenth century none of the major Native American societies that interacted with the British had existed a century earlier. "Each was an amalgam of survivors, refugees, and war captives produced by demo-graphic and military upheavals." The point is that, although these new iden-tities "arose in part from attempts to control and exploit, history was not made by the colonial masters alone." Africans and indigenous peoples "con-structed their own heritages, sometimes subverting and sabotaging the classi-fications imposed upon them, sometimes ignoring them altogether" (48). In other words, while white Britons rarely differentiated between non-western racial, ethnic or cultural groups, mixed or hybrid identities were forming around the globe and a variety of peoples were asserting their agency in the face of European colonialism and slavery.

By transforming the Indians of Steele's essay into a tribe of Black Car-ibs, Gilroy draws attention to the historical intermingling of Indians and Africans and the moment in history when these Black Caribs were resisting European oppression. Peter Hulme and Neil L. Whitehead explain in *Wild Majesty* that the Black Caribs, known as the Garifuna, had their origins in the early sixteenth century as a consequence of a wrecked slave ship or two, which may or may not have been Spanish. The surviving Africans, as well as escaped slaves from Barbados and some of the islands to the north, inter-married with the Carib population on St. Vincent. The Black Caribs and the so-called Red Caribs were two distinct but flourishing groups, although the Black Caribs were a much larger group. The British wanted to take the lands held primarily by the Black Caribs for sugar cane plantations, and in the late 1700s two wars were fought against the Caribs. In 1763, the Black Caribs and Red Caribs joined forces and prevented both the English and the French from taking over the island. However, the British eventually defeated the Caribs in the Second Carib War (1795–1796), and in 1797 the survivors were forcibly removed and exiled to the island of Roatan just off the coast of Honduras and in other parts of Central America.[23] Today, the Black Caribs celebrate their history and honor the heroes of the Second Carib War.

***

By exposing the psychological operations of the early eighteenth-century merchant-class male who got his name from Steele, Gilroy illustrates that, as with any other social and/or cultural identity, Britishness was always a "fragile and contested ideology of power" (Bayly 19). Inkle's final state-ment is, significantly, directed to his readers and utterly ambiguous: "As for Yarico, what is she now in my scheme of things? I cannot tell! I cannot tell!" (157). Is Inkle suggesting he *does not know* how Yarico has affected him and the narrative he produced? Or, does his declaration imply that he *will not* or *cannot* articulate the profound influence Yarico has had on the construction of his narrative and the *de*stabilization of his sense of Britishness? According to Gilroy's analysis of her own literary creation, by the end of the narrative Inkle is so "transformed by his experience with black people [that] he doesn't even know himself. His identity is zilch, gone" (Bradshaw 394). Indeed, it is apparent to the reader that at the end of the narrative Inkle is haunted by memories of Yarico and that, both literally and figuratively, he is a broken man. His sense of Britishness as a stable or fixed identity has not only been contested, it has become unhinged.

In the last interview before her death in 2001, Gilroy told Roxann Bradshaw, "When I write, I have a plan which is always an ethno-psychologi-cal plan, and in this plan I try to discuss experiencing identity. What identity is, and how we experience it, both emotionally and within a social group" (382). Gilroy usually writes about black women's oppression, in and out of slavery, contemporary and historical, and her work has served to teach peo-ple about the experiences of the oppressed, alienated and abandoned. In her other fiction, she gets into the minds of the aged (*Frangipani House*, 1986) and the young (*Boy Sandwich*, 1989). Inkle, who is British, white, male, and wealthy, seems an unlikely protagonist for her. But as Gilroy explains, Inkle "is not the model of a person," he is a model of different philosophies regarding black people, such as phrenology, theology, anthropology, social Darwinism, anglosaxonism and ethnology. As a friend of Gilroy's noted, Inkle "doesn't represent people . . . he represents a whole set of eighteenth-century beliefs about black people" (Bradshaw 392). When Gilroy arrived in London in 1951, she came face to face with a city and country full of Inkles who viewed foreigners as "sojourners, visibly and pathologically different."[24] Gilroy writes that the stereotypical identities thrust upon migrants "bore no relation" to their actual "feelings or interior lives," but they nonetheless contained the "crucial strands of an identity that had been historically constructed" for them. Gilroy subsequently realized that "Black people in a racist society are two people: the face and the real person who must exist in society" (*Leaves in the Wind* 4).

Gilroy persevered in the face of the racism and xenophobia she encountered in London and started a teaching career in 1953, earning the same year an advanced diploma in child development. In 1956, Gilroy acquired a bachelor's degree in psychology, with a specialization in ethno-psychology that she continued to pursue through both her 1979 Master's degree and 1987 Ph.D. in counseling psychology.[25] Gilroy also worked extensively with immigrant children and devoted herself to designing multicultural and remedial education plans, and she wrote school textbooks to "kill off the Eurocentric books foisted upon the children in order to set their places in the slurry at the base of the pyramid of achievement" (*Leaves in the Wind* 153). Gilroy's personal experiences with racism and work in ethno-psychology taught her that "Colour prejudice," which was the term used in the mid-twentieth century, "has many faces and in some people it is tucked away in a place of impenetrable darkness, emerging only to glow with irrational hate at the prospect of an encounter with someone different in creed, class and especially race." Another "face" of racism is Inkle, whose attitudes toward and beliefs regarding non-Europeans are extremely visible and dictate his actions. With the narrative she constructs for Inkle, Gilroy explores the psychology of racism that is as relevant today as for the eighteenth-century, and illustrates that racists are "unmindful of experience and bondaged by power-needs and ethnic falsehoods" (38). Gilroy's Inkle fails to learn from his experiences among the Caribs and, upon returning to England, he marries an aristocratic Englishwoman to perhaps cleanse himself of miscegenation, and devotes himself to the *anti*-abolitionist cause, perhaps to reenergize his sense of cultural supremacy or Britishness.

For Gilroy, it would have seemed as though little had changed when she arrived in England just after WWII. According to Winston James, the plight of black migrants might have been "less harrowing and prolonged had the British authorities taken measures to condemn and proscribe racist practices in the country." While the Pan-African Federation and the Pan African Congress had called for such measures as early as 1945, both Labour and Conservative governments refused to take action. Indeed, the Conservatives, from Churchill to Thatcher, were "far more interested in inflaming public opinion against black people rather than combating racism." Only after the 1958 riots did the Labour Party give serious consideration to anti-discrimination legislation, which yielded the "virtually toothless" Race Relations Act of 1965. The Race Relations Board was established to administer the Act, but even after it was strengthened in 1976 it was "too weak and far too late, given the urgency and seriousness of black people's suffering" (376–377).

As a member of the North Metropolitan Committee of the Race Relations Board, Gilroy dealt with blatant racism and helped create opportunities. But, as she explains in "Waltzing Across Four and Half Decades," today "economic racism has become subterranean." Racism "must be provable, and the only way to do this would be to place surveillance cameras where blacks are "negated, sedimented and persecuted each day 'just for fun'" (38). Thus one might argue that racism in the twentieth and twenty-first centuries is not unlike eighteenth-century ethnocentrism, just less visible.

Chapter Two

Novel Poetics and Pantomimes

Derek Walcott's Crusoe poems, *Pantomime*, and Daniel Defoe's *Robinson Crusoe*

Defoe's *Robinson Crusoe* appeared eight years after Steele's *Spectator No. 11* and, according to Catherine E. Moore, it is conceivable that "Defoe's imagination would have responded to and his memory stored away the little anecdote which appeared in the *Spectator.*" While Moore's suggestion that Defoe was influenced by Steele's essay is purely speculative, the similarities between Inkle and Crusoe cannot be ignored. Both are third sons of prominent families and young merchants seeking to improve their fortunes by participating in global commerce, and both are representative western males in their lust for power, control and profit.[1] In the beginning of Defoe's novel, Crusoe experiences his first mishap at sea and is imprisoned by pirates. While Crusoe eventually escapes from slavery with the help of Xury, a young *Moor*, he callously betrays Xury's loyalty by selling him to a Portuguese sea captain. Xury and Yarico differ in race and gender, but there is nevertheless a thematic similarity between these two anecdotes in that both Xury and Yarico are considered "savages" and treated as commodities by the Christian Englishmen whose lives they helped to preserve.[2] But unlike Gilroy, who transforms a periodical essay into a first-person captivity narrative to attack the sense of Britishness that contributed to, even enabled, colonial brutality, Walcott transforms Defoe's (Crusoe's) first-person narrative into verse and a dramatic work, thereby forcing two distinct reinterpretations of the figure of Crusoe, whom literary critics traditionally read as one of the first colonial minds in English fiction.

In his Crusoe poems, published in the mid-1960s, Walcott adopts Crusoe as a symbol of artistic isolation and highlights the moment that Crusoe the craftsman/artisan becomes Crusoe the writer and "saves his sanity" by writing a journal, which for Walcott is the first West Indian novel. But as Isidore Okpewho points out, although the figure of Crusoe served Walcott's early conception of the Caribbean artist "struggling to fashion something out of the apparent cultural vacuum in which he has been marooned," the figure itself—"derived as it is from a classic work of colonial fiction—comes saddled with a curious political baggage" that is not easily reconciled. Walcott invests so much in the figure of Crusoe as a "prototype of the Caribbean creative imagination"—"a focal point hardly redeemed by his equation with Columbus, Adam, even God"—that the "radical reader soon flinches" at what John Thieme refers to as the writer's "continued wrestling-match with European discourses" (44).[3]

The "excesses of the figuration" seem to have eventually dawned on Walcott, who revisited *Robinson Crusoe* in an entirely different way with his two-man play *Pantomime*, first performed in 1979. In this modernized variation of the personal relationship between Crusoe and Friday, which takes place on the island of Tobago, Walcott presents a white English hotel manager (Harry Trewe) and a local black employee (Jackson Philip) whose verbal jousting seemingly leads to, if not the dissolution of, a diminishing of their racial, class and economic differences. While postcolonial theorists typically view the Crusoe/Friday relationship as analogous to the colonizer's domination of the colonized and emblematic of Christianizing cannibals and converting people from "savagery," with *Pantomime* Walcott invites his readers and viewers to reinterpret this relationship as one that transcends colonizer/colonized and master/slave dichotomies.

Significantly, it is because Walcott's Harry and Jackson are rehearsing an English pantomime of *Robinson Crusoe* that an emotional bond develops between them and the roles of colonizer/colonized and master/slave are potentially neutralized. Walcott's play *Pantomime* subsequently functions as a commentary on the transformative and liberating potential inherent in the generic form of pantomime itself. While there is no evidence that Walcott is pointedly engaging with eighteenth-century English pantomimes, by revisiting the first pantomime of Robinson Crusoe to appear on a London stage, Richard Brinsley Sheridan's *Robinson Crusoe, or Harlequin Friday* (1781), through Walcott's *Pantomime* it is possible to (re)interpret this production as an example of theatricality and improvisation that allowed for the presentation—even celebration—of the possibility of transforming the material conditions of black peoples and race relations.

***

Walcott was born in the town of Castries, the capital of St. Lucia. Both of Walcott's grandmothers were said to have been the descendents of slaves, and both of his grandfathers were white. His father, a civil servant, painter and poet, died when Walcott and his twin brother, Roderick, were about a year old. His mother, a schoolteacher, was headmistress of the Methodist grammar school in Castries. Though his first language was a French-English patois, Walcott received an English education, which his mother encouraged by reciting English poetry at home and by introducing her children to European classics at an early age. After studying at St. Mary's College in St. Lucia, Walcott received a scholarship to study at the University of the West Indies in Jamaica, where he finished his degree in 1953. From 1953 to 1957 he worked as a teacher at schools on several Caribbean islands. In 1958 he accepted a Rockefeller fellowship to study theatre in New York, but in 1959 he returned to the Caribbean after discovering that there were few opportunities for black playwrights in the United States. That same year, Walcott embarked on a career as a journalist writing features for the Kingston *Public Guardian* and Trinidad *Guardian*, and he founded the Little Carib Theatre in Port of Spain, later the Trinidad Theatre Workshop, which produced many of his plays.[4]

But it was Walcott's poetry that initially earned him international acclaim. Although he arranged for his first collection of poetry, *25 Poems*, to be privately printed in 1948 when he was just eighteen years old, most critics consider *In a Green Night: Poems 1948–60* (1962) his breakthrough. According to Laurence A. Breiner, Walcott is the "first poet produced in some sense by the West Indies" (98). He was educated not abroad but at the University of West Indies in Jamaica, after which he took up residence in Trinidad. He published three volumes locally in three different colonies before Cambridge University Press introduced him to the English-speaking world at large. As Robert D. Hamner notes, Walcott rose from "colonial obscurity to international prominence as a direct result of his ability to assimilate and express the disparate elements of a rich social milieu" (2). Walcott's writings reflect the histories of slavery and indentured servitude and, along with these histories, the intermingling of European, African, Asian and Oriental languages and cultures. Patti Hartigan appropriately describes Walcott as a "man of many cultures, a polyglot of African, colonialist and Caribbean traditions, a self-described 'mulatto of styles.'"[5]

Walcott does, however, write in English, and in an interview with Edward Hirsch he declared that the English language is the "property of the imagination: it is the property of language itself." When asked how he thinks of himself and his own work in relation to "western" literary history, Walcott responded: "My generation of West Indian writers has felt such a powerful elation at having the privilege of writing about places and people for the first time and, simultaneously, having behind them the tradition of knowing how well it can be done—by a Defoe, a Dickens, a Richardson" (73). With regard to the West Indian writer's relationship to Africa, Walcott thinks too many people in the Caribbean "exploit an idea of Africa out of both the wrong kind of pride and the wrong kind of heroic idealism." Walcott believes that there is a "great danger in historical sentimentality" and, while the "whole situation in the Caribbean is an illegitimate situation," he sees "no shame in that historical bastardy." In order to mature, Caribbean writers cannot "sit moping or writing morose poems and novels that glorify a nonexistent past" (79).[6] In his seminal essay, "The Muse of History" (1978), Walcott acknowledges that there are those who write about history "through the memory of hero or of victim," but he believes this kind of "servitude" to the "muse of history" has "produced a literature of recrimination and despair, a literature of revenge written by the descendents of slaves or a literature of remorse written by the descendents of masters." For Walcott, "great poets" are those who reject altogether this "sense of history" and whose "vision of man in the New World is Adamic" (37). He adds that it is the "elemental privilege of naming the New World which annihilates history in our great poets . . . whether they are aligned by heritage to Crusoe and Prospero or to Friday and Caliban. They reject ethnic ancestry for faith in elemental man" (40). For Walcott, West Indian writers are in the position of Crusoe, "the namer," and it is precisely because Crusoe is "Adam," the "first inhabitant of a second paradise" ("The Figure of Crusoe" 36) that he is such an appropriate symbol for the West Indian writer.

Walcott's writings profoundly reflect the interconnectedness of history and art in the West Indies, and his life and works must therefore be contextualized with a brief review of the region's historic and artistic developments. After Christopher Columbus discovered the Caribbean in 1492, other European nations (especially England and France) joined Spain in the race to conquer the New World. The attempt by European colonizers to refashion the West Indies into a "wealth-generating" entity required a labor force, which led to the Atlantic slave trade and plantation slavery. A few hundred years later, once Europe determined that slave labor was no longer profitable, emancipated slaves found themselves thrust into economic slavery and, in the mid-nineteenth century, Indians and Chinese were imported as indentured servants. Other new "immigrants" included North Africans, Portuguese, Jews, Japanese and Syrians. Each group longed for their own homeland, and their own cultural "purities." In a paper entitled "Caribbean Dish on the Post-Colonial Supper Table," Daisal Rafeck Samad explains that those who came (or were brought) to the Caribbean, and who lived (or were made to live) in antagonism with each other, "shared like an unvoiced pain" the "consistent erasure of their humanity, the corrosion of the human person." By the

1930s and 1940s, "the stage was set for the only man-made culture on that scale in human history." After centuries, during which time human beings in the Caribbean were at once economic commodities and expendable, the "self was fragmented and unformed. And when self has yet to be created, society cannot labor it into being."[7] It is for this reason that V.S. Naipaul has spoken of the "storylessness," and Orlando Patterson the "historylessness," of the West Indies.

If West Indians are "psychically fragmented and culturally schizo-phrenic," as Samad proposes, how are they to represent themselves, their identities, and their condition? Colonial educations assured that white values and European civilization remained dominant and subsequently, since the outset of colonialism, writings produced in (and about) the West Indies exemplified a mastery of inherited mediums. The literary forms that Carib-bean writers inherited were the tools that enabled them to prove they were equal to Europeans, and imitation was the technique that allowed Carib-bean verse to be recognized as poetry. In addition, up until the 1920s, the principle themes of West Indian poetry were religion, patriotism (empire), and nature, all of which served to reinforce their connection to English poetry. Imitation continued to be the order of the day through-out the 1930s, but in the 1940s the trend shifted from representations of a pseudo England to representations of the West Indian landscape and people. Moreover, as Howard Johnson explains, by the 1940s a "national-ist consciousness among the middle-classes manifested itself not only in political activities but in a sense of cultural identity. The cultural divide between the middle and working classes narrowed as members of the intel-ligentsia celebrated Afro-Creole culture as authentic and non-European" (338). Such factors as the mystique of Africa, nationalism and socialism were subsequently invoked in the writings. By the 1950s, the tendency to imitate European voices and forms was overtaken by the tendency to write on behalf of narrow racial, ethnic or cultural allegiances. For example, the return to Africa movement was solidified by Marcus Garvey, which ulti-mately became the international movement known as Black Power. Those of East Indian descent looked to India, for what V.S. Naipaul referred to as an "Aryan" purity in *The Mimic Men*.

Yet West Indian writers of all races and cultural backgrounds also con-tinued to look toward Europe, especially England. Jean Rhys, C.L.R. James, George Lamming, Naipaul, Edward Kamau Brathwaite and Wilson Harris, to name just a few, immigrated to England.[8] Many of the works produced by West Indians since the mid-twentieth century have been explorations of what only became known as a West Indian "identity" after this literary invasion, when individuals from different islands found themselves categorized for the first time as "West Indian." But as Samad so poetically explains, there can be no such thing as an explicitly stated and agreed upon West Indian identity because the history of the region is

> too complex, the society too intricately heterogeneous, the psyche too fragmented and individualistic, the countries too scattered, shattered like a broken backbone, a discontinuous archipelago. There is no single tradition to hold things together, no all-consuming pattern of identity, no imprisoning or exclusionary cultural imperative; rather, the societies of the Caribbean are held together, paradoxically, by many traditions, each fractured and evolved into an entity quite unlike parent traditions, each informed and transformed by the other, each half-born, half-aborted; half-buried, half-excavated. It is upon the demanding economy of paradox that the conscience of West Indian society, psyche and art subsists.

Yet it is possible, as Lamming proposed in *The Pleasures of Exile* (1960), to locate three crucial events in British Caribbean history. The first is, of course, "the discovery," which "began like most other discoveries, with a journey; a journey inside, or a journey out and across." The second is the abolition of slavery and the "arrival of the East—India and China—in the Caribbean Sea" (36). The third important event is the "discovery of the novel by West Indians as a way of investigating and projecting the inner experiences of the West Indian community" (37). At the time, the second event was approximately a hundred and fifty years behind him, and the third, he claims, was hardly two decades old.

But Walcott, one of the few West Indian writers to remain at home, posits a much earlier moment of origin for the West Indian novel by embracing Crusoe as a credible metaphor for the situation of the West Indian writer. In the poem "Crusoe's Journal," Walcott writes: "out of such timbers / came our first book, our profane Genesis / whose Adam speaks that prose / which, blessing some sea-rock, startles itself / with poetry's surprise, / in a green world, one without metaphors" (ll. 10–15). Walcott's identification is rooted in the fact that Crusoe is a castaway against his will on a Caribbean island, just as African slaves were forcibly transplanted from their homes to islands of the West Indies. Walcott's personal identification with Crusoe as a castaway is perhaps most explicitly exemplified in the first lines of his poem "The Castaway": "The starved eye devours the seascape for a morsel / Of a sail. / The horizon threads it infinitely" (ll. 1–3). Walcott's narrator is acutely aware of his isolation and loneliness, and he recognizes that all that is available for consumption is emptiness, nothingness. According to Paul Breslin, Walcott's speaker "desperately awaits the approach of a ship, bringing sustenance of a wider world. But no ship appears" (106). As in his poem "The Sea is History" (1979), in which Walcott writes that "the ocean kept turning blank pages" as it is "looking for history" (ll. 24–25), in "The Castaway" the sea is a metaphor for historical erasure. By depicting Crusoe as isolated on a deserted beach and oppressed by the desolate conditions of his surroundings, Walcott alludes to the moment in Defoe's text when Crusoe ponders the wreckage of the ship and wonders how, given its distance, he could have possibly gotten to shore: "I cast my Eyes to the stranded Vessel . . . I could hardly see it, it lay so far off" (35). Later, after surveying the layout of the island, he determines that amongst the necessities for setting up a "Settlement" he requires "a view of the Sea, that if God sent a Ship in Sight, I might not lose any Advantage for my Deliverance" (44). In both cases the image of a ship, whether real or imagined, whether present or absent, makes Crusoe all the more conscious of his remoteness and seclusion.

In his poem "Crusoe's Journal," Walcott illustrates that in this space Crusoe becomes the archetypal West Indian artist because his "intellect appraises / objects surely, even the bare necessities of style / are put to use / like those plain iron tools he salvages / from shipwreck, hewing a prose / as odorous as raw wood to the adze" (ll. 4–9). Moreover, "his journals / assume a household use; / we learn to shape from them, where nothing was" (ll. 54–56). Crusoe's journal becomes for Walcott the first West Indian novel and, as Neloufer de Mel notes, "his is the first Adamic example of the artist turning a loss of history and tradition into privilege, as he names the landscape and its people with imagination and awe" (136).[9] The isolated Crusoe, who in "Crusoe's Island" is "howling for a human voice" (l. 35), mirrors Walcott's own sense of an alienated existence on St. Lucia as a mulatto, a Methodist in a predominantly Catholic country, the son of middle-class parents by virtue of education and profession in a community stricken by poverty and, later, lone director of the Trinidad Theatre Workshop who was ostracized by friends and betrayed for forging his own creative direction.[10] Walcott's identification with Crusoe's struggles on the island and will to survive is evidently deeply personal.

The appeal of *Robinson Crusoe* for Walcott, as opposed to Shakespeare's *The Tempest* is likely due to the fact that Crusoe merely finds himself on an uninhabited island. Unlike Prospero, he neither wrangles territory from indigenous peoples nor violently asserts his authority. Moreover, Crusoe saves Friday from death at the hands of "cannibals," and Friday's gratitude and humility distinguish him from Caliban, who represents forced servitude. However, while Friday supposedly volunteers his servitude to Crusoe, and Crusoe does not call him his "slave," Crusoe does not hesitate to teach Friday to call him "Master," to follow orders, and convert to Christianity. Walcott attempts to reconcile these historical contaminations, or what he refers to as the "political baggage" associated with Crusoe, by insisting upon his protean nature. In "The Figure of Crusoe," he writes that Crusoe is

> Columbus because he has discovered this new world, by accident, by fatality. He is god because he teaches himself to control his creation, he rules the world he has made, and also because he is to Friday, a white concept of Godhead. He is a missionary because he instructs Friday in the uses of religion; he has passion for conversion. He is a beachcomber because I have imagined him as one of those figures of adolescent literature . . . and finally, he is also Daniel Defoe, because the journal of Crusoe . . . is Defoe's journal. (35–36)

Walcott does acknowledge that after Friday's arrival Crusoe "stops becoming a writer, hermit, saint, and becomes . . . a master. He reverts to what he has been taught and becomes self-righteous on such subjects as God, civilization, art and human nakedness. And of course race." Yet rather than see this as a problem for his adaptation of Crusoe as a symbol of the West Indian writer, Walcott asks his readers to allow him the leeway to make Crusoe "various, contradictory, and as changeable as the Old Man Of the Sea." In his poetry, Walcott opts to see Crusoe's "several shapes" which, for him, "represent various problems organic to West Indian life" (35).

However, Walcott is apparently only able to identify with some of Crusoe's "shapes," such as Crusoe the writer and craftsman as opposed to Crusoe the master and missionary. In order to accommodate the glaring contradictions in the figure of Crusoe in "Crusoe's Journal," he switches from speaking as Crusoe to speaking from Friday's subject position:

> Like Christofer[11] he bears
> in speech mnemonic as a missionary's
>   the Word to savages,
> its shape an earthen, water-bearing vessel's
>   whose sprinkling alters us
> into good Fridays who recite His praise,
>   parroting our master's
> style and voice, we make his language ours,

converting cannibals
we learn with him to eat the flesh of Christ. (ll. 16–25)

The fact that Walcott speaks from both subject positions suggests he identifies with *both* Crusoe and Friday. However, in his Crusoe poems, he seems to privilege Crusoe over Friday, which is one of the reasons critics have attacked his work.[12] But as Stephen Breslow writes, the merit of such criticism is entirely compromised by the fact that Walcott has shown his commitment to exploring "purely regional" Caribbean themes, racism and discrimination, "the lowest as well as the highest strata of society," and the "bounteous beauties of the islands" (268). There are also those critics who defend Walcott's privileging of Crusoe, such as de Mel, who argues that it is "rooted in his admiration of Crusoe the craftsman, the survivor, whose language is English, which is his own" (138). It can also be attributed to his own sense of alienation from those whom he refers to in "Crusoe's Journal" as "Friday's progeny, / The brood of Crusoe's slave" (ll. 101–102). The poem concludes with Walcott's speaker claiming: "Nothing I can learn / From art and loneliness / Can bless them as the bell's / Transfiguring tongue can bless," (ll. 114–117). To be an artist in isolation who positions oneself as a god or an Adam is to find oneself alienated from humanity, from the human beings whom the artist loves, and it is for this reason, as much as any other, that Walcott's speaker "labors at his art" (l. 18).

Walcott's identification with Crusoe as an artist in isolation forces a reinterpretation of the figure of Crusoe for contemporary readers. As he claims in "The Figure of Crusoe," Crusoe's survival is "a triumph of will" (40). While Defoe's Crusoe utilizes tactics that are instigated by his fear of being consumed by "savages" and wild beasts and aided by the western tools he salvages from the wrecked ship, his survival is ultimately fueled by his will to survive in isolation. Despite his claims that he would not have been able to survive without having the European provisions that he salvaged from the wrecked ship, what he considers the "Necessaries of Life," it is Defoe's Crusoe's absolute acceptance of his isolation—and decision to begin a journal—that enables him to work through and even overcome his despair. In fact, Crusoe's first writing exercise is to "set good against Evil." Although he claims to register these observations "impartially, like Debtor and Creditor," and he interprets his inventory of the good and evil that has come upon him within a religious (distinctly Protestant) context, he also manages to comfort himself by recording his experiences, thoughts and feelings, by setting down his "Condition" in writing. In doing so, Crusoe recognizes that, even though he has been "cast upon a horrible desolate Island, void of all Hope of Recovery," he is "alive, and not drown'd." He also acknowledges that, although "divided from Mankind, a Solitaire, one banish'd from humane Society," he is not "starv'd and perishing on a barren Place" (49). While seemingly convinced that there is "scarce any Condition in the World so Miserable," he is aware that there is "something *Positive* to be thankful for." What is so crucial about Crusoe's realizations is that they prompt him to give up "looking out to Sea" (50), and to begin his life anew on the island, in the New World.

Crusoe's journal begins with a list of such fears as being "devour'd by wild Beasts, murther'd by Savages," and "starv'd to Death for Want of Food" (52). He then offers detailed descriptions of how he labored to preserve himself against these threats by building secure lodgings, renovating the cave to store his provisions, planting and killing food, and even making a candle. When Crusoe becomes ill with fever, he has a dream that stimulates his desire to repent. He claims: "Conscience that had slept so long, begun to awake" (66). In this moment of awakening, Crusoe sees the world around him as if he is newly born, and wonders who made the sea, earth, sky and air. Crusoe's musings about the existence of God prompt him to turn to the bible for education and spiritual direction. After ten months, and at last satisfied that his habitation is secure, Crusoe begins to explore the island. He discovers running brooks, meadows, tobacco, sugar cane, and all kinds of plants, trees, flowers and fruits. He reports: "the Country appear'd so fresh, so green, so flourishing, every thing being in a constant Verdure, or Flourish of *Spring*, that it looked like a planted Garden" (73).

Yet the wonder and awe Crusoe experiences as he surveys "that delicious Vale" (73) and the "Fruitfulness of that Valley" (75) are mixed with a "secret Kind of Pleasure" (73). Crusoe imagines that "this was all my own, that I was King and Lord of all this Country indefeasibly, and had a Right of Possession; and if I could convey it, I might have it in Inheritance, as completely as any Lord of a Manor in *England*" (73). At the end of his fourth year on the island, he writes with conviction: "I was Lord of the whole Manor; or if I pleas'd, I might call myself King, or Emperor over the whole County which I had Possession of" (94).[13] Thus the figure of Crusoe with whom Walcott identifies for his humble beginnings, ingenuity, craftsmanship and will to survive, and who, according to Walcott, only "stops becoming a writer, hermit, saint, and becomes, *by necessity* [my emphasis], a master" when Friday arrives, actually envisions himself as a "master" long before Friday's arrival, and even before he sees the infamous footprint.

Nonetheless, by revisiting Defoe's novel through Walcott's essay and Crusoe poems it is it is evident that Crusoe is "Adam," because he creates an entire world via a pattern of naming or, in a sense, by writing it into being. As Maximillian E. Novak explains in "Friday: Or the Power of Naming,"

Crusoe's island is "nameless" until he names it the "Island of Despair." Unlike Columbus, "he does not have to contend with a previous system of names that have to be conquered or translated." Crusoe makes himself "King," and his "Subjects" are, initially, his dog, his cat, and his parrot. He expands his cave and calls it his "Castle." He creates a "Country Seat," which he also refers to on different occasions as his "Country-House," "Sea-Coast House," or simply his "Bower." He can be whatever he names himself, be it "King" or "Emperor." At other times, depending on what occupation he is engaged with, he is a "mere Pastry-Cook," "bad *Carpenter*, and "worse *Tailor*." Novak determines that Crusoe's naming, his creation of a new world, is the "activity of his imagination." While Crusoe has certainly put in time and labor in building and farming it also the case that he "creates all and possesses all as much by the power of naming as by his labor" (120). When the "cannibals" arrive, they invade *Crusoe's* world.

Crusoe's fear of "savages" could be due to the influence of such captivity narratives as those that were produced in the seventeenth and eighteenth centuries by Europeans, in which the narrator enacts revenge and attempts to recover a position of cultural supremacy by drawing on stereotypes to represent his captors, such as the one Gilroy constructs for Inkle. Yet even though fantasies of being captured and eaten torment Crusoe and, later, he becomes violently ill upon seeing the remains of the cannibals' feast, he does not plan to attack and kill them. According to Crusoe, this would "justify the Conduct of the *Spaniards* in all their Barbarities practis'd in *America*, where they destroy'd Millions of these People" who, despite their apparent barbarity, were "a very innocent People" (124). To do so would be "meer Butchery, a bloody and unnatural Piece of Cruelty, unjustifiable either to God or Man" (125). Defoe's Crusoe does not even dream about committing an act of aggression but, instead, dreams that when one of their victims escaped he smiled upon him, encouraged and assisted him. Of course, also in this dream the escaped savage becomes his prisoner and his "Pilot," showing Crusoe the way to the mainland. But even though Crusoe suspects his "Deliverance" may require that he attack "a whole Caravan of them" in order to save one, and dread and terror cause him at times to "think of nothing" but how he might "destroy some of these Monsters" (122), he is troubled by the "Lawlessness of it." He claims: "my Heart trembled at the thoughts of shedding so much Blood" (144). When his dream comes to pass he does end up shooting and killing two of the victim's "Enemies," but he gives the "poor Creature" all the "Signs of Encouragement" that he can think of, and "smil'd at him, and look'd pleasantly" (147).

However, as Novak points out, despite the fact that the story Defoe *wants to tell* is of the "advantages of exploiting foreign lands and of a good relationship between colonizer and indigenous population" (114), it is Crusoe's fear of savages that prompts him to think of himself as a "master." He thoroughly enjoys thinking of the prospect of acquiring two or three savages and making them "entirely Slaves to me, to do whatever I should direct them"(145). Crusoe's sense of himself as a "master" is solidified when he interprets Friday's acts of gratitude—kneeling, kissing the ground, laying his head upon the ground, taking Crusoe by the foot and setting his foot upon his head—as being "in token of swearing to be my Slave for ever" (147). Shortly thereafter, Crusoe becomes the new name he gives himself when he determines that Friday repeated the same "Signs" of "Subjection, Servitude and Submission" to let him know that he would "serve me as long as he liv'd." Crusoe "made him know his name should be Friday" and, in turn, "taught him to call me *Master* and then let him know that was to be my name; I likewise taught him to say, YES and NO and to know the Meaning of them" (149). In addition, as Novak asserts, by "renaming this handsome, twenty-six-year-old savage, Crusoe assumes possession of him in the same way that Columbus assumed possession of the land by his namings" (117). Thus with Friday's arrival Crusoe switches from using language harmlessly in isolation for the purpose of creating a new world for himself to using language as a means of domination and for the purpose of sustaining a position of power. Crusoe's agenda in teaching Friday to speak English, to understand the words "yes" and "no," at least at first, serves Crusoe's mission of weaning Friday off human flesh, teaching him to wear clothing and keep house like an Englishman, and converting him to Christianity. In short, Crusoe's agenda in teaching Friday the English language is to render him capable of understanding and following orders.

When Walcott produced his Crusoe poems in the mid-1960s, writers were just beginning to adopt the figures of Crusoe and Friday (and Prospero and Caliban) as emblematic of colonizer/colonized and master/slave relations. While Walcott identifies with Crusoe as a castaway and artist in isolation, he also acknowledges the political implications of Defoe's literary figures by drawing attention to the fact that Crusoe sees himself as a godlike figure, and that he embodies middle-class dreams of upward mobility and the British empire's desire for power, mastery and wealth. In fact, Walcott's poems reflect his awareness that Defoe's novel served as a virtual blueprint for the pursuit of individual progress and colonialism because Crusoe brings imperialist ideologies and English cultural behavior *to* the island, where he alone transposes them onto or reconstitutes them within an entirely new space, which for Europeans was the New World.

***

While Defoe's Crusoe fancies himself a "master" and exploits Friday as an indentured servant, he also frequently refers to Friday as "loving" and "sincere." This is not to refute that Crusoe—colonizer, slave trader and missionary—is one of the first colonial minds in English fiction. Nor is it the case that Friday, because of his subjugation, represents anything other than the natives of America, Asia, and Africa who were brutally oppressed by European imperialism, colonialism and slavery. As postcolonial critics generally recognize, the moment that Crusoe instructs Friday to call him "Master" he becomes, like Yarico, a political symbol of colonial exploitation and racial injustice. However, Friday proves to be such a wonderful companion that Crusoe begins to enjoy life on the island, so much so that he is not sure he wants to leave. Friday's personality is appealing to both Crusoe and the reader because he exhibits a charisma that is in stark contrast to Crusoe's lack of emotion and, as time passes, Crusoe undergoes moral growth and transformation as a consequence of the friendship and emotional bond he develops with Friday. The fact that this Englishman grows to love Friday, whom he initially considers an illiterate cannibal, suggests that Defoe may have wanted his readers to acknowledge Friday's humanity.

Crusoe's relationship with Friday incites him to acknowledge that all God's creatures are created equal. He concedes that God has "bestow'd" upon non-Europeans the "same Powers, the same Reason, the same Affections, the same Sentiments of Kindness and Obligation, the same Passions and Resentments of Wrongs; the same Sense of Gratitude, Sincerity, Fidelity, and all the Capacities of doing Good, and receiving Good, that he has given to us." Not only does Crusoe realize that Friday is an equal human being in the eyes of God, he suspects that Friday might even be a better Christian, and his observations of Friday make him all the more aware of "how mean a Use" Europeans make of God's gifts. When Crusoe realizes that the year he spent with Friday was the "pleasantest Year of all the Life I led in this place" (154), he determines that he would be content to stay on the island forever with his new companion. According to Crusoe, Friday

> was the aptest Schollar that ever was, and particularly so merry, so constantly diligent, and so pleas'd, when he cou'd but understand me, or make me understand him, that it was very pleasant to me to talk to him and now my Life began to be so easy, that I began to think to my self, that could I but have been safe from more Savages, I cared not, if I was never to remove from the place while I lived. (152)

Crusoe's contentment with his immediate circumstances is somewhat surprising, given that he spent twenty-three years contemplating his escape from the island.

But when Crusoe begins to teach Friday about Christianity, Friday's inquisitiveness makes Crusoe conscious of his own lack of knowledge, and he confesses to his readers that, in the process of teaching his new companion, he learns from him: "in laying Things open to him, I really inform'd and instructed myself in many Things, that either I did not know, or had not fully consider'd before." In fact, in the company of Friday Crusoe takes much more pleasure from his religious and spiritual education than he did when he was alone: "I had more Affection in my Enquiry after Things upon this Occasion . . . I had great Reason to be thankful that ever he came to me: My grief set lighter upon me, my Habitation grew comfortable to me beyond Measure" (159). Crusoe changes significantly as a consequence of his relationship with Friday, as his state of mind and attitude toward his island home are in every respect improved. It is not his own religious or spiritual development, nor Friday's, that transforms Crusoe, but rather his conversations and friendship with his new companion. In fact, for the first time in the entire narrative Crusoe admits that he is completely happy and he even develops a great sense of gratitude: "In this thankful Frame I continu'd all the Remainder of my Time, and the Conversation which employ'd the Hours between *Friday* and I, was such, as made the three Years which we liv'd there together perfectly and completely happy, *if any such Thing as compleat Happiness can be form'd in a sublunary State.*" (159). Of course, regardless of whether readers and critics opt to view Friday as a slave, servant or friend, or all at once, there is no question that Crusoe mediates Friday's actions and interprets his behavior for his readers and, consequently, we are inhibited from accessing Friday's thoughts about the white man who saves his life.

Unlike such revisions or rewrites of *Robinson Crusoe* as J.M. Coetzee's *Foe* and Michel Tournier's *Friday*, in which Crusoe's failure to understand and respect Friday, and Friday's victimization and lack of voice, are emphasized, with *Pantomime* Walcott suggests that Crusoe and Friday hold the potential to understand and respect each other. *Pantomime* is the story of Harry Trewe, a retired actor who came to Tobago from England to run a resort named Castaways Guesthouse for British tourists. At the heart of the play is Harry's attempt to solicit his handyman, Trinidadian and retired calypsonian Jackson Phillip, to perform a "Christmas panto" of *Robinson Crusoe* for hotel guests when the holiday season begins. The English Harry is, like the figure of Crusoe, a "castaway" and, also like Crusoe, he seems to symbolize British imperialism and white economic power.

When Jackson first enters, Harry speaks to him as if life imitates art: "Friday, you, bring Crusoe, me, breakfast now. Crusoe hungry" (95). But Walcott's Jackson is a much stronger character than Harry, and he responds to his employer by saying, "Mr. Harry, you come back with that same rake again? I tell you, I ain't no actor, and I ain't walking in front a set of tourists naked playing cannibal. Carnival, not canni-bal" (96). Jackson's refusal to play Friday as he is instructed incites Harry to propose that they experiment with the Robinson Crusoe plot. "We reverse it," he suggests. "We could work up a good satire, you know, on the master-servant—no offense—relationship. Labor management, white-black, and so on . . ." (109). But Jackson thinks his idea "is shit," and sees none of the humor that Harry does in the idea of a "black man playing Robinson Crusoe" and a "half-naked, white, fish-belly man playing Friday" (111). When Harry insists that the genre of pantomime allows for such improvisation, a point to which I will return, Jackson concedes and makes his first order of business changing Friday's name: "Robinson obey Thursday now. Speak Thursday language. Obey Thursday gods" (114). But Harry is not entertained, and even less so when Jackson invents his own language: "If you want me to learn your language, you'd better have a gun" (117). Jackson thoroughly enjoys Harry's agitated reaction to his improvisation, so much so that he takes it a few steps further by suggesting that, if he is to play a "black explorer," Harry should play a "white sea bird." Harry responds to this idea contentiously by saying, "What sea bird? I'm not going to play a fekking sea bird" (120). Jackson's comment is indubitably a reference to the albatross of Samuel Taylor Coleridge's *Rime of the Ancient Mariner*, and this moment foreshadows the scene in the second act when Harry tells his "story" to Jackson and is relieved of the oppressive guilt he carries around with him. Despite Harry's protestations, Jackson proceeds to act out his version of the story, which is about a Crusoe figure who gets shipwrecked in a rowboat and, immediately upon crashing onto the sand, kills a goat (which he thinks Harry should play!) to make a parasol and a hat.

As Jackson's improvisations become more elaborate, Harry becomes increasingly more disconcerted and warns Jackson that he will call the whole thing off. Harry then attempts to gain control of the situation by insisting that Jackson put an end to his farce, giving Jackson orders to clear away the breakfast dishes and threatening to fire him. But Jackson refuses to leave "in the middle of a job," and declares: "You see, it's your people who introduced us to this culture: Shakespeare, *Robinson Crusoe*, the classics, and so on, and when we start getting as good as them, you can't leave them halfway" (124). Thus their rehearsal ultimately evolves into what Bruce King describes in his biography of Walcott as a "debate about European and Caribbean culture and behavior" (361), and also West Indian creativity. When Harry demands that Jackson stop improvising, Jackson responds:

> Here am I getting into *my* part and you object. This is the story . . . this is history. This moment that we are now acting here is the history of imperialism; it's nothing less than that. And I don't think that I can—should—concede my getting into a part halfway and abandoning things, just because you, as my superior, give me orders. People become independent. Now, I could go down to that beach by myself with this hat, and I could play Robinson Crusoe, I could play Columbus, I could play Sir. Thomas Drake, I could play anybody discovering anywhere, but I don't want you to tell me when and where to draw the line! (125)

Jackson's point is that, like the figure of Crusoe in Walcott's poems, he can be whatever or whomever he *names* himself.

Harry eventually confesses that the problem with Jackson's improvisation is that it "could get offensive . . . if you take this thing seriously, we might commit Art, which is a kind of crime in this society." As opposed to offering people "something light," a little "entertainment," they would be doing something that would make their audience "think too much." It is as if, watching Jackson, Harry realizes the irony of performing the story in reverse:

> This cannibal, who is a Christian, would have to start unlearning Christianity . . . he'd have to be taught by this—African . . . that everything was wrong, that what he was doing . . . for nearly two thousand years . . . was wrong. That his civilization, his culture, his whatever, was . . . *horrible*. Was all . . . wrong. Barbarous, I mean, you know. And Crusoe would then have to teach him things like, you know, about . . . Africa, his gods, pantamba, and so on . . . and it would get very complicated. (126)

The irony would not, of course, be lost on the audience. But Harry evidently finds this scenario unthinkable, as he again resorts to treating Jackson like a servant, like a Friday, in an attempt to wrest back from him creative and social control. But the story of how Walcott came to write *Pantomime* suggests that the point of the play is not limited to an analysis of racial conflict in the Caribbean. Walcott wrote *Pantomime* while he was staying at a hotel in Tobago managed by Arthur Bentley, a former British actor who moved to the West Indies after his marriage fell apart. Apparently Bentley asked Walcott to write something that would provide his guests an evening's entertainment. The idea for the play came to Walcott while he listened to the banter between Bentley and one of his employees. In *Derek Walcott and West Indian Drama*, King explains: "Although the situation involved a white English hotel manager and a local black employee, there was an equality in the exchange of repartee that dissolved the racial, class, and economic differences. This was Walcott's idea of the Caribbean" (295).[14]

In fact, when Hirsch asked Walcott in 1986 whether this play is a parable about colonialism, Walcott maintained that *Pantomime* was not about "black anger" and "white racial guilt." Rather, he sees it as an investigation of what happens when two different character types are thrown together:

> The point of the story is very simple. There are two types. The prototypical Englishman is not supposed to show his grief publicly. He keeps a stiff upper lip. Emotion and passion are supposed to be things that a true blood Englishman avoids. What the West Indian character does is try to wear him down into confessing that he is capable of such emotion and there's nothing wrong in showing it. Some sort of catharsis is possible. (108)

Walcott acknowledges that inside the play there is a "point in which both characters have to confront the fact that one is white and one is black. They have to confront their history. But once that peak is passed, once the ritual of confrontation is over, then that's the beginning of the play" (108). Thus one might argue that the beginning of Act 2 is actually the beginning of the play, perhaps specifically the moment when Harry says, "So let's have a drink, man to man, and try and work out what happened this morning" (134). As the two men sit facing each other, Harry consumes more and more whiskey and begins to divulge more and more information about his past. He confesses to Jackson that he has sunk his whole life savings into the hotel, and he alludes to the fact that he is haunted by "a brilliant actress who drank too much, and a car crash at Brighton after a panto" (136), which was a panto of Robinson Crusoe. This is the "albatross" that hangs around his neck.

When Harry admits that he is afraid he might be "prejudiced," Jackson forces him to see that it is his grief and loneliness that are bothering him: "'Tain't prejudice that bothering you, Mr. Harry; you ain't no parrot to repeat opinion. No, is loneliness that sucking your soul as dry as the sun suck a crab shell. On a Sunday like this, I does watch you . . . Walking round restless, staring at the sea. You remembering your wife and your son . . . You ain't get over that yet?" (136). Jackson thereby accuses Harry of being the isolated Crusoe whom Walcott depicts in his Crusoe poems, the castaway whose loneliness sends him "howling for another voice." Jackson then challenges Harry by directly confronting him about his emotional paralysis: "You drive so careful you make your car nervous" (137). Jackson also points out that, although Harry imagines they are speaking to each other as equals, in actuality the two of them are always acting, and the "boss-and-Jackson" business is as much a play as the panto they are rehearsing: " . . . two of we both acting a role here we ain't really believe in, you know. I ent think you strong enough to give people orders, and I *know* I ain't the kind who like taking *them* . . . We faking, faking all the time. But man to man, I mean . . . that could be something else" (139). In other words, they are always playing the identity constructions of white "master" and "black" servant or slave that are portrayed in Defoe's novel.

As the action progresses, Jackson goads Harry into acknowledging and expressing his emotions. Harry finally reveals that he came to the West Indies after his ex-wife Ellen left him, and that, because she was driving drunk, she is responsible for the death of their son. At the end of the play, Jackson holds out a photograph of Harry's wife, enabling Harry to finally, although virtually, confront her. Jackson, now playing the role of the Englishwoman Ellen, asks Harry what she has done. Harry, losing all control, cries out: ". . . you're a silly selfish bitch and you *killed our son!*" (160). The emotion of the scene continues to escalate as Ellen, played by Jackson, threatens to kill herself and asks, "Will you forgive me now, or after I jump?" (163), to which Harry responds by shouting: "*Ellen! Stop! I forgive you!*" Then, having obviously experienced a catharsis, Harry calmly confesses: "That's the real reason I wanted to do the panto. To do it better than you ever did . . . You wiped the stage with me." When Jackson, who has been acting as Ellen, speaks as himself, he reminds Harry that they were supposed to be playing Robinson Crusoe, and that "Crusoe must get up, he must make himself get up. He have [sic] to face a next day again." He then shouts: "*I tell you: man must live!*" (164). Through Jackson, Walcott reminds his readers and viewers that the inherent message in the story of Robinson Crusoe is survival, or how the will to survive is actualized.

After Harry and Jackson engage in this playacting, Harry feels the burden of his past lift and, accordingly, he quotes Coleridge's *Rime of the Ancient Mariner*: "The albatross fell off and sank / like lead into the sea" (ll. 290–291). Jackson therefore occupies a position comparable to Coleridge's saint, who takes pity on the mariner and blesses him. As a direct result of Jackson's influence and encouragement, Harry is cleansed of the remembrances that have haunted him and the guilt from which he has suffered, and even alleviated of his loneliness.[15] According to Breslin, at the conclusion of the play both Jackson and Harry have given each other something: "Jackson's contribution is the more obvious one: he has been the catalyst in exorcising Harry's bitterness at his ex-wife and in breaking down his characteristically English emotional inhibition." But Harry has reignited in Jackson his awareness that "Caiso is [his] true work" (170). Breslin concludes that each man

> has kindled the theatricality of the other, and theatricality reveals itself as a transforming power. Throughout the mythical reanactment of the traumatic origins of West Indian colonial history, Jackson and Harry are able to change the script and throw the burden of the past from their shoulders. Starting with familiar roles, familiar masks, they improvise until they find ways to shed their historically imposed roles and communicate 'man to man.' (126).

Thus through improvisation and theatricality, social hierarchies and racial conflicts are seemingly dissolved or neutralized for this modern-day Crusoe and Friday.

One of the most crucial scenes in *Pantomime* for understanding how Walcott transforms Defoe's novel from an imperialist narrative into a liberating narrative is when Jackson kills the parrot. Jackson knows that Harry's excuse for the parrot's tendency to say "Heinegger, Heinegger" is that an old German named Herr Heinegger used to own the guesthouse, and that it only sounds like a racial insult because of "his accent . . . He's a Creole parrot." This does not, however, inhibit him from experiencing the parrot's mimicry as a flat-out racial slur. When Jackson proposes "perforating his arse by firing squad," Harry responds: "The war's over, Jackson! And how can a bloody parrot be prejudiced?" Jackson's answer? "The same damn way they corrupt a child. By their upbringing. That parrot survive from a pre-colonial epoch, Mr. Trewe, and if it want to last in Trinidad and Tobago, then it go have to adjust." But in Act II, Jackson finally takes the matter into his own hands. Dressed as Crusoe, he throws a take-out box across the floor to Harry's feet in which he has placed the dead parrot. He says, "One parrot, to go! Are you eating it here?" Harry, after calling Jackson a "son of a bitch," picks up the parrot and throws it into the ocean, and then calls Jackson "a blood savage." Jackson, acting as Friday, defends his actions by saying: "Me na strangle him, bwana. Him choke from prejudice." When Harry taunts Jackson by acting as the parrot—he "crouches, tilts his head, shifts on his perch, flutters his wings . . . squawks"—Jackson, as Crusoe, declares: "You people create nothing. You imitate everything. It's all been done before" (156–157).

By killing the parrot Jackson demonstrates his refusal, as Patrick Taylor argues, to "accept Crusoe's vision of the servant," and thus to see himself as either "a cannibal from a race of backward sub-humans" or as a "good" Friday who "adopts the master's values." More specifically, rather than imitating or mimicking *Robinson Crusoe*, Jackson explodes the myth of submission that Defoe illustrates in his novel by having his Crusoe tell us that the "savage" bowed down and placed his new "master's" foot upon his head. The supposed submission of the non-European world served to justify imperial expansion, colonial conquest and slavery and, according to Taylor, this "myth was and is the core of an ideology keeping slaves, peasants and workers in their set place. It has endured for more than three hundred years" (294). Moreover, Jackson contests the charge of mimicry that Europeans usually aim at the colonized. As Breslin explains, here the "charge of mimicry boomerangs," as the parrot, a stock emblem of mimicry, "is identified not with West Indians but with Europeans." The implication here is that "European racism is itself a form of mimicry, a mindless acceptance of received attitudes" (121).

In Defoe's novel, Crusoe kills the parrot to teach Friday a lesson about guns and their capacity to kill animals for food. According to Carol Houlihan Flynn, shooting the goat, no matter how flashy the display of powder and power, can be rationalized as a way to replace human with animal flesh. But killing the parrot is an act of luxury. Even Crusoe seems to recognize the gratuitous nature of his deed, for on Crusoe's island, parrots are made "not to be eaten, but to speak" (156). Crusoe's Poll cries, repeatedly, "Poor Robin Crusoe, Where are you? Where have you been?" If Crusoe were to answer, he would have to answer, killing parrots to educate the savage. But the act of killing the parrot is "gratuitous" because, in doing so, Crusoe eliminates the only other voice on the island. Crusoe had captured and taught the parrot to speak out of desperation to hear another voice, but in actuality this voice is really just an echo of his own. The parrot therefore represents the European tendency to propagate its own voice and prejudices. The implication in Crusoe's act of killing the parrot is that he puts an end to the practice of reproducing himself and creates space for a dialogue with another human being, that of the native Friday.

***

By having Harry and Jackson rehearse a Christmas panto of *Robinson Crusoe*, and by portraying the liberating potential of theatricality and improvisation, Walcott invites his readers/viewers to revisit the form of eighteenth-century English pantomime. In 1969, David Mayer III wrote in *Harlequin and His Element* that the eighteenth-century English pantomime was a

> highly topical form of dramatic art offering audiences immediate and specific comment on the issues, major and minor, of the day. Disguised in its exotic and traditional ornamentation, the pantomime held up an imperfect mirror to its audiences. The audiences saw themselves, their countrymen, the ambitions and triumphs of their nation, the pitfalls that an unwary people might tumble into. They saw their achievements glorified and their failures ridiculed. (2)

English pantomimes can thus be considered the "Art" that, according to Walcott's Harry, would make people think.[16] Prior to the first *Robinson Crusoe* Christmas pantomime, which was performed in 1781 at the Theatre-Royal, Drury Lane, the main story and the Harlequinade were kept separate. But in Richard Brinsley Sheridan's *Robinson Crusoe*, the characters from the main story are revealed after the transformation scene to be stock pantomime characters. Sheridan's production ran for thirty-eight nights, which was an extremely long run for a pantomime and therefore evidence of its popularity. While there is no evidence that Walcott is engaging specifically with, or even alluding to Sheridan's *Robinson Crusoe*, or any other eighteenth- or nineteenth-century pantomime of Defoe's infamous story, by revisiting this production through Walcott's *Pantomime* it becomes readily apparent that the genre itself allowed for the kind of social and political critique—and transformations of stereotypes and identity constructions—that might not have been socially acceptable if conveyed through other artistic forms.

The anonymous author of "A Short Account of the Situations and Incidents Exhibited in the Pantomime of Robinson Crusoe at the Theatre-Royal, Drury Lane" stresses Sheridan's adherence to Defoe's *Robinson Crusoe* by juxtaposing summaries of each scene with the corresponding sections from the novel.[17] The author evidently seeks to demonstrate that the pantomime is "Taken from the Original Story." Sheridan does seem to aim at realism, at least in the first part of the production. In scene i, Crusoe descends from his habitation "exactly according to the history" in "theatrical dress" that is "conformable to his own account of it" (4). The author also points out that in this scene is "exhibited the melancholy way in which this desolate mariner contrived, by a wooden calendar, to keep an account of his silent solitary life" (6–7). While none of Philippe-Jacque de Loutherbourg's set designs for the pantomime survive, John McVeagh surmises that his opening scenery, which would certainly have represented the cave, the palisade and the tree stump, "would have aimed to strike by minute detail and picturesque appeal—a mixture of realism and romance" (138). However, Thomas Linley's published music for Sheridan's production has survived. [18] McVeagh determines that the music for the first scene "conveys a serene but serious mood: gentle oboe with pizzicato accompaniment on strings" (13), and thus the anonymous author's assessment of the scene's mood as serious is correct: "Crusoe's isolation, marking of the passage of time and dedication to a work schedule are emphasized" (138).

Scene ii takes place on a different part of the island, in a "grove near the sea-shore, where Crusoe is working on two boats." The scene represents his "long labour and final disappointment in the first," and his "more successful work" in the second (7–9). While Crusoe is pursuing his work of building a boat out of the trunk of a tree, his lost parrot reappears and startles him by calling his name. Then, Crusoe sees the footprint in the sand and the "first terror of the savages breaks in on his mind" (10). Scene iii opens with a view of the sea and shows the "arrival of the savages in their canoes with their prisoners, and among the rest was *Friday*, whose escape and refuge" is described in detail in Defoe's novel (11). As the "savages" prepare to kill Friday, he breaks free and escapes. Scene iv takes place in a grove in the woods on a new part of the island. Crusoe enters from one side and Friday from the other, with the "savages" in pursuit. When Crusoe fires his gun, Friday falls down as if dead and the "savages" retire "in the utmost consternation."[19] Crusoe then calls to Friday, who approaches him in fear but eventually kneels down, kisses Crusoe's foot, and places it on his head as a token of submission, exactly as in the novel. While the emphasis is evidently still upon fidelity to the novel, McVeagh suggests that Sheridan "highlights themes likely to appeal to a 1781 audience: exotic settings, the savagery-civilization clash, castaway survival, life and death struggles, Spanish-English disputes over empire" (140), themes also present in Defoe's novel that contributed to its popularity.

Scene v is set at the "bower," or Crusoe's country house, which is described as follows: "This, his second plantation, was of a different nature from his fortified tent." In addition, the "inclosures for his cattle are here exhibited" (13–14). The scene is filled with birds of all different species and, when Crusoe raises his gun to bring one down, once again frightening Friday, Friday falls to his knees and kisses the gun in worship. He then goes for water but quickly returns pursued by the savages.[20] In scene vi, "savages" arrive "with more prisoners," but when Crusoe and Friday fire at them the savages run away.

Although the anonymous author of *A Short Account* states that Crusoe's plan is to "surprise the savages and the assistance that Friday gave to rescue the victim are conformable to the history"(14–16), among the abandoned prisoners in Sheridan's production are the *commedia del'arte* characters Pantaloon and Pierot. According to McVeagh, "this addition to Defoe is intended to unify. Sheridan is looking forward to the harlequinade in Part II in which Crusoe plays no part, and seeks to make the break seem less stark. The novel's equivalent scene is the rescue of the Spanish prisoners, conflated with that of the rescue of Friday's father" (140). In scene vii, Crusoe and his company's supper is disturbed by "signal guns," which gives them "the first notice of some ships having approached the island" (17). Friday and Pierot are sent to investigate, and return with the news of an approaching ship. Scene viii shows an "English ship at anchor near the island" (18). Crusoe observes as the sailors bring their prisoners ashore and then disperse to explore the island. He then reveals himself, learns their story, and provides them with arms. Scene ix takes places in a "woody part of the island." Crusoe enters with Friday, and then "dispatches him to observe the rest of the crew, who had now landed in quest of their companions" (19). The separated groups eventually reunite, a contest of some sort ensues, with the results being that the mutineers agree to surrender and promise to obey the Captain. A "reconciliation follows," followed by the *Song*, after which Crusoe and all the characters go off in the long-boat. The act concludes with the ship sailing away after the firing the signal gun.

Significantly, the anonymous author of *A Short Account* reports: "The *Story* being no longer pursued in the remainder of the representation," it is only necessary to add that Friday, "being invested with the powers of the Harlequin," and after the traditional chase scenes and antics, "receives his final reward in the hand of Columbine" (20). However, what happens in part two of Sheridan's *Robinson Crusoe* is crucial, for the story is no longer focused on Crusoe but, rather, on Harlequin, or Friday transformed, as he strives to win the hand of Columbine. The fact that the actual title of this production is *Robinson Crusoe, or Harlequin Friday*, and the storyline strays from the original when Friday is released from servitude and transformed into Harlequin, suggests that Sheridan's production may have ultimately, although perhaps inadvertently, conveyed an abolitionist message, especially since Harlequins in eighteenth-century pantomimes always wore a black mask.

In *Harlequin Britain: Pantomime and Entertainment, 1690–1760*, John O'Brien devotes an entire section of his book-length study to exploring the "extent to which eighteenth-century Britons might have been able to take Harlequin's black mask as a racial sign, a referent to Africans, and what that might have meant in performance" (xx).[21] O'Brien proposes that the extent to which Harlequin's black mask might be read as a racial sign "gains a certain urgency" when the fact that the period of pantomime's greatest popularity, the 1720s and 1730s, were years during which Britain's participation in the slave trade markedly increased. It was not until the 1760s that the "moral implications" of Britain's involvement in the trade "prompted the emergence of a substantial abolitionist discourse, one that would dramatically increase the frequency and intensity with which African persons were individually and collectively constructed as objects of public knowledge" (123). In the 1720s, there was a strong black presence in London and, as *The Daily Journal* for April 5, 1723 claimed: "Tis said there is a great number of Blacks come daily into this City so that 'tis thought in short Time, if they be not suppress'd, the City will swarm with them."[22] Moreover, images of blacks were everywhere, especially advertisements. O'Brien notes that there were also black-faced performances of such theatrical roles as Othello and Oroonoko. Thus English Harlequins "came to prominence in a period when other black faces suffused the public imaginary" (126). Moreover, many Britons had clear associations with Africans, either as servants or because of their involvement in the slave trade, although none of these contexts "seem to have encouraged Britons to consider the relationship between real and represented Africans consciously or critically" (127). However, Afro-British writers played on this distinction both consciously and critically in their works, which I discuss in chapter four.

O'Brien points to two myths of origin for the black-masked Harlequin. The first is that he descended from masked characters in Roman drama who represented African slaves, and the second is that he originated in the town of Bergamo and represented "a bumpkinish servant from the countryside," the dark mask being a "mark of the rural peasantry" (131).[23] While these myths seem to be contradictory, they both speak to the way that Harlequin "was cast in the public sphere as a representative of common folk—playful and mischievous, occasionally a petty criminal, articulating desires through the body rather than by speech" (132). Yet to demonstrate that by the mid-eighteenth century Harlequin's blackness was a racial signifier, O'Brien examines David Garrick's *Harlequin's Invasion* (1759). Garrick's text "contains the first explicit description from within a pantomime itself that would identify Harlequin as an African, as it twice refers to him as "that Blackamoor man."[24] O'Brien argues that Garrick's identification of Harlequin as a Blackamoor positions Harlequin "as the ethnographic Other against which Britishness can be defined," and that what is most important about this "openly nationalist" pantomime produced in the middle of the Seven Years' War is that

Harlequin is cast as an "alien presence on British soil—he is both African *and* French." Significantly, this Harlequin functions as the "embodiment of a *principle* of national identity that needs to be displaced by the most powerful of all the theatrical figures that might articulate the British nation—William Shakespeare" (135). At the end of the pantomime, Shakespeare banishes Harlequin from the stage. After this, Harlequins could readily be racialized as Africans, as such titles as *Harlequin Mungo* (1788)—"mungo" being a typical or generic name for an African, which I also address in Chapter Four—and *Furibond, or Harlequin Negro* (1807).

Thus it seems likely that in Sheridan's 1781 production of *Robinson Crusoe* Harlequin's black face would also have had racial implications. Therefore, just as Yarico evolves from an Indian maiden into an African in the mid-eighteenth century and was, by the end of the century, a symbol of both colonial oppression and sexual exploitation of African women, Friday evolves from a native Carib to an African and, given the date of Sheridan's production, could be viewed as representative of the plight of the slave and a call for abolition. In Part II, the Harlequinade, the audience follows Harlequin through a series of escapades as he strives to win the hand of Columbine. The Harlequinade is set in Spain because, at the end of Part I, Crusoe and company had set out to take the Spanish prisoners home. Sheridan thus introduces some national satire into the entertainment, as Spain was at the time in the British news because of disagreements over the Falklands. The first scene opens in Pantaloon's house, where Columbine, her lover and her mother learn from Pierot that Pantaloon has arrived on shore. Scene ii takes place in Cadize quay, where everyone celebrates the reunion. Crusoe then bids the company farewell and sets sail for England and out of the pantomime.[25] The center of interest now shifts from Crusoe to Friday, as Harlequin, and Columbine, who grow enamored with each other in accordance with typical pantomimes.

The Harlequinade itself is difficult to reconstruct, as there is little surviving detail about it. However, according to reviews, in scene ii Friday is discovered by Pierot on his knees kissing Columbine's hand, and consequently turned out of Pantaloon's house.[26] Two magicians then meet Friday in a grove where they transform him into Harlequin. According to McVeagh, it is likely that Friday's outer clothes were removed to reveal the Harlequin dress and he was, concurrently, given his magic bat. Moreover, the magicians explain that they had wrecked Pantaloon on the island for revenge, having been threatened by him with the Inquisition.[27] Harlequin dances a solo dance entitled "Harlequin Happy," in which he demonstrates his pleasure at the transformation. In scene iv, Harlequin gains admission to Pantaloon's house disguised as a friar (or, according to one review, a nun). In scene v, Harlequin hides Columbine in a convent, or in another summary, two friars lure her to their cloister. Harlequin gains entry by taking the place of a young girl hidden inside a truss of straw, which is being carried on a monk's back labeled "food for convent."[28] This is followed by a series of comic episodes, which may or may not have included a friars' drinking scene. After the convent drama, there is a chase sequence, which ends with Harlequin being caught and handed over to the Inquisition. Harlequin is sentenced to death and he walks to the stake with a lighted torch accompanied by other victims. But when they are all about to be burned, a magician reappears and transforms the prison into a garden. Finally, Pantaloon consents to the marriage of Harlequin and Columbine, and the entertainment concludes with a dance.

McVeagh suggests that Friday (rather than Crusoe) is chosen to become Harlequin because Crusoe would have been perceived as too old to perform as Columbine's lover, and because a "contrast may be intended between [Crusoe's] rationality and material power and Friday-Harlequin's magic tricks, which are the subject of the rest of the pantomime." More simply, as the harlequinade gets underway, "sober realism yields to fantasy and fun" (143). However, it is also conceivable that Friday is chosen because, by transforming him into Harlequin, he is released of his servitude to Crusoe. Thus as in Walcott's *Pantomime*, in which humor and theatricality allow for socio-political critique, in Sheridan's production of *Robinson Crusoe*, humor and theatricality allow for what could be interpreted as the liberation of an African slave, and thus abolitionist sentiment. Moreover, Sheridan's production is as much a commentary on the brutality of the Spaniards as Defoe's novel, although, because it points directly to the Inquisition, this is brought up to date.[29]

With *Pantomime*, Walcott brings the story of Robinson Crusoe even more up to date. Despite his insistence that the focus of the play is not on race relations, the relationship between his modern-day Crusoe and Friday can be viewed as a commentary on the black experience in the British Caribbean. According to Johnson, by the early 1900s the "deteriorating material conditions for the working classes and the static position of blacks at the base of the race-class hierarchy prompted a class and racial consciousness," which was expressed "not merely in spontaneous protest but also in the formation of organizations to improve labour conditions and promote a sense of black pride and identity as an essential component of racial upliftment" (325). At the same time, and despite attempts by Trinidadian writers in the inter-war years to produce a distinctly West Indian body of literature, which was published in *Trinidad* (1929–30) and the *Beacon* (1931–33, 1939), in most colonies national consciousness was still limited to the middle class. In the post-war years, the modification of political and economic reforms did not reorder existing social and economic structures and, in most colonies, members of the "white elite . . . continued to exercise effective power" (340). Throughout the British Caribbean, "colonies advanced to independence without a disruption to the long-entrenched social structure, with its colour/race correlation" (344).

While Walcott's portrayal of Harry and Jackson seems to suggest a neutralization of racial and social hierarchies, it is not as idealistic as it seems. By having Jackson recommit to Calypso, and declare that "Caiso" is his "true work," Walcott points to the fact that in Trinidad, although Calypso and Carnival eventually came to define the national culture, it had "previously been the cultural expression of the working class," and "served to stimulate class and race consciousness" in the Caribbean (338). Jackson is well aware that there is still much work to be done. The play concludes with Jackson singing and, when Harry joins in, Jackson stops and declares: "Wait! Wait! Hold it! . . . Starting from Friday, Robinson, we could talk 'bout a raise?" (*Fadeout*). Despite the emotional bond that develops between Harry and Jackson, and the cathartic experiences their friendship yields, they are still in a master/servant relationship reminiscent of Defoe's Crusoe and Friday.

Chapter Three

Satire's Spectacles

Wole Soyinka's "Gulliver" and
Jonathan Swift's *Gulliver's Travels*

Soyinka produced his retrospection of *Gulliver's Travels* while imprisoned by the Federal Military Government of Nigeria for denouncing the military dictatorship and campaigning for a cease-fire in the war against Biafra. Not surprisingly, his poem "Gulliver," included in a section of his prison poems (*A Shuttle in the Crypt*, 1972) entitled *Four Archetypes*, is a scathing critique of neocolonial tyranny and totalitarianism throughout history. According to Lubomir Dolezel, revisions of classic works confront the "canonical proto-world by constructing a new, alternative fictional world." Of the three distinct types of revisions—transposition, expansion and displacement—the notion of transposition is particularly applicable to Soyinka's "Gulliver." Transposition "preserves the design and the main story of the protoworld but locates them in a different temporal or spatial setting, or both. The proto-world and the successor world are *parallel*, but the rewrite tests the topicality of the canonical world by placing it in a new, usually contemporary, histori-cal, political, and cultural setting" (206). By dramatizing himself as Gulliver in late-1960s Nigeria, Soyinka reveals that Gulliver's experiences in Lilliput are analogous to the events that gave rise to his imprisonment. Yet Soyinka makes Swift's legacy entirely his own by reintroducing Gulliver as a *political* prisoner, or prisoner of conscience, who is as much a victim of a corrupt totalitarian regime as the writer himself.[1] In doing so, Soyinka investigates the roots of tyranny and depicts the method with which dictatorships con-trol their subjects by convincing them that their subjugation is due to their own weaknesses rather than the government's domination. By creatively doc-umenting the crimes against humanity he experienced in Nigeria, Soyinka delivers the message that the world cannot be silent as totalitarian regimes pledge "extinction of their [own] kind" (l.77).

In addition to being a victim of an oppressive regime, like Gulliver in Lilliput, Soyinka's narrator is a witness to human rights violations. Thus

Soyinka also identifies with Gulliver in Laputa and Lagado, whose observations provide an alternative perspective on tyranny. Soyinka's simultaneous engagements with Parts I and III of *Gulliver's Travels* reflect Leon Guilhamet's claim that Parts I and III are thematically "linked in that they both discover a single source of evil for corruption and vice in the government of nations" (156). For example, just as the Lilliputian Emperor in Part I represents how "unmeasurable is the Ambition of Princes" (40), the Laputian King in Part III "would be the most absolute Prince in the Universe, if he could but prevail on a Ministry to join with him" (161). However, while Swift's Gulliver observes the political structures of Laputa and scientific experiments in Lagado with detached neutrality, Soyinka's narrator is neither detached nor neutral. According to Tanure Ojaide, Soyinka "seems to write with a motive . . . a determination, as a witness to get down a record of the abuses of the violators of his person and society," and he "uses his particular experiences to expose the evil nature of his prosecutors" (164). Thus in addition to the figure of Gulliver, Soyinka identifies with the eighteenth-century writer himself, whose works, according to Edward Said, can be defined by their attention to "human aggression or organized human violence" (84).

Soyinka and Swift's writings comparably exemplify the kind of critical vision that induces consciousness and which, consequently, totalitarian regimes throughout history and around the world fear, censor, and endeavor to destroy. Just as Soyinka protests war and oppression in "Gulliver," Swift designed his anti-war pamphlet *The Conduct of Allies* (1711) to persuade the reading public toward sanctioning an end to the War of Spanish Succession. Just as Soyinka denounces totalitarianism from behind the mask of a fictional persona in "Gulliver," Swift speaks from behind the guise of a Dublin drapier in *The Drapier's Letters* (1721) to mobilize Irish resistance to the importation of Wood's halfpence, which would have been devastating to Ireland's economy. Carole Fabricant explains that these works were "not only urgent responses to crises immediately at hand, but also attempts to lay the groundwork for a future differing in significant ways from the present" (198). Similarly, Soyinka's prison writings are responses to the immediate crises in Nigeria and call for a different future. However, while Soyinka demonstrates that Swift is capable of speaking to contemporary concerns, his engagements with Swift's writings reveal such contradictions in Swift's political thought as his crusade against tyranny but disdain for revolutionary action.

***

Soyinka's determination to expose and reconcile segmentation in societies around the globe fuels what critics refer to as his "aesthetic and political radicalism." As Biodun Jeyifo points out, for nearly half a century Soyinka has been one of Nigeria's "uncompromising and vigorous human rights campaigners, and perhaps the fiercest and most consistent opponent of the African continent's slew of dictators and tyrants," and his prison writings remain inseparable from what Jeyifo refers to as his "sustained and relentless activism in furtherance of the protection of democratic rights and egalitarian values" (7). Any discussion of the works Soyinka produced while in solitary confinement must therefore take into consideration the historical events leading up to, and the material circumstances surrounding, their production.

In January 1966, during a military coup led by left-leaning Igbo officers, the First Republic was overthrown and Prime Minister Alhaj Sir Ahubakar Tafawa-Balewa was abducted and assassinated. The immediate reasons for the first military action concerned the nationwide disillusionment with their politicians, who were not only corrupt and selfish but also unable to maintain law and order and guarantee the safety of lives and property. General Ironsi, an Igbo, emerged as head of state and formed a military government. Yakubu Gowon became the army chief of staff. In the Eastern Region, C. Odumegwu Ojukwu was appointed governor. In July 1966, there was a counter coup led by a group of officers from the North. Most top-ranking Igbo officers, including Ironsi, were killed, and General Gowon was installed as Head of State. In late September and early October, more rioting and Igbo massacres took place in the North, and many Igbos fled to the Eastern region. On 27 May 1967, in order to prevent a threatened secession by the Eastern Region, General Gowon decreed that the four regions of Nigeria be split into twelve federal states, dividing the Eastern Region into three separate parts. Despite these efforts, on 30 May, the leaders of the Eastern Region unilaterally declared the region an independent nation, giving it the name Republic of Biafra. On 6 July, fighting broke out between Biafran and federal troops and, on 9 August, Biafran forces invaded the Midwest, captured Benin, and advanced to Ore in the West, threatening both Ibadan and Lagos. On 10 August, Gowon announced that what had previously been a "police action" against succession was now Civil War.[2]

Three weeks into the Nigerian Civil War, Soyinka issued an appeal for a cease-fire in the *Nigerian Daily Sketch*. He claimed that General Ojukwu had made a miscalculation, and that the Federal Military Government needed to reexamine its acts of war as it would be responsible for the massacre in the North of the Igbo people.[3] At the end of August, as Soyinka was returning from a visit with General Ojukwu, the Federal Military Government of Nigeria arrested Soyinka for conspiring with the Biafran secessionists. According to Derek Wright, Soyinka was "detained on the trumped-up accusation of having given active support to the enemy by assisting with the purchase of jet aircraft for the rebel leader" (133).[4] A forged confession of his guilt was produced and, although he was never formally charged or brought to trial, Soyinka was imprisoned for almost two years between 1967 and 1969; the Civil War ended in 1970. In his prison memoirs, *The Man Died* (1972), Soyinka explains that his arrest was prompted by the following activities:

> . . . my denunciation of the war in the Nigerian papers, my visit to the East, my attempt to recruit the country's intellectuals within and outside the country for a pressure group which would work for a total ban on the supply of arms to all parts of Nigeria; creating a third force which would utilize the ensuing military stalemate to repudiate and end both the secession of Biafra, and the genocide-consolidated dictatorship of the Army which made both secession and war inevitable. (19)

Soyinka's visit to Biafra was one of a series of interventions planned by the Third Force, of which he was a key member. According to Jeyifo, the Third Force's "objective was to avert war by neutralizing the equally compromised and reactionary leadership of the 'federalists' and the 'secessionists.'" Soyinka made no secret of his visit to Biafra, even though at this particular time "such action was considered highly treasonous by the Nigerian federal military regime, with its large clutch of fractious, rabidly anti-Biafran military and civilian zealots" (7). As Soyinka told Gates in 1975, his mission to the secessionist region was not "clandestine," as the "propaganda machinery" of the Federal Military Government labeled it. It could, to a certain extent, be labeled a "peace mission" (50). Moreover, his "association and collaboration" with the group known as the Third Force was "dictated by a conviction that the roots of the Civil War were not to be found in the act of secession of the Igbos or even in the hideous massacre of the Igbo people; but that they reached far deep into the very fundamental disjunction within the total society" (52).

Soyinka spent nearly two years of his incarceration in solitary confinement, deprived of books, writing materials, and human companionship, and this experience taught him the unlimited possibilities of human survival. In an essay entitled "The fourth stage," first published while he was in prison, Soyinka writes:

> Nothing but the will . . . rescues a being from annihilation within the abyss . . . Only one who has himself undergone the experience of disintegration, whose spirit has been tested and whose psychic resources laid

under stress by the forces most inimical to individual assertion, only he
can understand and be the force of fusion between two contradictions.
The resulting sensibility is also the sensibility of the artist, and he is a
profound artist only to the degree to which he comprehends and expresses
this principle of destruction and re-creation. (150)

As Gates explains in "Being, the Will, and the Semantics of Death," it is the
human will with which Soyinka "the artist and Soyinka the activist are both
concerned: the integrity of the will and a fundamental belief in its capacity to
structure and restructure the world in which we live." It is Soyinka's regard for
the will "in the face of terror, combined with the unqualified rejection of the
indulgence of pity, and a belief in the communality of individual struggle, that
most characterizes Soyinka's metaphysics" (67).

With the exception of two or three poems in the section "Poems of bread
and earth," Soyinka wrote all the poems in *A Shuttle in the Crypt* while in solitary
confinement. Knowing it is not healthy for any human being to feed entirely on
his or her own mind without any replenishment from other sources, Soyinka
devised all kinds of mental exercises to preserve his sanity. For example, the poet
imagines himself as a "shuttle," which he identifies in the Preface to *A Shuttle
in the Crypt* as "a unique species of the caged animal, a restless bolt of energy, a
trapped weaver-bird yet charged in repose with unspoken forms and designs."
The act of identifying with this "essence of innate repletion" was for Soyinka "a
natural weapon to employ against the dangers of an inhuman isolation. It was
never a mere poetic conceit; all events, thoughts, dreams, incidental phenom-
ena were, in sheer self-protection perceived and absorbed into the loom-shuttle
unity of such an existence" (vii).[5] Subsequently, as Niyi Osundare proposes, *A
Shuttle in the Crypt* can be read as a "testimony to a personal anguish, the psy-
cho-mental struggle against a vegetable existence." It is a "psychological odyssey,
the travails of the shuttle in the skull-ridden vault of thought-killers" (195).

Prison narratives and other representations of detention reflect the
actual historical experiences of their authors and, according to Werner
Sedlak, if we deny them this reference "our reading of these texts would
deprive them of their political and human impact" (42). Thus one must
approach Soyinka's prison writings with awareness that they were produced
while in solitary confinement. In *The Man Died*, Soyinka explains that his
prison memoirs are "not a textbook for survival but the private record of one
survival," and therefore it has the capacity to "refresh the world's conscience
on the continuing existence of the thousand souls held under perverted
power" (25). Soyinka's prison poems testify to his individual suffering
and will to survive, and they serve as reminders of the countless political

prisoners and prisoners of conscience who continue to fight for their lives by whatever means necessary. Soyinka survived in prison by writing, secretly, in any way he could. The act of writing itself became a means of survival, a way to maintain his sanity, a way to enact his will.

In *The Man Died*, Soyinka recounts the moment he stole a pen from the breast pocket of a prison doctor: "To write! To be able to set down thoughts on paper . . . but most importantly, it was occupation. A pen and I would be *doing* something. Time would be largely or minutely eroded" (193).[6] After acquiring a writing tool, he scribbled on toilet paper, cigarette wrappers, and between the lines of books that were smuggled in to him.[7] In his introduction to the section of *A Shuttle in the Crypt* entitled *Prisonettes*, Soyinka explains that each of these poems had to be "short enough and as self-containing as possible to remain in his head until, at night-time or in a slack moment of surveillance" he could transfer it to the inside of a cigarette packet. Moreover, as he told Jane Wilkinson, "it was necessary, while I was in prison, to try and distance myself from the immediate environment. That was also a process of sanity, to think in terms of distancing me from the reality, and connecting with *other*, larger symbols" (157). Among these *other*, larger symbols are Soyinka's *Four Archetypes*—"Joseph," "Hamlet," "Gulliver" and "Ulysses"—which operate collectively to give universal validity to the events in Nigeria during the Civil War. At the same time, as Peter Sabor notes, because each of Soyinka's "heroes is a falsely treated wanderer," each poem alludes to Soyinka's individual "plight" (45).[8]

The title of Soyinka's "Gulliver" directs immediate attention to his explicit engagement with *Gulliver's Travels*, and the opening lines reinforce this engagement at the level of narrative:

> Once upon a ship-(of state) wreck, where
> The sun had shrunk the world at last to a true
> Stature of deserving—the ant for unit–
> I lay on earth tide-flung, obtruding
> Miles of heart and mind, an alien hulk
> Into a thumb assemblage. (ll. 1–5)

Here, Soyinka alludes to the Nigerian state wrecked by crises and the political conflicts that led to his imprisonment. According to Antony Johae, "'once upon a' is invoked parodically not to indicate the beginning of a children's story (which Swift's novel is often taken to be) but to signal the poet's adult incursion into a political conflict (extrinsically, the Biafran War), an incursion that will cost him his freedom for over two years" (30). Soyinka's references to Gulliver's enormous size function metaphorically to convey the writer's sense of himself as worlds taller than his captors, who arrogantly consider themselves big and powerful, but whose small physical size (like Swift's Lilliputians) reflects their narrow vision, small-mindedness and immorality. When Soyinka's narrator claims that "Miles of heart and mind" are "obtruding" (ll. 4–5) and his feet are "scaled as mountains" (l. 7), he reiterates his sense of himself as an "alien hulk" in the "thumb assemblage." Like Swift, Soyinka uses antitheses to convey the contrast between prisoner and captors.

By depicting himself as having been forcefully restrained, Soyinka alludes to the process with which totalitarian regimes control the lives of their subjects, which includes systematically suppressing dissent by terrorizing the masses via military action and secret police. In Soyinka's poem, "alien minds / Must learn recumbent positions" (ll. 10–11), and thus only by feigning passivity and conformity will his narrator—who asserts his autonomy—avoid further punishment. Soyinka's narrator's sense of himself as much too big for his environment reflects what the reader can only imagine was the poet's actual experience of his physical body—and his overactive mind—while in solitary confinement. In his poem "Live Burial" he describes his jail cell as measuring just "Sixteen paces / By twenty-three. They hold / Siege against humanity / And Truth / Employing time to drill through to his sanity" (ll.1–2). "They" are his captors, and they endeavor to destroy their captive's mind by confining him in such an agonizingly claustrophobic space. In "A letter to Compatriots," which served as an introduction to the first edition of *The Man Died*, Soyinka writes: "I testify to the strange, sinister, byways of the mind in solitary confinement, to the strange monsters it begets. It is certain that all captors and gaolors know it; that they create such conditions for those whose minds they fear" (12). For totalitarian regimes to remain in power and maintain domination over their subjects they must destroy the minds of those they perceive as a threat to their stability.

With "Gulliver," Soyinka exposes that Swift's Lilliputians restrain (and eventually imprison) Gulliver because they fear him for reasons other than his enormous physical size. For example, he challenges their authority when he attempts to liberate himself from their restraints. When Soyinka's narrator succumbs to "A brief / Impulse to unguided knowledge" (ll. 11–12), when he thinks for himself and takes action, his defiance is greeted with "A shower of needles, full-fanged, venom-bodied" (l. 13). In Swift's text, Gulliver relates the following account of his experience:

> I discovered the Methods they had taken to bind me; and . . . with
> a violent Pull, which gave me excessive Pain, I loosened the

Strings . . . in an Instant I felt above an Hundred Arrows discharged
on my left Hand, which pricked me like so many Needles; . . . When
this Shower of Arrows was over, I fell to groaning with Grief and Pain;
and then striving again to get loose, they discharged another Volly larger
than the first. (8)

Swift's Gulliver is a captive who is virtually paralyzed and unrelentingly tortured for acting on his innate awareness that his fundamental human right—
personal freedom—has been violated. When Soyinka's narrator reports that
he experiences the "shower of needles" as "full-fanged" and "venom-bodied"
(l.13), he draws attention to Swift's Gulliver's pronouncement that he "fell
groaning with grief and pain" (8). While the reasons for his physical pain
are obvious, why does he experience grief? Soyinka's poem implies that the
brutal attack is emotionally as well as physically painful for Gulliver because
it has come from people who utilize whatever means available to them to
clamp down on insurgence. He grieves because his captors, who are fellow
human beings, are manifestly devoid of humanity.

Gulliver's account of his transport to the Temple that will serve as a jail
cell is seemingly neutral. He nonchalantly reports: "while the whole Opera-
tion was performing, I lay in a profound Sleep, by the force of that soporifer-
ous Medicine infused into my Liquor" (13). According to Guilhamet, the
"fact that he is a prisoner under threat of imminent death does not seem to
enter into Gulliver's assessment of his situation" (143). However, by portraying his imprisonment as a journey to a mythological underworld, Soyinka invites the reader to see what Gulliver does not, which is that his life is
threatened from the outset: "Wheels approached, / They bore me through
the famished blades / As dead the living come into necropolis / Corded to
a span of tumbrels, drugged (ll. 15–21). In addition, Soyinka highlights the
fact that Gulliver has been drugged: "They quenched my fleshly thirst / In
draughts of Lethe, and I was plunged / Deep in mindless trance" (ll. 15–17).[9]
By alluding to the mythic underworld river Lethe, which upon consumption
induces forgetfulness, Soyinka reveals that the Lilliputians, like the Federal
Military Government, use particularly devious methods of control to sub-
due their prisoner's body and numb or alter his mind. By revisiting Swift's
account of Gulliver's imprisonment through Soyinka's, the reader learns that
the Lilliputians attempt to blind Gulliver long before they accuse him of
treason and sentence him to have his eyes put out.

The Lilliputians' deceitful methods exemplify what for Soyinka is the
fundamental methodology of imposing and maintaining tyranny, which is
the practice of inhibiting subjects from seeing that their oppression is due to

government coercion. Yet unlike Swift's Gulliver, Soyinka's narrator knows that the charges against him are false, that the Federal Military Government removed him from circulation to immobilize his political activism, and that their agenda in placing him in solitary confinement is to destroy his mind. With "Gulliver" Soyinka shows that, despite Gulliver's ignorance, the Lilliputians enchain and incarcerate him to curb his resistance to their domination. Swift's Gulliver's description of his imprisonment is remarkably detailed and, as with Soyinka's narrator, and the writer himself, he is confined in an extremely small space:

> The great Gate fronting to the North was about four Foot high, and almost two Foot wide, through which I could easily creep. On each side of the Gate was a small Window not above six Inches from the Ground: Into that on the Left side, the King's Smiths conveyed fourscore and eleven Chains, like those that hang to a Lady's Watch in *Europe*, and almost as large, which were locked to my Left Leg with six and thirty Padlocks. (13–14)

Moreover, unbeknownst to Gulliver, the Lilliputians turn their prisoner into a spectacle as a means of imposing their power. Across the highway, the Emperor and "many principle Lords" ascend a "Turret" to "have the opportunity" of viewing him, but he cannot see them. In addition, approximately ten thousand "Guards" are assigned to keep watch over him (14). Given that the Lilliputians watch Gulliver from a "Turret," their penal system is comparable (at least until Gulliver begins entertaining visitors) to Jeremy Bentham's Panopticon, a building with a tower at the center from which it is possible to see each prisoner's cell. Bentham determined that "power should be visible but not verifiable." The prisoner can always be seen and always see the tower, but never knows from where he is being observed. In the central tower, one sees everything without ever being seen.[10] As Michel Foucault has argued, the Panopticon induces "in the inmate a state of conscious and permanent visibility that assures the automatic functioning of power" (470), which differs from force or violence because it involves restricting or altering an individual's will.

Soyinka's Lilliputians are not only comparable to Swift's because they represent actual governments but also because they utilize comparable methods of quelling disaffection and resistance. Swift's depiction of Gulliver's imprisonment reinforces his politically-motivated satire of state-sponsored terrorism and physical coercion, which was administered by the Whigs after the death of Queen Anne in 1714 and geared toward wiping out political dissent. As Kathleen Wilson explains in *The Sense of the People*, "the free reign given to Whig loyalists, troops and militiamen to harass and assault— or even kill—Tory and Jacobite demonstrators in the post-succession years was only one aspect of the draconian measures employed by successive Whig administrators to keep order and stamp out disaffection." In addition to these invasive government measures, "house arrests" and the use of "networks of informants and spies" were also legitimized (98). Only when the Lilliputians determine that it would be impossible for Gulliver to "break loose" do "they cut the strings that bound [him]." But Gulliver nonetheless experiences "as melancholy a Disposition as [he] had in [his] life" (14).

Swift's Gulliver's melancholia is likely due to the fact that the Lilliputians have dehumanized him, which is comparable to how the Federal Military Government of Nigeria treated their political prisoners during the Civil War. In his prison memoirs, Soyinka recounts being shackled with "chains the likes of which I had seen only in museums of the slave trade," at which time he thought: "I defined myself as a being for whom chains are *not*, as, finally, a human being" (39).[11] Soyinka is further dehumanized when he is confined to what he describes as "an animal cage" (80). As soon as he found himself in this "cage" and under twenty-four hour surveillance Soyinka realized that he was "more than ever at the mercy of the state propaganda machine" and, therefore, if he did not find a way to smuggle out a statement he would end up like the thousands of other political prisoners who had simply vanished. So, he "commenced an exploration into the mind of the enemy and future dangers," and "watched, waited and schemed" (81).

In "Gulliver," Soyinka dramatizes his investigation of his captors: "I schooled me / In their ways, picked a wary course /Through egg-shell structures. I looked above /Their draughty towers, peered within /Secret chambers, and marveled at their councils" (ll. 23–27). Unlike Swift's Gulliver, who is seemingly oblivious to his captors' lust for supremacy, Soyinka's readily identifies his captors as "Peacock vain, manikin cruel, sycophant" (ll. 23–24). However, to read Swift after Soyinka is to recognize that, despite his apparent naïveté, Swift's Gulliver does instinctively know he has been unjustly detained. He tells the reader: "the first Words I learnt, were to express my Desire, that [the Emperor] would please to give me my Liberty; which I every Day repeated on my Knees" (19). In fact, Gulliver is consumed with desire to obtain his freedom, and he devotes much of his time to drafting requests and submitting them through the proper channels. Like Soyinka himself and other prisoners of conscience, Gulliver uses "Words," as opposed to violence, to plead for his freedom.

In addition to identifying with Gulliver's actual imprisonment and sub-jugation, Soyinka identifies with the fact that Gulliver gets himself in trouble for attempting to *serve*. When Soyinka's narrator "decried an earthly burn," he "squelched the puny flames in fountains / of urine" (ll. 42–44). Just as Soyinka considered his visit to Biafra a "peace mission" rather than an act of treason, Gulliver considers his act of urinating on the palace an "eminent Piece of Service."[12] But unlike Gulliver, who is surprised by the Lilliputians' response to his constructive, although apparently illegal, act, Soyinka's narra-tor sees and understands the psychology of his captors' cruelty so profoundly that their response is not entirely surprising: "In such surrounds, in truth of fire, / was it a wonder I would sagely err?" (ll. 37–38). In other words, it is not surprising to him that this totalitarian regime considers *wise* activities— such as working closely with such writers/activists as Christopher Okigbo and Victor Banjo, both of whom supported the Biafra secession, and advo-cating arbitration as opposed to war—as treasonous. While Soyinka is never formally charged, he is imprisoned for allegedly conspiring with the Biafran secessionists to overthrow the Federal Military Government. Thus he identi-fies with Swift's Gulliver, who is charged with treason for putting out the fire "maliciously, traitorously, and devilishly, by discharge of his Urine" (56). By drawing a parallel between the charges brought against Gulliver and his own arrest, Soyinka denounces the Federal Military Government's response to his peace mission and indicates that it is as absurd as the Lilliputians' response to Gulliver saving the palace.

In a later verse, Soyinka exposes that Gulliver's encounter with judicial corruption is comparable to his own experience just after his arrest when, as he explains in *The Man Died*, "All was secrecy" (73):

Indictments flowed at secret sessions
The palace deed re-echoed, concluding–
Imprimis: Unless by aid of Secret Powers
No human bladder could eject such potent
Piss to douse sidereal flames. Thus,
Imprimis: A blasphemer who dared mistake
Cosmic conflagration for mundane disaster, and–
For paradox: An arsonist for dwarfing
Flames of Lilliput with stark reflection. (ll. 81–89)

As in Swift's text, after "secret sessions" the council determines it is illegal to take action without permission from "Secret Powers." Soyinka's narrator is also charged with being a "blasphemer," for making accusations against those in power, which can be read as an allusion to the Federal Military Government's hostile response to Soyinka's journalistic writings. According to James Gibbs, Soyinka's "instinct, or perhaps his 'intuition' prompted him to point out and vilify those who were exploiting the confusion and chaos into which [Nigeria] had been swept. These are the very men whom he later accused of *creating* the confusion and chaos." In "Let's Think of the Aftermath of this War" (*Daily Sketch* 4 August 1967), Soyinka describes these men as: "the now familiar brigade of professional congratulators, opportunists, patriots and other sordid racketeers who are riding high into positions of influence on the wave of hysteria and tribal hatred" (242).[13] The paradox, then, is that Soyinka is accused of being an "arsonist" for attempting to abate political conflicts by drawing attention to the discord and violence that the Federal Military Government initiated.

As the poem progresses, Soyinka's narrator further ridicules his captors for being the aggressors and declaring war:

> The seasons passed of peace, winds gathered
> To a storm within an egg-cup.
> Excavating scrolls in long forgotten archives
> They stretched the warps of mind to rigid poles
> Of opposition, blared the martial note:
> From Us the Lilliwhite King Lillypuss
> To You obfuscating Blefuscoons
> From Us the Herrenyolk of Egg
> To you Albinos of the Albumen . . . We Declare . . . ! (ll. 63–69)

By specifically referencing Swift's "Big-Endians" and Little-Endians," the two great empires of Lilliput and Blefuscu that have "been engaged in most obstinate war for six and thirty Moons past" (36), Soyinka reiterates his association of Lilliput with Nigeria and Blefuscu with Biafra.[14] The parallels between Lilliput/Blefuscu and Nigeria/Biafra are certainly striking. Biafra is the Eastern Region of Nigeria and, similarly, Blefscu is Northeast of Lilliput. During the Civil War, the Federal Military Government put severe restrictions on communication and the importation of goods to Biafra, which ultimately led to widespread starvation and disease, and made it illegal to visit Biafra. In Swift's text, during the war "all intercourse between the two Empires" is "strictly forbidden . . . upon Pain of Death; and an Embargo laid by our Emperor upon all Vessels whatsoever" (38). When Soyinka's narrator asserts that he "pledged reversion of [his] strength / To arbitration; they pledged extinction of their kind" (ll. 75–76), he alludes to his own non-violent activism and his captors' calculated act of genocide, and points directly to Swift's Gulliver's statement: "And I plainly protested, that I would never be an Instrument of bringing a free and brave People into Slavery" (41).

However, Swift's Gulliver only realizes that the Lilliputians have made a slave of him so as to enslave the Lilliputians when he goes to war on their behalf and dons his spectacles to protect his eyes. When Gulliver first arrived in Lilliput, he was subjected to a meticulous search of his pockets but managed to retain "a Pair of Spectacles" and a "Pocket Perspective," devices for enhancing vision or aiding impaired vision (23).[15] In 1978, Pat Rogers wrote that Gulliver is "perhaps the first bespectacled hero in English literature" (179), and from the start his character is an extension of Addison and Steele's *Mr. Spectator*, who claims in *Spectator No. 1* to "live in the World, rather as a Spectator of Mankind, than as one of the Species." According to Rogers, "sight" in *Gulliver's Travels* ultimately comes to "express the ordeal of consciousness" (186). Thus just as *Mr. Spectator* is a literary device for raising the consciousness of Addison and Steele's readers, Gulliver (with his spectacles on) is a literary devise for raising the consciousness of Swift's readers. In other words, what Gulliver sees when he puts on his glasses is perhaps exactly what Swift wants his readers to see. For example, the next time Gulliver mentions his visual aids is when he reports that he used the Pocket Perspective to view the Blefuscudian's Fleet and, out of concern for his eyes, put on his spectacles and "thus armed went on boldly with my Work in spight [*sic*] of the Enemy's Arrows" (39). Regardless of Gulliver's rationale for putting his spectacles on, once he does he realizes that the Emperor's objective is "nothing less than reducing the whole Empire of *Blefuscu* into a Province, and governing it by a viceroy; of destroying the Big-Endian Exiles, and compelling that People to break the smaller end of their Eggs; by which he would remain sole monarch of the World" (40).

Gulliver had confessed earlier that he needed his spectacles to correct a "Weakness" of his eyes and prior to this moment he mistakenly viewed the Lilliputians as non-threatening. For example, by having his narrator claim, "They lodged me in a hall of sorts," Soyinka refers to Gulliver's comment, "In this Edifice it was determined that I should lodge" (12). Gulliver's assessment of the Temple as lodgings, as opposed to a prison, indicates that he is oblivious to the gravity of his situation. Soyinka also points to the absurdity of Gulliver's desire to gain the Emperor's and his courtiers' respect, despite their tiny physical stature:

> I pledged my strength anew
> To service of the state,
> Enticed the court

Statesmen, minions and nobility
To grace my temple home. They trod a measure
On the dais of my handkerchief
The king excelled in skating on a mucus
Rink—indeed we passed the rapid days
In feasts of love, in mirth and mutual service. (ll. 52–60)

In Swift's text, Gulliver enthusiastically participates in the Lilliputian social system, naturally supports the authority of the Emperor, and admires the Emperor's military display and pageantry.[16] By having his narrator declare, "I could not choose but serve" (l. 70), Soyinka points to Swift's Gulliver's naïve agreement to defend the Emperor and State "against all Invaders" (37). But when Gulliver goes to war on their behalf and puts his spectacles on to protect his eyes, he *sees* for the first time his captors' greed, ruthlessness, and lust for supremacy; in other words, he experiences (albeit temporarily) a sharpening of *perspective*.[17] Subsequently, he tries to divert the Lilliputian Emperor from his "Design, by many Arguments drawn from the Topicks of Policy as well as Justice" (40). Gulliver's attempts to reason with the Emperor and initiate arbitration with the Blefuscudians are unsuccessful and, like Soyinka, he is charged with treason.

Debates ensue regarding how to punish Gulliver, and the compromise that is reached is to spare his life but blind him. Thus the Lilliputians will put his girth and strength into the service of the State, but *see for him*.[18] When Gulliver learns that the "Sentence of putting out [his] eyes" is what will be "entered into the Books" but that the government also intends to put into effect a "Secret" sentence, which is the "Project" of starving him to death (60), he resolves to escape to Blefuscu. He confesses to the reader that his primary motivation for running away is the preservation of his "Eyes" and his "Liberty," but he also recognizes that he "durst not rely on so dangerous a Decision, in so critical a juncture, and against such Powerful Enemies"(61).[19] Here, Gulliver seems to be very much aware of the injustice and corruption of the Lilliputian judicial system. But he quickly remembers the "Favours" he received from the Emperor "with gratitude," and does not believe that "his Majesty's *present Severities acquitted me of all past Obligations*" (61). The moment of acute vision Gulliver experienced when he declared that he would "never be an Instrument of bringing a free and brave People into Slavery" is short-lived. Unlike Soyinka's narrator, Swift's Gulliver is unable to see that, by taking his *eyes*, the Lilliputians endeavor to prevent him from *thinking* and *acting* for himself, and from being *conscious* of the fact that his oppression is due to the government's coercion rather than his own weaknesses.

In Soyinka's "Gulliver," what his narrator *sees* when they "pardon him to lose his sight" (l. 102) is his captors' calculated attempt to destroy his mind and suppress his consciousness. For dictatorial regimes, to destroy vision is a "proven cure for all / Abnormalities of view—foresight, insight / Second sight and all solecisms of seeing—called Vision" (ll. 103–106). Soyinka's poem stops here, with the threat to Gulliver's vision, which seems to suggest that he is engaging only with Gulliver's Voyage to Lilliput, specifically the charges against him, and that, while Swift's Gulliver manages to escape his oppressors, Soyinka's narrator is forced to endure the punishment imposed upon him. However, the very production of "Gulliver" testifies to the fact that Soyinka continued to be a witness and thus retained his vision while in solitary confinement.

***

By portraying his narrator as a witness who observes and documents abuses of power and crimes against humanity, Soyinka conveys his identification with Gulliver in Laputa and Lagado who, rather than being an object of satire and an unwitting victim, witnesses and records how governments maintain domination and suppress the autonomy of their subjects. Thus in addition to forcing a reinterpretation of Swift's Gulliver in Lilliput as a prisoner of conscience, Soyinka forces a reinterpretation of Gulliver in Laputa and Lagado as an author who witnesses, records his observations, and offers an alternative perspective on the theme of Part I: tyranny and government corruption. When Soyinka's narrator studies his captors, he sees their unreserved quest for hegemony and, by concurrently engaging with Parts I and III of *Gulliver's Travels*, Soyinka draws attention to the thematic link between these two sections. [20]

Soyinka's narrator reports that his captors' narcissism is so out of control that they have even ordered the universe to reduce itself to match their tiny size and the planets to orbit around their "sun"—the king:

> The world was measured to a dwarf
> Sufficiency; the sun by state decree
> Was lowered to fit the sextant of their mind
> And planets sighted lower to turn
> In calculable grooves, in orbits centred
> On the palace of the Sun of suns
> Man-Mountain, King of Lilliput,
> Lord and Terror of a thimble universe! (ll. 29–36)

Here, Soyinka once again uses antithesis to represent the relationship between captor and captive. However, as Johae astutely observes, while the name "Man-Mountain" is given to Swift's Gulliver by the Lilliputians "in recognition of his awesome size," in Soyinka's poem this title, "among other synonymous kennings of eulogistic function," is assigned to the King of Lilliput. In fact, there is nothing in the poem to indicate that the Lilliputians treat Soyinka's narrator with the "wonder" and "astonishment" that Swift's Lilliputians treat his Gulliver (34). At the same time, Soyinka's narrator observes that his captors exercise and exert control over their subjects by manipulating the natural world, and thereby alludes to the Laputian-controlled movement of the floating island. When Swift's Gulliver first encounters the floating island he observes—with wonder and astonishment—that the center of the island is a "chasm, from which the Astronomers descend into the Astronomers Cave," and that the "Place is stored with a Variety of Sextants, Quadrants, Telescopes, Astrolabes, and other Astronomical Instruments. But the greatest Curiosity, upon which the fate of the Island depends, is a Loadstone of prodigious size" (158). Not only is movement of the island determined by this giant magnet, but "it is in the Power of the Monarch to raise the Island above the Region of the Clouds and Vapours" and "he can prevent the falling of Dews and Rains whenever he please" (156). Thus like Swift, Soyinka dramatizes tyranny as scientific experiments taken to outlandish extremes.

Most of the ideas that Swift presents in Part III are based on reports published in the *Philosophical Transactions of the Royal Society* during the last third of the seventeenth century and first quarter of the eighteenth century, up to and including material published in 1726, the year Swift composed Part III. Swift's floating island is at once a critique of scientific experimentation, specifically the Royal Society's development of William Gilbert's study of magnetism (*De Magnet*, 1600), and a condemnation of colonialist exploitation and oppression, specifically England's domination of Ireland. Soyinka's embedded allusion to the floating island suggests that Swift's allegory of England's domination over Ireland—like his allegory of England's war with France in Part I—is applicable to the material conditions of the Nigerian Civil War. For example, the Laputians' first response to rebellion is to cut the people off from natural resources:

> If any Town should engage in a Rebellion or Mutiny, fall into violent Factions, or refuse to pay the usual Tribute; the King hath two Methods of reducing them to Obedience. The first and mildest course is by keeping the Island hovering such a Town, and the Lands about it; whereby he can deprive them of the Benefit of the Sun, and the Rain, and consequently afflict the Inhabitants with Dearth and Diseases. (161)

Similarly, during the Nigerian Civil War the Federal Military Government's first response to Biafran secession was to impose severe economic sanctions, including a blockade of the Eastern Region's air and seaports, a ban on foreign currency transactions, and a halt to all incoming post and telecommunications. Not only were the Biafrans unable to import food and medical supplies, relief organizations were unable to supply aid to people on either side of the fighting.

According to John J. Stremlaw, the "starvation of the Biafrans was not an accident, or a mischance, or even a necessary but regrettable by-product of war. It was a deliberately executed and integral part of Nigerian war policy" (195). Dan Jacobs, who served as Executive Director of the Committee for Nigeria-Biafra Relief, asserts that the "sheer horror of children starving—or being deliberately starved—made this one of the most emotional events of our time." Jacobs adds that, a few months after the war began, "there arose confusion as to who was at fault, and what could be done about it, as to who was blocking food relief and causing the starvation. Nigeria, by imposing the blockade? . . . Biafra, because General Ojukwu insisted on unreasonable conditions for entry of relief, as he needed the starvation to sustain the world's compassion and support for Biafran independence?" After the war, Jacobs embarked on his own investigation of why relief organizations encountered so much resistance, which led him to the conclusion that the "Nigerians were starving the Biafrans," but it was the British, who were supplying increasingly more arms to the Nigerian government as the war progressed, who covered it up (5).[21]

Alfred Obiora Uzokwe explains that the deliberate starvation of the Igbo people was not the only means that the Federal Military Government used to "break the spirit of Biafra and cow her into submission." When the war started, it was believed that the rules of conventional warfare would apply, and that air raids and military assaults would only be targeted at army formations. But as "things progressed, it became clear that Nigeria was determined to break all the rules of conventional warfare; they bombed civilians with reckless abandon and the havoc they were causing in civilian enclaves was utterly gruesome! The testament to the carnage they left in their wake could be seen all over Biafra—maimed children, men and women with missing body parts, destroyed residential buildings, cratered highways with skeletal remains littered all over them and the constant smell of death" (90). Nigerian War Policy included killing Igbo civilians by bombing crowded marketplaces, and murdering officers in the Eastern Region in "ritualistic, brutal ways" (Jacobs 24).[22]

Thus Swift's Gulliver's description of the Laputians' methods of suppressing rebellions is shockingly prophetic. Along with cutting off natural resources, rebels are "pelted from above with great Stones, against which they have no Defense." If the rebels "continue to be obstinate," the Laputian king will drop the Island "directly upon their Heads, which makes a universal Destruction of both Houses and Men (161–162). The Laputian king is "seldom driven" to this last resort, and his advisors rarely advise him to take such action, for "fear of breaking the Adamantine Bottom, in which Case it is the Opinion of all their Philosophers, that the Load-stone could no longer hold it up, and the whole Mass would fall to the Ground" (161–162). The general sense here, as Turner suggests, is that if the English government is too oppressive "it will fall" (332). In the twentieth century, the sheer bloodiness of the Nigerian Civil War, the massive destruction of Biafra, and the colossal death toll (estimated at more than two million) all indicate that the Federal Military Government had absolutely no reservations about being too oppressive.

In another verse, Soyinka once again engages simultaneously with Parts I and III of *Gulliver's Travels* to portray the Federal Military Government's despotism. This verse is more obviously an engagement with the scene in Gulliver's Voyage to Lilliput in which the court hygienists deliberate on "waste disposal" and warn that a decomposing corpse of that magnitude could cause "plagues" and "infections":

> From a capital doom, the saving thought
> Was waste disposal—how rid the state
> Of carrion weightier than the court and state.
> The Court Hygienists voiced a dread
> Of plagues, infections, cautioned—Hold!
> A cult of septic hydrants may derive
> From such a monumental corpse, springing
> To douse orthodoxies of state and power
> In rank corrosive draughts! (ll. 90–98)

Yet this verse can also be read as an engagement with Gulliver's tour of the Academy of Lagado which, like Swift's floating island, is at once a critique of the Royal Society and an allegory for the way in which a colonized people are oppressed by the union of scientific speculation and imperial power. Soyinka alludes here to one professor's plan for "discovering Plots and Conspiracies against the Government," which is to have "great Statesmen" examine the diet of "all suspecting Persons; their Times of eating . . . with which Hand they wiped their Posteriors; to take a strict View of their Excrements, and the Colour, the Odour, the Taste, the Consistence, the Crudeness, or maturity of Digestion, form a Judgement of their thoughts and Designs." The reasoning behind this plan is that "Men are never so serious, thoughtful, and intent, as when they are at Stool." The professor proposes that, if someone is contemplating the "best Way of murdering the King," their "Ordure would have a Tincture of Green; but quite different when he thought only of raising an Insurrection or burning the Metropolis" (182).

By engaging with Swift's grotesque depiction of state-sponsored terrorism to dramatize how totalitarian regimes clamp down on political activism, Soyinka exposes that Swift's rendering is actually more realistic than absurd. Just as Swift's "political Projector" views variations of excrement as evidence that the person who evacuated it was contemplating regicide or rebellion, Soyinka's captors believe that what comes out of the bodies and minds of political activists will "douse orthodoxies of state and power / in rank corrosive draughts." Given that a "draught" is also a move in the game of checkers, the implication here is that what comes out of political activists will instigate counter-attacks. As in Swift's text, it is the political activist's *live* body and *active* mind that are deemed threatening and need to be eliminated or destroyed. Soyinka's captors' concern, however, is that the presence or discovery of a "monumental corpse," a dead political activist, will cause what this regime considers "plagues, infections." In other words, the disappearance or death of an insurgent would be bad publicity, and is as damaging to their reputation and stability, if not more, than the political activist's activism. In order to avoid public backlash—locally and globally—the compromise that is reached is to keep this world-renowned writer/activist alive, but physically remove him from circulation and destroy the mind from which revolutionary thoughts and "aesthetic radicalism" spring.

In *The Man Died*, Soyinka reports that soon after his arrest an "examiner" angrily accused him of leaking information to the foreign press: "'How is it that the foreign papers are already carrying news of your arrest? . . . How could they have known and why all this publicity?'" (43). He then warns Soyinka that such publicity would not be in his best interest, and he charges the foreign press, rather than their own treatment of prisoners, with being corrupt, deceitful, and malicious: "'They are already insinuating that you are being ill-treated. I hope you realize that all this publicity is not helping your case one bit . . . we know you are a world-famous figure, but these foreign papers are naturally mischievous. Any opportunity to slander the authorities . . . '" (44). An hour after this interrogation, orders were given to transfer Soyinka to Kiri-kiri Prison. In addition, the Federal

Military Government countered by distributing propaganda. After Soyinka stood his ground and refused to be examined by a government doctor during a hunger strike, "the police (and the government) panicked" and "rushed to the press" with a release that reported, 'He sleeps well, eats well, is allowed to see his own doctor . . . '" (67).

Shortly thereafter, the Federal Military Government released another press release: "A famous Nigerian Playwright, Head of Drama and Lecturer in English of the Lagos University, Mr. Soyinka . . . has been ominously connected with espionage activities for the rebel leader Odumegwu-Ojukwu against the Federal Military Government." Soyinka has "admitted in a statement" that he was involved in attempts to overthrow the government, but has since "changed his mind on this" (*The Sunday Post*, 29 October 1967). According to Soyinka, the image such a report leaves in the reader's mind is that he signed a "confession" but is now a "repentant traitor" and "happy, contented and relaxed, glad to have the whole thing off his chest. The Military machine had some highly efficient experts on public psychology working on his affairs" (72). Once the problem of how to dispose of Soyinka's body is settled by arresting and imprisoning him, the police and government embarked on the project of destroying his mind by transferring him first to Maximum Security Prison and then to Kaduna, where he was placed in solitary confinement, which for Soyinka was equivalent to being buried alive.

But as I mention above, the very existence of "Gulliver" proves that Soyinka managed to maintain his sanity and write while in solitary confinement. Unlike Swift's Gulliver, who reports that he was "ill entertained" while visiting the Academy of Lagado and that thinking of the political Projectors makes him "melancholy" (179), Soyinka documents his encounters with government corruption, as well as his own personal physical and mental abuse, to expose evil and tyranny. Subsequently, his poem functions like a political tract. Moreover, by engaging with *Gulliver's Travels*, Soyinka points to the fact that this text, as George Orwell argues in "Politics vs. Literature: An Examination of *Gulliver's Travels*" (1962), represents the author's "extraordinarily clear pre-vision of the spy-haunted 'police State,' with its endless heresy-hunts and treason trials, all really designed to neutralize popular discontent by changing it into war hysteria" (84). Swift attacks that aspect of totalitarianism which "is not merely to make sure that people will think the right thoughts," but which will "make them *less conscious*" (85). Soyinka, similarly, exposes that the Federal Military Government endeavored to suppress their subjects' consciousness as a means of imposing authority and maintaining dominance.

For this Nigerian writer and political activist, Swift's legacy is his life-long crusade against organized human aggression. As Said determines, Swift's body of work includes

> commentaries on such disparate issues as war itself (about which he never had a good word to say; a remarkable fact), conquest, colonial oppression, religious factionalism, the manipulation of minds and bod-ies, schemes for projecting power on nature, on human beings, and on history, the tyranny of the majority, monetary profit for its own sake, the victimization of the poor by a privileged oligarchy. (84)

It is therefore conceivable that Soyinka's "Gulliver" is at once an engagement with what Andrew Varney refers to as Swift's "savage indictments of the prac-tice of European warfare in *Gulliver's Travels,* and of the corrupt and selfish interests that prompt it" (31), and with his political pamphlet, *The Conduct of the Allies; and of the Late Ministry, in Beginning and Carrying on the Present War* (1711). Swift had previously indicted the "war-mongering" Whigs and the corruption of their "great general," the Duke of Marlborough, in print. As editor of the *Examiner* and chief Tory propagandist, Swift devoted a series of anonymous articles to justifying Tory strategies to end the war with France and secure peace with Europe.[23] But his most substantial and effective anti-war treatise is *The Conduct of the Allies*, which was published by the govern-ment in November 1711 and sold over ten thousand copies in two months (McMinn 21). *The Conduct of the Allies* can be viewed as a "political tri-umph," as it helped prepare public opinion for the Treaty of Utrecht within two years, and it is a powerful example of how a written text can successfully raise the reading public's awareness of government corruption and contribute to ending a war.

In a letter to Stella dated 30 October 1711, Swift announces that he was "to-day in the city concerning some things with a printer . . . I won't tell you now; but the ministers reckon it will do [an] abundance of good, and open the eyes of the nation, who are half bewitched against peace" (*SW* ii. 402). In a letter dated 30 November 1711, he informs Stella that he "had been all this afternoon with the printer, adding something to the second edition . . . the pamphlet makes a world of noise, and will do a great deal of good: it tells an abundance of most important facts which not all are known" (*SW* ii. 429). A third edition was printed on December 2, and a fourth on December 6. But Swift's pamphlet was effective not only because it was timely and reached so many people, but also because of his rhetoric. He prefaces *The Conduct of the Allies* with a declaration that "no reasonable man, whether Whig or Tory . . . can be of the opinion for continuing the war . . . unless he be a gainer by it . . . [or] be very ignorant of the kingdom's condition, and by what means we have been reduced by it." Regarding the latter possibility, he thinks it "highly necessary that the public should be freely and impartially told what circumstances they are in, after what manner they have been treated by those whom they trusted so many years with the disposal of their blood and treasure, and what the consequences of this management are likely to be, upon themselves and their posterity" (*SW* iv. 303). In the main section of the pamphlet, Swift provides the information that the Whigs withheld as evidence that "England ought no more to have been a principal in this war than Prussia, or any other power" (*SW* iv. 313). Despite the fact that *The Conduct of the Allies* was Tory propaganda, Swift positions himself as bipartisan by appealing to both Whigs and Tories. Moreover, he puts his readers on the defensive, as no one would want to be viewed as a "gainer" by the war, and simultaneously creates an alliance with them by demonstrating that the government has lied and taken advantage of them.

Swift explains that The War of the Spanish Succession (also known as Queen Anne's War) was primarily about maintaining the balance of power in Europe, and about trade. As King Charles II of Spain had died without an heir, the issue of who would inherit the Spanish kingdoms became extremely contentious, with both the French Bourbons and Austrian Habsburgs vying for the Spanish throne. Charles II had bequeathed his possessions to the Duke of Anjou, a grandson of King Louis IV, who became Philip V when he ascended the throne. In an attempt to secure French hegemony in Europe, King Louis cut off England and the Netherlands from Spanish trade and, as Swift reveals, there were those in England who favored the war because, with Philip as King of Spain, "we could have no security for our trade . . . nor any hopes of preserving the balance of Europe, because the grandfather would in effect be king, while his grandson had but the title" (*SW* iv. 314). So, "without taking time to consider the consequences . . . we hastily engaged in a war" (*SW* iv. 315). To pay for the war, taxes were raised, and for ten years this "artificial wealth of funds and stocks" had been in the hands of those who were "plundering the public." In fact, there was now corruption in "every branch of government" (*SW* iv. 317). Swift eventually comes around to directly attacking the Duke of Marlborough's "appetite for wealth and power" (*SW* iv. 350).[24] Thus as Oakleaf explains, Swift exploits "contemporary anxiety about the growing power of speculative capital," disparages the Whigs as a "subversive faction serving the treacherous forces of godlessness (dissent) and credit," rallies support for the Tory government's policy of extricating Britain from the war, and exposes that "avarice tainted" the Duke of Marlborough, who was considered a national hero for his "spectacular military success" (34).

While it is reasonable to suggest, given that with "Gulliver" Soyinka exposes the Federal Military Government's corruption and brutal war tactics, he identifies with Swift's anti-war sentiment and use of a written text to influence public opinion toward peace, he could not possibly identify with Swift's partisanship and the fact that he was a paid political pawn. Although Swift had for a long time associated with the Whigs, in 1710 he was courted and eventually secured as an ally by Robert Harley, the leader of the Tory majority in the House of Commons. He put his writing skills at the Tory party's disposal, and was financially compensated for such propagandist writings as *The Conduct of the Allies*. Moreover, the grave irony for any discussion of how Soyinka engages with Swift's anti-war campaign is that, with the end of the War of Spanish Succession came the Treaty of Utrecht, which gave England a monopoly on the Slave Trade. In the early eighteenth century most slaves were being taken from the west coast of Africa, or what is now Nigeria.

After the death of Queen Anne and the Tories fell from favor, Swift returned to Ireland, where he served as Dean of St. Patrick's Cathedral in Dublin for the remainder of his life. Although he was fairly quiet for several years, in the 1720s he became a fervent defender of Irish rights. According to Nigel Wood, it was while Swift was in "exile" in Ireland that he developed a "self-image of the embattled outsider" and, with the publication of his *Drapier's Letters*, which inspired the Irish to reject the importation of Wood's halfpence, Swift became (like Soyinka) a "threat to centralizing power" (13). Thus rather than the earlier Swift, Soyinka identifies primarily with the Swift of the 1720s, who during this time produced numerous political tracts about Ireland, as well as *Gulliver's Travels*.[25] While there is no evidence in "Gulliver" that Soyinka is engaging with *The Drapier's Letters*, the fact that he engages with *Gulliver's Travels*, in which Swift includes an account of the Lindalino rebellion, an allegory of Ireland's successful anti-Wood campaign, enables speculation.[26] Perhaps more suggestive is the possibility that Soyinka identifies with Swift's utilization of a fictional persona who is a fellow sufferer or victim to incite non-violent resistance to government oppression. Letter I of *The Drapier's Letters* is addressed to the "tradesmen, shopkeepers, farmers, and country-people in general, of the kingdom of Ireland," whom M.B. Drapier addresses as his "brethren, friends, countrymen, and fellow-subjects," and for whom he "ordered the printer to sell it at the lowest rate." The general purpose of this letter is to inform the Irish masses of the law: "You are not obliged to take any money which is not of gold or silver . . . Much less are you obliged to take those vile halfpence . . . by which you must lose almost eleven pence in every shilling" (*SW* vi. 371). In Letter II, Swift as Mr. Drapier speaks both *on behalf of* and directly *to* those to whom he had addressed the first letter, and he critiques the printer to whom he addresses this letter for circulating misleading information. In the first two letters, Mr. Drapier presents himself as successful shopkeeper who, although economically secure, is ultimately concerned for the rights of the common people.

In Letter III, addressed to the "Nobility and Gentry of the Kingdom of Ireland," Mr. Drapier adopts a slightly different persona, as he presents himself as a "poor ignorant shopkeeper, utterly unskilled in law," who will critique "The Report by the Committee of the Lords relating to Wood's halfpence," which is clearly propaganda, "by plain reason, unassisted by art, cunning or eloquence" (*SW* vi. 404). The self-deprecating persona Swift adopts here is clearly for the purpose of not alienating his upper-class readers, and is remarkably comparable to the rhetoric later utilized in slave narratives: "Were not the people of Ireland born as free as those of England . . . Does not the same sun shine upon them? And have they not the same God for their protector? Am I a freeman in England, and do I become a slave in six hours by crossing the channel?" (*SW* vi. 405). The first three letters dwell on arguments against Wood's halfpence, derived from their alleged inferiority in weight and value, and Swift lashes out against Wood himself for his avarice and lack of principles. Subsequently, the Irish Houses of Parliament took action by addressing the English government about the scheme, and Irish people of all religious and political allegiances, and all social classes, formed associations as they joined together in refusing to accept the halfpence. Letters V, VI and VIII are for the most part follow-ups to the victory and include additional details about how the cause was won.

But it is in Letter IV, the most well known of *The Drapier's Letters*, which is addressed to the "Whole People of Ireland," that Swift articulates his real concern: Ireland's independence from British rule. Here, he boldly attacks the English government for binding the Irish to laws of a Parliament in which Ireland had no representation. As Sir Walter Scott explains in his "Life of Swift" (1824), "the alarm was instantly taken by the English government . . . a proclamation was issued, offering a £300 reward for the discovery of the author of the Drapier's fourth letter, described as a wicked and malicious pamphlet, containing several seditious and scandalous passages, reflecting upon his majesty and his ministers, and tending to alienate the affections of his good subjects in England and Ireland from each other" (296). Mr. Harding, the printer of *The Drapier's Letters*, was thrown into prison and threatened with prosecution. One of the passages selected as evidence that he was deserving of prosecution reads: "Those who come over

hither to us from England, and some weak people among ourselves, whenever in discourse make mention of liberty and property, shake their heads,
and tell us, that 'Ireland is a depending kingdom;' as if they would seem by
this phrase to intend, that the people of Ireland are in some state of slavery or
dependence different from those of England" (*SW* vi. 445).[27] Harding's family urged him to inform against the author, but he apparently replied that he
would "rather perish in jail before he would be guilty of treachery and baseness." According to Scott, this exchange took place in Swift's presence, "who
sat beside them in silence," and "came and departed without being known to
anyone but Harding" (297–298). The grand jury ultimately brought down
a verdict of "*ignoramous*," and the bill against Harding was eventually dissolved.

In the sixth *Drapier's Letter*, the Dean pleads the cause of the Drapier,
and in certain passages it seems as though he is no longer anxious to conceal his identity. The surrender of Wood's halfpence marked the end of the
first significant struggle for Ireland's independence, and the Drapier/Swift
became known as the liberator of Ireland. While Swift avoided direct prosecution because of his anonymity, Soyinka did not enjoy the same fate. But
Swift's refusal to remain silent on the issue of England's oppression of Ireland
is perhaps, above all else, the reason Soyinka identifies with him. As he writes
in *The Man Died*, "The Man dies . . . in all who keep silent in the face of
tyranny" (13). In fact, this is likely the reason Soyinka's engagements with
Swift are so extensive. In his satirical play, *Requiem for a Futurologist* (1983),
he rewrites Swift's "Bickerstaff prank" and, according to Sabor, Soyinka's pervasive motif of cannibalism is a look back at *A Modest Proposal*.

But by transforming the generic forms of Swift's writings, Soyinka
distances himself from Swift and exposes the contradictions in his political
thought. For example, while Soyinka condemns Britain's colonialist policies
he concurrently blames the victims of economic oppression for contributing to their own subjugation by being either lazy or squandering what little
they possessed. Swift's attitudes toward the relationship between rulers and
their subjects are likewise at odds. In a letter to Archbishop King dated 18
May 1727 he writes: "My Lord, I have lived, and by grace of God will die,
an enemy to servitude and slavery of all kinds: And I believe, at the same
time, that persons of such disposition will be the most ready to pay obedience where it is due" (*SW* xvii. 111–112). Moreover, Swift wholly supported
hereditary rights of monarchs and "passive obedience" but concurrently
believed that if a King becomes a tyrant his subjects have the right to wish
for a better one. Perhaps the most crucial difference between Soyinka and
Swift is the fact that Swift abhorred dissent and revolution. According to

Frederick V. Bogel, Swift, as well as John Dryden, Alexander Pope and Samuel Johnson, were writing with the memory of the late seventeenth century in mind. They regarded the revolution of the 1640s as a "singular fracturing of order: a fall into regicide, a dismantling of centralized authority, and a splintering of consensus into sectarian waywardness." With the restoration of the Stuarts in the 1660s and the Bill of Rights in 1688–89, this "fall was redeemed" (16). Nevertheless, they "frequently deride the wish to overthrow existing forms and institutions" and "satirize—with merciless intensity—the revolutionary transformation that is really replication, the 'new order' that unwittingly reproduces the old" (17). Similarly, in his critique of neocolonial tyranny and brutality in Nigeria, Soyinka illustrates that the "new" military dictatorship was actually a replication of the "old" colonial rule.

Of course, these canonical English writers were hardly strict conservatives. Pope was a Roman Catholic during a time of intense anti-Catholic sentiment, and it is well known that Johnson offered a toast "to the next insurrection of the Negroes in the West Indies" in the company of Oxford scholars long before abolition was popular. Swift, as I have discussed, was a staunch anti-colonialist and critic of British rule in Ireland. Moreover, while Bogel contends that for Swift the "recourse to revolutionary innovation" and the "decisive break from traditional forms" (16) were to be avoided at all costs, Soyinka's engagements with Swift expose that Swift's aesthetics—his innovative form of political satire, his use of a fictional persona—were indeed revolutionary, just not calls for revolution.[28] But as Dustin Griffin contends, this is due to the form itself and, "despite the fears of political authorities from ancient to current times, it has not been convincingly shown that satire has the power to encourage the actions or alter the attitudes of its readers" (54). Soyinka exposes that a satire such as *Gulliver's Travels* is incapable of stimulating material change because the protagonist is the amusing object of Swift's satire. The appeal of *Gulliver's Travels* for early eighteenth-century readers can in part be attributed to not only its humor but also its readily identifiable allusions to, and critiques of, actual people and events, which in turn generated an alliance between the author and his readers and an opposition between his readers and the objects of satire. Subsequently, readers endorse the author's judgment and fail to develop compassion for Gulliver, who is offered to the reading pubic as deserving of his victimization and abuse in Books I and II because of folly and blindness, and deserving of his (self-imposed) alienation at the end of Book IV because of his overblown pride. If Gulliver is responsible for his own oppressed condition, then the strongest response readers would have is the desire to not be like Gulliver. Yet Soyinka, as a *reader*, both aligns himself and distances himself from *both* the object of satire and the author. As a *writer*, he conveys identification with Swift's object of satire by reintroducing Gulliver as a fellow victim of oppression who has been *unjustly* abused by a corrupt and tyrannical government and who, like the author himself, documents his suffering for twentieth-century readers. Soyinka thus establishes a tri-way alliance between author, narrator and readers and, by also dislodging humor, empowers his text to encourage the actions and alter the attitudes of his readers.

***

In "Swift's Political Legacy: Re-Membering the Past in Order to Imagine the Future," Carole Fabricant addresses the question of how far "we can (or ought) to go in making a figure from the past our contemporary, capable of participating in current debates" (181). She considers, among other examples, Orwell's "Jonathan Swift: An Imaginary Interview," in which Orwell imagines encountering Swift on the streets of London during World War II. Orwell takes advantage of the opportunity to comment on the "contemporaneity" of *Gulliver's Travels* by critiquing Swift for being "too hard on humanity" and even his own country. He then accuses him of preferring Louis XV's France, "which is almost like preferring Hitler's Germany" (113). While Orwell attacks Swift for not thinking better of the common people than their rulers, and not being in favor of increased social equality, according to Said what Orwell is unable to realize is that "one can be steadfastly opposed to tyranny" and "not have a well-developed position on representative institutions." Swift is a product of his time, and we cannot expect him to "think or act like a prototype of Orwell" (77). Nor can we expect him to think and act like a prototype of Soyinka.

Unlike Orwell, Soyinka is very much aware of the fact that, although there are commonalities in their attitudes regarding totalitarianism, oppression and global conquest, Swift is not our contemporary. As Fabricant concludes, Swift's "legacy is valuable precisely because it *isn't* a readymade product waiting to be neatly labeled and passively consumed . . . Swift's legacy takes on life and meaning only to the extent that we make it our own" (200). While Swift may have predicted with shocking accuracy the omnipresence of violence and government-sanctioned terrorism in the modern world, Soyinka is not suggesting with his "Gulliver" that we turn to Swift for advice on how to reconcile contemporary issues. Rather, he is showing us that what he has learned from Swift *as a writer* is to experiment with a variety of literary forms and not to be silent in the face of tyranny.

Soyinka continues to be a champion of human rights on the African continent and around the globe. In a talk entitled "Human Rights and

Cultural Alibis" (29 November 2001, University of Pennsylvania), Soyinka declared that the "gates of hell" are thrown open whenever the strong overtake the weak and the innocent. While all sectors of humanity are entitled to equal time and equal space, within every culture it is still possible to find minds that are not divorced from the craving for power and arguments for enslavement and genocide. According to Soyinka, the irony is that Judeo-Christian religions are founded on principles of universal peace but people are hiding behind the cloak of tradition, often disguised as religion, and abandoning moral obligation. This abandonment of morality has, in Soyinka's view, nurtured "monsters," inhibited cultures from understanding each other, and turned our world into a graveyard.

As Alison Brysk explains in her introduction to *Globalization and Human Rights*, there are a variety of psychological, social, economic and political patterns that put societies "at risk" of human rights violations. These generally include: "authoritarian government, civil war, strong ethnic cleavages, weak civil society, power vacuums, critical junctures in economic development, and military dominance." Above all, the study of human rights teaches us that human rights violations usually reflect a "calculated (or manipulated) pursuit of political power, not inherently evil or ungovernable passions" (4). Jonathan Glover similarly argues in *Humanity: A Moral History of the Enlightenment* that the "psychology of the human species can be seen as having a strong propensity both for getting trapped into conflict and also for cruelty and mass killing. Twentieth-century wars, massacres and genocides come from combining this psychology with modern technology" (413), which Swift prophesied in *Gulliver's Travels*. While keeping the past alive in our memories and via narratives may help prevent the repetition of atrocities, it is evident to contemporary observers that the past is very much alive today in the form of an *inhumanity* that stretches back to the eighteenth century.

Yet Soyinka's call for a new culture, a "culture of dignity," is also profoundly reminiscent of the Enlightenment's liberal values of tolerance, individualism, respect for human rights, and hope for a peaceful and more humane world. While criticism of the Enlightenment's totalizing historical narratives is both fashionable and warranted, and postcolonialism and postmodernism typically define themselves against the Enlightenment's absolutist, repressive, colonialist and racist thinking, a dialogue with the eighteenth century nonetheless continues to exist. Soyinka seemingly defies political correctness by turning to the Enlightenment and calling for the kind of enlightened consciousness in the twentieth and twenty-first centuries that, according to Said, was Swift's greatest contribution to political thought.

Chapter Four

Visual and Textual Narratives

David Dabydeen's *A Harlot's Progress* and
William Hogarth's *A Harlot's Progress*

The starting point for Dabydeen's *A Harlot's Progress* is Hogarth's pictorial story of an innocent Yorkshire country girl, Moll Hackabout, who travels to the city to earn a living but is ultimately destroyed by its commercialism. Dabydeen's protagonist, whom he names Mungo, is the black slave-boy from Plate 2 of Hogarth's satirical series thirty years after the prints first appeared. Mungo is now the oldest black resident of London, and he is in the process of telling his life story to a "Mr Pringle," Secretary of the Committee for the Abolition of Slavery, in exchange for food, clothing and the occasional shilling. But Mungo refuses to give Pringle the "story" he wants to hear, which can in part be attributed to his acute awareness of how he has been represented visually by and for white British society. According to Mungo, Pringle "hungers for understanding as to the link between barracoon and brothel, rank nigger and perfumed pet. He seems to believe that one moment I was a dusty black child playing in a sand-dune, crinkle-mouthed from the sun, then many rivers later I found myself in an English boudoir, a feathered turban on my head, my skin polished as bright as my teeth, and I am rollicking and sipping at Moll's lush bosom" (4).

With the narrative he imagines for one of "Hogarth's blacks," Dabydeen exposes that Hogarth's representations of blacks in Britain, however satirical or ironical, and however contrary to his intentions, defaced individual and cultural identities and perpetuated racial ideologies. Moreover, by engaging with eighteenth-century Afro-British writings, Dabydeen points to the contradiction inherent in texts produced by Africans in Britain for publication. If Mungo consents to have his narrative constructed for him, he will be complicit in sustaining the presumption that Africans are incapable of participating (as equals) in western culture. If he fictionalizes his narrative in order to adhere to a formula, he would be employing a tactic that, if discovered by his contemporaries, would discredit his eyewitness account of the evils of slavery. But by placing Mungo as a servant in the "Montague" household, Dabydeen links his protagonist to Afro-British writer Ignatius Sancho, who worked for the 2nd Duke of Montagu, and whose *Letters* (1782) defy categorization and serve as evidence that Sancho exercised his literary agency. In his writings, Sancho does not succumb to the linearity that was considered a necessary aspect of slave narratives because it demonstrated that Africans were capable of rational thought.

By naming the abolitionist "Mr Pringle," Dabydeen also draws attention to—and critiques—the circumstances surrounding the production of *The History of Mary Prince*, which was designed to serve as propaganda for the abolitionist campaign. Prince dictated her *History* to Susanna Strickland, after which Strickland and Thomas Pringle "pruned it into its present shape" (preface) and added supplementary documents validating the text's authorship and authenticity. By repudiating Pringle's plan to produce a straightforward narrative of sin and redemption, Mungo contests the practice of having his identity (as an African) constructed for him. Of course, by naming his protagonist "Mungo," a common name (like Sambo) given to Africans in the eighteenth century, Dabydeen conveys that white society has already attempted to obliterate his individual and cultural identity, and that he is expected to behave like—even *be* like—the stock slaves depicted in the period's dramatic works. Dabydeen is perhaps specifically alluding to Isaac Bickerstaff's *The Padlock* (1768), which tells the story of an African in Spain who is at once a comical or farcical servant and a victim of cruel subjugation, and whose colloquial speech differs significantly from such early dramatic representations of a "Noble Savage" as Oroonoko and Yarico. But Dabydeen's Mungo refuses to be an object of amusement for white readers, and by revisiting this eighteenth-century drama, as well as the pantomime entitled *Harlequin Mungo*, through Dabydeen's novel it is possible to discern the subtle ways in which Africans in dramatic productions of the period can be interpreted as symbols of oppression, and whose very depictions serve to contest the identities imposed upon them. Thus while Dabydeen's novel may seem to represent the "writing back" tradition, given that he gives voice to one of Hogarth's black figures, he actually parodies the conventions of the slave narrative and draws on the more improvisatory forms of Sancho's *Letters* and the pantomime.

***

Dabydeen was born in 1955 in Berbice, Guyana, which was a British colony predominantly inhabited by Indians and some Africans until 1966. Dabydeen's family moved several times during his childhood to avoid race riots between Indo-Guyanese and Afro-Guyanese and, at the age of ten, Dabydeen moved to the capital city of Georgetown to further his education. In 1969 Dabydeen moved to England, where he earned a Bachelor of Arts with Honors from Cambridge in 1978, and a Ph.D. in eighteenth-century literature and art from the University of London in 1981. Between 1982 and 1987, Dabydeen continued his studies at Oxford and Yale, lecturing on Caribbean Studies. Today, he directs the Centre for Caribbean Studies at Warwick University, where he is a Lecturer at the Centre for British Comparative Cultural Studies. Dabydeen is also Guyana's Ambassador-at-Large and a member of UNESCO's Executive Board.

In a 1989 interview with Wolfgang Binder, Dabydeen explained that his parents would not have seen England as "an Utopia, or an El Dorado in reverse, but certainly as a place where jobs were plentiful and the people hospitable." What they discovered, conversely, was that they were "unwanted." As an Asian student in a boy's school, Dabydeen felt pressure to integrate so as not to be seen as different or "defined as 'other,'" but by the 1980s he began to feel proud of his Asian-Caribbean heritage. In his first collection of poetry, *Slave Song* (1984), which won the Commonwealth Poetry Prize and Cambridge University Quiller-Couch Prize, Dabydeen recreates Guyanese Creole: a mixture of French, Spanish, and African dialects. In each of these fourteen poems, the poetic persona inhabits the men and women—slaves and indentured servants—who worked the cane fields of Guyana. To illuminate the accent, emotion, culture, and language of the cane fields for a wider audience, Dabydeen adds critical notes to each poem, in which he includes a glossary of words and expressions and a "translation" of the poem into Standard English. He also includes historical prints of slave and plantation life and thus, like *A Harlot's Progress*, *Slave Song* reflects his interest in the complex relations between historical documents, visual representations and literary creations.[1]

Dabydeen's first novel, *The Intended* (1991), which won the Guyana Prize for Literature, is a semi-autobiographical account of growing up in London. The title, an allusion to Kurtz's "intended" in Conrad's *Heart of Darkness*, conveys Dabydeen's continued focus on the history and continuing impact of slavery and colonization. In *Heart of Darkness*, Kurtz leaves his "intended" and journeys into the Congo; in *The Intended,* a young "brown" boy leaves a poor home and country (Guyana) and comes to England. The novel is set, for the most part, in London, although there are flashbacks to Guyana and glimpses of Oxford. *The Intended* is primarily an exploration of identity and survival strategies in twentieth-century England, where the immigrant narrator is taken to be an Indian but has no knowledge of India.

While the narrator is a West Indian, the "real" West Indian is presumed to be black, an African-Caribbean. Initially, the focus of the novel is the narrator's desire to assimilate, to succeed in British terms by going to Oxford, becoming a famous writer, and marrying an upper-class white woman. But the focus ultimately shifts from the narrator's struggle to become white to his struggle to become black.

Dabydeen's protagonist's sense of disillusionment reflects the writer's own experience. According to Winston James, the "root cause of the disillusionment and growing bitterness among black Britons was the clash of two logics within British imperialism—that of the Empire and that of the metropole." At home in the Caribbean, black people were taught that they were British and came to think of themselves as British. "They imbibed even such obscene jingoistic tunes as 'Rule Britannia,' which they sang, not only without objection but also with genuine pride" (377). Subsequently, they saw their movement to Britain as "internal migration," not as immigration. But the "logic of the metropole" was more powerful and overrode the "logic of the Empire." The British ruling class saw black people as colonials, and as such as inferiors. In the colony they could be British, but *not* in Britain, the "white man's country, the home of superior beings" (378). For many migrants, as Philip D. Morgan and Sean Hawkins explain, the experience of racism led them to identify as Africans. "This sense of being African was a cultural and political reaction against racist exclusion from full imperial citizenship" (4). Moreover, as Margery Fee suggests, while Dabydeen's novel is a "fairly straightforward, realist *Bildungsroman*, "its deliberate messiness" serves to counter the "iron cage of racial absolutism and hierarchy, the dominance of Standard English, and the ideal of clarity, order, and homogenous identity" (87). Its "structural peculiarities" derive from a "profound although tortured identification with blackness," and seem to reflect the "implied author's allegiance" to a Guyanese and West Indian black identity (69).[2]

Dabydeen's scholarly writings, like his poetry and fiction, and like the non-fiction and creative works produced by the other postcolonization writers in this study, are deeply personal. His interest in eighteenth-century British art developed because, as he told Binder, he could not look at it without finding something of himself or, if not himself, of the people that he came from. In his first book on the subject, *Hogarth's Blacks: Images of Blacks in Eighteenth Century English Art* (1985), Dabydeen highlights the marginal black figures in Hogarth's canvases and seeks to determine why they are there, how they contribute to the total narrative, and what Hogarth was saying about the black presence in England.[3] It is an "attempt to show that English art has a dimension of blackness to it; in other words, and on a personal level, that [he] belonged to British society" (164). Dabydeen begins his study by arguing that the sheer number of black figures in British art dating back to Elizabeth I serves as evidence of the widespread black presence in England, but the way in which blacks in Britain are depicted reflects the anxiety with which whites responded to this presence.[4] Seventeenth- and eighteenth-century English paintings reinforce a hierarchy of power relationships, as blacks are usually relegated to the margins and shown doing menial tasks. In portraiture, blacks appear as servants, almost always looking up in awe at their masters and mistresses, or as "pets" sharing the same lowly status as animals. Hogarth's *Wallaston Family* exemplifies the practice of commissioning an artist to include a black figure as a token of a family's affluence and colonial business interests.[5] In this group portrait, he is "barely more than a glob of paint, a shadowy figure with no personality or expression," and thus he is not represented as an "individual in his own right" (21). Images of Africans in British art recorded and maintained racial definitions and boundaries, and it is these representations of black figures with which Dabydeen, as a West Indian migrant of Asian descent, identifies.[6]

Dabydeen begins his discussion of Hogarth's satires by examining the examples Hogarth provides in his *Analysis of Beauty* manuscripts (1750) for the theory that judgments about beauty depend upon "custom, Fashion, perswasion and delusion." Hogarth claims, "the most remarkable instance, that is given in support of this is, that the Negro who finds great beauty in the black Females of his own country, may find as much deformity in the european Beauty as we see in theirs."[7] Such statements indicate that Hogarth was extremely knowledgeable about philosophical and scientific debates regarding Africans, and also that he recognized their humanity. Dabydeen uses *An Analysis of Beauty* as a springboard for his argument that Hogarth's blacks "amount to more than an erudite nod at artistic conventions, they are very much part of the narrative of his paintings and prints" (52). Each black figure is a "key to unlocking Hogarth's narrative puzzles" (9) and, significantly, "a yardstick, as well as a stick with which to beat the whites" (130). As Peter Sabor notes, Dabydeen "brings a new perspective to bear on Hogarth's art, treating blacks as observers and interpreting scenes through their eyes" (288).[8]

But in another review of *Hogarth's Blacks*, S.E. Ogude criticizes Dabydeen for reading "more into the prints than the facts can support." While Ogude credits Dabydeen for seeing the African in eighteenth-century British art as an "appendage of the upper class," whose "social value was not greater than that of the lapdog or the marmoset with whom he was generally associated," he disagrees with Dabydeen's view that Hogarth's black figures differ from other artistic renderings of the period.[9] Ogude contends that it is a mistake to see the black figures in Hogarth's works as carrying the "burden" of his satire, which he thinks would be just as forceful if the servants were white. But for Dabydeen, it is *because* the servants are black that Hogarth's critique of white society is so forceful. However, Dabydeen does acknowledge that Hogarth's black figures are stereotypical. At the conclusion of *Hogarth's Blacks*, he asserts that Hogarth "consciously employs current myths and stereotypes about blacks, relating to their sexuality, paganism, primitivism, and simian ancestry, so as to comment on the morality of the English aristocratic class." While Hogarth's "contempt was intended for whites," and each black figure "employed as a satirical device," because he gave validity to myths about Africans his works "reflected or reinforced racism among his white contemporaries" (130–131).

Fourteen years later, Dabydeen approached Hogarth's satirical series creatively with a fictional text, rather than an academic one. Just as Walcott seems to address the criticism of his Crusoe poems with *Pantomime*, with *A Harlot's Progress* Dabydeen seems to address the criticism of *Hogarth's Blacks*. Dabydeen not only produces a narrative for one of Hogarth's black figures to illustrate his conviction that Hogarth endowed each of them with their own narrative, he also imagines, appropriately, that such a narrative would include disdain for the artist himself. According to Dabydeen's Mungo, Hogarth "lied" about him, Moll, and the Jew, and his refusal to accommodate Mr. Pringle's desire for a story is rooted in his conviction that whatever words he utters will be "misconceived." He tells the reader: "You have, as evidence of this, Mr. Hogarth's prints" (273). Toward the end of his narrative, Mungo recounts the story of how he came to be one of "Hogarth's blacks." Hogarth visited the stable where Mr. Gideon (the Jewish, and supposedly "quack," doctor) was attending to prostitutes dying of venereal disease. Mungo thought at first that he was an emissary of Lord Montague, whose household he had run away from out of fear of being sold to a West Indian merchant. When he "smelt paint upon him, not death," he greeted him respectfully and brought him a stool to sit on as well as some water. But Hogarth did not even acknowledge Mungo, "thinking his action no more than a slave's duty. Nor did he have money to give." Prior to leaving, Hogarth gave him a Christian Bible, "as if a pagan needed neither bread nor soup nor silver like other humans, but only nourishment for his soul" (271). The implication here is that Hogarth upheld the same attitudes toward Africans as those reflected in the period's portraiture, such as the notion that natural savagery could be tamed by force, education and Christian conversion. Such portrayals concurrently imply that Africans are inherently savage and therefore incapable of rising above their lowly status of slave, servant or pet.

Mungo also recalls that Hogarth "promised to represent us in the best light, to immortalize us by his art" (271–272). The dying prostitutes consequently opened up to him, vying with each other for his attention; they trusted him. Mungo wonders: "Did he betray their faith out of malice? Or for money, an account of sensationalism being more marketable than the sacred in our age of Commerce?" (272). Mungo thus alludes to the fact that the success of Hogarth's *A Harlot's Progress*, like Swift's *Gulliver's Travels*, was in part due to his satirical portrayals of easily-recognizable, actual people who had recently been involved in titillating scandals. In Plate I, for example, Moll is greeted from the York stage by the high-powered bawd and notorious brothel owner, Mrs. Elizabeth (Mother) Needham, while the infamous rake and "rape-master of Britain," Colonel Charteris, enthusiastically looks on with his hand thrust suspiciously into his pants. In the spring of 1730, Colonel Charteris was convicted for raping his servant Anne Bond and condemned to die, although he never faced the gallows and received a royal pardon with the assistance of an aristocratic friend.[10] In addition, in the spring of 1731 Sir John Gonson, the Westminster magistrate who was considered the scourge of Drury Lane, had arrested Mother Needham. Hogarth borrowed Moll's surname from highwayman Frances Hackabout, who was hung, and Kate Hackabout, the highwayman's sister, who was arrested in one of Gonson's brothel raids. Needham (d. May 1731) and Charteris (d. February 1732) exemplified the corruption of social life and were widely featured in the satirical works of the period.

According to Mungo, despite the "seeming realism of his art," Hogarth "lied" about the prostitutes by broadcasting "their lives as everyday and bleak, evoking nothing more worthy than pity in the viewer" (272), and about Mr. Gideon by representing him only as the Jew who whored Moll, so that "you, dear reader, will be roused once more to ancient hatred of the Jew." Hogarth also lied about Mungo, who claims, "I wanted him to make me ordinary, for that is what a Negro is, an ordinary man and woman" But Hogarth represented the African Mungo as a "servant to Moll and to the oldest profession. And servant too to the Jew, who was the oldest Jew in the book, in terms of his cunning, his hoarding of coin, his purchase of Christian women" (273). In other words, Hogarth portrayed the prostitutes, Jew, and African in accordance with the era's dominant social and racial myths, and these stereotypical images became widespread because "a dozen ballads and a dozen pirated versions of his pictures appeared, cheap enough for mass purchase." At one time, only the very rich could afford slaves, but because of Hogarth the African was "possessed, in penny image, by several thousands." Consequently, the African became "an historic and memorable figure in the birth of democracy in the British realm . . . A Negro, a devil. A Negro, a creature of mischief. A Negro, a thing of lawlessness" (275). Dabydeen is evidently commenting here on how print capitalism and cultural production facilitated and contributed to the mass production and dissemination of stereotypical imagery that fueled—and continues to fuel—racism. [11]

Mungo's response to the way in which Hogarth represented him reflects Michael D. Harris's claim in *Colored Pictures: Race & Visual Representation* that "African American [and Afro-British] responses to the oppressive presence of derogatory imagery and stereotypes suggest that this presence was fortified by power and affected the lives of people in complicated but tangible ways" (252). By having Mungo relentlessly criticize Hogarth, Dabydeen exposes just how powerful Hogarth's image of the black slave-boy in Plate 2 of *A Harlot's Progress* was at the time it appeared, and how detrimental it has been for race relations, despite the fact that Hogarth likely utilized the image to help illustrate Moll's subjugation. While the presence of a liveried, turbaned black child carrying a teakettle suggests that Moll has been seduced by the glitter of a life of wealth and comfort and is attempting to raise her social status to that of aristocratic women, she has apparently fallen quickly from the hands of noblemen and into the hands of an unattractive but wealthy Jewish merchant. As Uglow points out, Moll "seems in control" but, like the servant, "she too is a slave and a pet, ministering to a rich man's desires" (202). The presence of the black slave-boy serves to reiterate that Moll's social status, as a prostitute, is no different from that of her supposedly inferior servant.

The presence of the black servant also reinforces the Jew's status as a merchant whose wealth comes from his participation in the slave trade and colonial commerce. In *Hogarth's Blacks*, Dabydeen determines that the black boy bearing the tea-kettle, being an emblem of colonial wealth, suggests that the Jewish merchant is "a slave dealer in two ways: he is the polite keeper of courtesans like Moll who are slaves to his pleasure, and he also deals in Africans, who are slaves to his profit." One can presume from the details of Plate 2 indicating his wealth, particularly his art collection, that the Jewish merchant is either directly involved in the slave trade and profits from the sale of Africans to the colonies, or he works African slaves on his West Indian plantation and profits by trading in such products of their labor as tobacco, sugar, rum, brandy and tea. Thus the "money that finances the Jewish merchant's art collecting . . . and his elegant lifestyle is derived from a process of brutalization and exploitation" (114).[12]

In "Black people in Hogarth's criticism of English culture," Dabydeen explains that the "whole of the *Harlot's Progress* series describes the human degradation from the commercial spirit operating in society. The cash nexus had replaced human relationships, and the 'progress' of Moll Hackabout exemplifies the brutal materialism of the Age" (47). Moll's "progress," or rather, deterioration, is clearly represented in Plate 3, in which she is shown living in a slum in Drury Lane. The Jewish merchant has discarded her, her marketability has been further reduced because she has contracted syphilis, and she is consequently forced to prostitute herself to criminals and sexual deviants. The fact that she will continue to decline is represented by the presence of Justice Gonson, who appears in the background contemplating her arrest. Plate 4 depicts Moll's committal to Bridewell prison, where she beats hemp along with thieves and other prostitutes. In Plate 5 she is reduced to abject poverty and dying of venereal disease. In Plate 6, a mock vigil is held for Moll, who is dead at age twenty-three.

In his *A Harlot's Progress*, Dabydeen places the black slave-boy—rather than Moll—at the epicenter of Hogarth's multiple and overlapping stories. He thereby demonstrates that, as much as his presence underscores Moll's and the Jew's stories and serves to mock white society, the image of a turbaned and livered slave-boy serving tea, who surely has his own story and experiences irrespective of his current condition and status, served to reinforce for Hogarth's contemporaries the African's status as an "exotic" possession. When Dabydeen's Mungo arrives in England, Lord Montague purchases him as an anniversary gift for his wife, who is distraught over the death of her pet monkey. Lady Montague renames the boy Perseus and orders her other servants to dress him in "suitable clothes" and "Medusa's silver," thinking all the while of her poor monkey—who was named Medusa. Lady Montague's choice of a name for Mungo is particularly intriguing, as in Greek mythology Perseus beheaded Medusa. The servants shave his head and wrap it in a turban, for he is to be "remodeled into a fantastic land creature, part Indian (his turban), part English coxcomb (his suit), part Chinese (his slippers), with a small Arabian scimitar strapped to his side" (207). According to Beth Fowkes Tobin, in eighteenth-century portraits and conversation pieces the figure of a black servant is frequently a boy or an adolescent male dressed in livery and wearing either a turban or a skullcap. "Both head coverings are exotic and allude to the Turkish, Moslem, and Mughal cultures of the Levant, northern Africa and the Indian subcontinent." This conflation of Arabic, African and Indian origins is typical and what seems to matter is not that these servants are African, Muslim or Indian but that "they are exotic, that they originate in tropical, fertile, and remote lands. Their status as exotics is reinforced by the frequency with which they are associated in prints and paintings with the consumption of foreign luxury goods such as sugar, tea, tobacco, and coffee, all commodities associated with the dark others of the world" (27). Like black servants in eighteenth-century portraiture, Dabydeen's Mungo is put on display as one of the family's most unique, valuable and exotic possessions.

When Lady Cardew arrives with her own servant in tow, Mungo (Perseus) is "stunned by his appearance. He is richly appareled, with a lace cravat, its fringed ends appearing through a buttonhole; a snuff-coloured velvet coat with gold buttons and a red velvet waistcoat trimmed with gold. He is also black." This black page stands behind his Mistress's chair and "remains composed as befits his years of training, and the particular status bestowed upon him by Sir Joshua Reynolds. For he figures in Reynolds' much-admired portrait of the Cardew family, serving chocolate to the gathering. Lady Cardew had attired him in true finery for the occasion and made him put on his most dignified face as he served, to show the quality of his devotion to them" (219). Consequently, he had "acquired a degree of fame among the black servants who worked in lesser households and were therefore lucky even to get into the cheaper canvases of a Mortimer or Smith, or even into a Hogarth print. He was a Reynolds black, and behaved accordingly" (222). This scene seems to suggest that during the eighteenth century there was a hierarchy of black servants based on how they were represented, in portraits or in prints, and on who painted them.[13] By having Lady Cardew's black servant boast that he is a "Reynolds' black" and imagine that he is superior to Mungo, who would later become a "Hogarth's black," Dabydeen draws attention to the fact that behind representations of Africans are multiple, and even contrasting, narratives.

This is not to suggest, however, that Africans were always portrayed stereotypically. According to Rayahn King, unlike Hogarth, "whose use of violet pigments when painting black faces results in a grayish skin tone, the brick-red of [Ignatius] Sancho's waistcoat in [Thomas] Gainsborough's portrait [painted in Bath in 1768], combined with the rich brown background and Sancho's own skin color, make the painting unusually warm in tone as well as feeling." Moreover, Gainsborough's image of Sancho is "notably vivacious and shifting in mood. Sancho's expression seems both amused and quizzical as if Gainsborough has captured him on the verge of speech or laughter" (28). In addition, unlike lesser servants Sancho is not wearing livery or holding an object. He is instead dressed in a fashionable waistcoat and necktie, and portrayed in a "gentlemanly 'hand-in-waistcoat' pose," which seems to confirm Sancho's position and reputation as a "respectable Englishman" (29). As opposed to a smudge of black paint, or as an "exotic" or "pet," Gainsborough represents Sancho as an individual unto himself. However, while Sancho's intelligence and wit "would have reflected well on his master," his "skin color alone" made him an "exotic asset." As Caretta points out, "black men were especially desired as servants in wealthy households—particularly in the public roles of butler and valet—because they were associated with the exotic riches of the empire and thus served as the most obvious indicators of the status of their owners or employers" (xii). It is this desire that most likely prompted Sancho's employer, the 2nd Lord Montagu, to have Gainsborough paint a portrait of Sancho, richly though "not exotically dressed" (21).

The same desire is satirized in Hogarth's 1746 print *Taste in High Life*, which includes an exotically-dressed black boy whom nineteenth-century commentators thought was Sancho, although it is now generally believed that Hogarth and Sancho never met. Yet by placing Mungo in the home of Lord and Lady "Montague" as a servant, and by having him control the production of his own narrative, Dabydeen links his narrator to Sancho who, although represented visually as an "exotic asset," represented himself and exhibited his literary agency in his *Letters*. As Caretta and Philip Gould suggest in *Genius in Bondage*, Sancho "might serve as an emblem" of the black writers in late eighteenth- and nineteenth-century Britain who "achieved identities" by the "very act of authoring their texts" (1–2).

***

Sancho was born on a slave ship a few days after it sailed from the coast of Guinea for the Spanish West Indies. His mother died on board of disease and his father, rather than endure slavery, committed suicide shortly thereafter. Sancho's owner took him to England when he was approximately two years old and left him in the hands of three sisters in Greenwich whose "prejudices," according to Sancho's biographer Joseph Jekyll, had "unhappily taught them that . . . African ignorance was the only security for his obedience, and that to enlarge the mind of their slave would go near to emancipate his person."[14] Sancho accidentally met the Duke of Montagu, who had a house in Blackheath, and, according to Caretta, the Duke was so "impressed with Sancho's intelligence that he frequently brought him home, encouraged him to read by giving him books, and unsuccessfully tried to get Sancho's mistresses to support his education" (x). When the Duke died in 1749, Sancho ran away from his mistresses and sought protection from the Duke's widow, who, as Jekyll notes, initially "dismissed him with reproof," causing Sancho to consider suicide. But the Duchess "secretly admired his character" and eventually "consented to admit him into her household," where he remained until her death in 1751.

As Caretta explains in his introduction to Sancho's *Letters*, Sancho's situation was one of the "relatively rare instances in which the theory of the ideal master-servant relationship coincided with actual practice" (xi). The "ideal master" supervised the education and spiritual development of the servants, and "in theory" looked after the material welfare of the servants beyond the years of service. Indeed, the Duchess of Montagu left Sancho seventy pounds and an annuity of thirty, although he quickly squandered his savings and inheritance on gambling, women, and the theater. In fact, it is widely reported that Sancho spent his last shilling to see David Garrick play the role of Richard III. While Mungo's experiences in the "Montague" household are in no way comparable to Sancho's experiences in the Montagu household, the fact that he receives a classical education from Lady Montague can be read as a reference to the education that Sancho received from his patron/employer. Lady Montague introduces Mungo (Perseus) to Greek myths and Roman fables. She gives him a tour of the family's possessions, explains the origin of books, and teaches him Latin, the notation of music, and the historical and religious subjects of the family's paintings. Throughout his narrative, as in Sancho's *Letters*, Mungo's classical education is always apparent: he quotes Latin (7), teaches Betty about Euclid and geometry (107), uses Newton's computations and Dryden's couplets as analogies for England (111), and lectures to the reader about the interconnectedness of religion, mercantilism and politics (142–145).

In 1758 Sancho returned to the Montagu household and, while working for the 2nd Duke of Montagu, the Duke's son-in-law, he became acquainted with Laurence Sterne and David Garrick, produced and published musical works, all of which are dedicated to members of the Montagu family, wrote two plays, which are unfortunately lost, and even dabbled in acting.[15] Sancho's reputation as a "man of letters" began with the publication of his introductory letter to Sterne (1766), in which he urges him to write about the oppression of Africans.[16] When he was no longer able to work for the Montagus because obesity and illness rendered him unfit to be a valet, the Duke helped Sancho and his wife Anne establish a grocery shop specializing in tobacco, sugar and other small goods near their residence in Westminster. Sancho died in 1780 from complications due to gout, and two years later Frances Crew published his letters, many of which were written while he was running the shop. Crew explains in an editorial note that her "motives for laying them before the publick were, the desire of shewing that an untutored African may possess abilities equal to an European." Unfortunately, this note (inadvertently) implies that Sancho did not consciously contribute to the production of his own text, and thus it denies his agency as a human being and (black) writing subject.

Although early critics read Sancho as an Uncle Tom figure and, all too reductively, as obsequious, these claims have since been widely disputed.[17]

In their introduction to Sancho's *Letters*, Paul Edwards and Polly Rewt write that, while Sancho gives the impression in his letters that he is "wholly assimilated" into the lifestyle and values of "polite" English society, he also displays "tensions and contradictions on matters of race," and, although he had no memory of Africa, he was "acutely conscious of his racial origins" (3). Brycchan Carey takes this one step further when he argues that it is possible to detect strategies of protest in Sancho's writings. Drawing on Markman Ellis's claim that Sancho's letters are "[w]ritten in the self-conscious and refined mode of sentimentalism," Carey determines that Sancho's *Letters* was "consciously constructed and deployed, both by Sancho himself and by his editor, in the form of an epistolary novel of sentiment illustrating the immorality of slavery." Thus Sancho's *Letters* should be seen "not as peripheral or unique but, rather, as fully integrated into the literature of the early abolition movement" (82–83).[18] While more work needs to be done with regard to the place of Sancho's *Letters* in abolitionist literature, it is indisputably the case that the *Letters* is as much a literary production as it is a historical document.

By constructing a narrative for Mungo that, as Wallace notes, "defies logic, linearity, and reason," Dabydeen engages with Sancho's *Letters*, which is, according to Ellis, "chronologically incoherent and incomplete . . . [and] miscellaneously eclectic" (81). Although Pringle demands "a beginning," Mungo proposes that he "had many beginnings." The reader is privy to several different versions of, for example, how he acquired the markings on his forehead. In one version, the Headman of his village "branded him with the sign of sin" for venturing into the katran bush, or rather, trespassing in the spaces of the dead, which made their ancestors depart in anger and leave the village vulnerable to attack. While Mungo claims, on the one hand, that he only understood the "peculiar sign, called *peia*," when he arrived in England because his people "were ignorant of mathematical formulae" (30), he also explains that *peia* was their native word for the bush, which "howls eternally, like a soul condemned to the habitation of fallen angels." At one point Mungo asserts that *peia* is "an obvious corruption of the Greek *pi*, which we also signify as TT" (31), and backs up his claim that the sign of *pi* on his forehead is evidence that he is an "imprint of a lost tribe of Greeks" with a story of how the Greeks, having wandered off the path from North Africa, ended up in the bush. At first they massacred whole tribes, but eventually they settled down and bestowed their civilization "unto their brightest slaves and mulatto offspring" (32). Mungo concedes that Pringle will deny that his forehead bears the sign of Greek learning and say instead that Captain Thistlewood was "marking his property by branding his initials into my flesh," because "it is true that he stamped his foot upon my neck to stop me from wriggling so as to better brand my forehead with his initials" (75). When he tells Betty that he inherited the sign of *pi* on his forehead from the Greeks, she knowingly declares: "That's Thistlewood's mark. All it means is that you've been breached and made accustomed to men. It is his way of signaling to men with special tastes that you are a special boy" (123). In yet another version, the ghosts of his village tell him that they had marked his "forehead in preparation for . . . manhood" (65) because his father was too sick from grief over the death of his mother in childbirth. The advertisement for his sale in a London newspaper accordingly reads: "Handsome in demeanour but for some slight tribal scarring on his forehead" (164).

While π is indeed the sixteenth letter of the Greek alphabet, and also a symbol for the transcendental number that expresses the ratio of the circumference to the diameter of a circle, in printing the word "pi" refers to an amount of type that has been jumbled or thrown together at random. Or, more generally, it means to jumble or mix up. Thus π is an appropriate symbol for Mungo's narrative in which, as Wallace points out, the "past and present, here and there, living and dead, truth and lies, exist side by side" (239). Throughout the novel, Mungo talks to the ghosts of his village as if they exist alongside the living, and their stories conflict with each other's as well as with Mungo's. For example, they insist at one point that the "tribe was content" and that there were "ceremonies of love" by which they lived, "each with each and in communion with the gods of earth and sky" (65). Yet at other times they discuss the cruelty with which the tribe treated women, such as maiming and casting out widows beyond childbearing age. Even their status as alive or dead is called into question. Kaka, the village beggar, wonders if the gods will forgive the ghosts "now that they are all dead," and immediately after saying this Captain Thistlewood "cuffs his head with such force that it cracks open" (95). Manu, who is also supposedly already dead, beats off a sailor, runs to the side of the ship, and "shouts out defiantly the name of our village" before he plunges into the sea. Later in the novel, the ghosts claim to have died from such maladies as diarrhea, cholera, dysentery, and/or fever, which conflicts with their already conflicting claims that they died during the attack on their village and as a result of brutal beatings on the slave ship. In addition to countless others, both told and untold, these are the individual stories that constitute the "story" of the Atlantic Slave Trade.[19]

Mungo's stories of his experiences in London are similarly jumbled and represent the "story" of Africans in Britain during the eighteenth century, which is likewise comprised of multiple, intersecting stories. While he is with Betty, who prepares him for auction, and thus prior to his sale to Lord Montague, Mungo speaks English fluently and is evidently well educated, although later he tells the reader that when he arrived at the Montague household his "mind was as yet unsyllabled" (185). When Mungo recounts the stories of Betty and Mary, who each in their own way reflect Hogarth's Moll and both used to work for the Montagues, it is virtually impossible for the reader to locate any truths. Was it Mary who *"came to town in York wagon . . . looking for work* (128), or Betty who abandoned her family and arrived in London on the Yorkshire wagon? Is Mary alive, or was she hanged? If she was hanged, was it for prostitution or for stealing? If it was for stealing, was it for stealing the handkerchief and silver box from the Montagues, or for stealing soap from Thistlewood to make a few extra pennies? Or was it Betty who stole the soap but blamed it in on Mary? Did Mary steal a handkerchief from the Jew, who may or may not have been her keeper, or did Mungo steal a handkerchief from Lady Montague? Or was it Betty who lost her position as a senior servant in the Montague household for stealing a lace handkerchief and a silver box? Was it Betty who loved the Jew and was jealous of his relationship with Mary? Or did the Jew discard Mary, after which she tried to get revenge by stealing the handkerchief, getting herself hanged, and thereby making him remorseful? Was there even a handkerchief at all? Was there no Mary at all, except for the baby, "which Betty bore for the Jew, and out of shame strangled it, cleansing it first in her washing-tub of sin, and baptizing it Mary?" (142)

But it is while he is with Betty that Mungo has a flashback of the voice of Captain Thistlewood demanding, "'Where is your village?'" He remembers that he could not understand the words at the time, but that he pointed in its direction, knowing intuitively that they would kill or capture everyone and he would not have time to warn them. Betty tells him that it is foolish to blame himself for leading the slavers to his village, for he was only a small boy and terrified by their appearance. Is his "responsibility" for the massacre and enslavement of his villagers a "truth" that must be suppressed if his narrative is to be published as abolitionist propaganda? Mungo develops such compassion for Betty that, consequently, he begs the reader: "Remember her by *my* testimony, and not by the descriptions of thief and sinner that Mr Pringle will furnish of her" (168). With his representations of Betty and Mary, Dabydeen engages with Hogarth's depictions of the lower/working class. Mungo asks the reader to believe his version, as opposed to the one that Pringle will write, because, like Hogarth, Pringle will not take into account the tragedy of their lives and will, subsequently, represent them as common thieves deserving of punishment. Mungo further implicates the reader when he asserts, "I free her into your care" (169). Dabydeen thereby suggests that readers and viewers have a responsibility to (re)interpret the images disseminated by writers and artists, as these images are extensions of the artist's and writer's attitudes and prejudices rather than representations of authentic experiences.

Dabydeen reinforces his illustration of how all people embody multiple stories, and that stories about particular events are dependent upon the perspective of the teller and the occasion of the telling, with his depiction of how Lord Montague came to purchase Mungo. In what is most likely Pringle's version of the Montagues, the reader learns that Lady Montague is an esteemed hostess and devoted to her husband's ambassadorial duties. Lord Montague, in return, brought her exotic gifts from overseas, including a parrot purchased at a Spanish port and a monkey from North Africa. "He had long resisted the idea of a pet Negro, such as kept by many of his friends, out of a vague moral qualm. He was contemptuous of the world of commerce, particularly the West Indian merchants whose manners were as unbecoming as their traffic in human bodies" (188). It was while in this frame of mind that Lord Montague went to Johnson's Coffee House to purchase Mungo, with awareness that what caught his eye about the advertisement was Captain Thistlewood's name. Two months earlier, Lady Montague had informed him that Captain Thistlewood had "shackled some forty slaves," and "ordered them to be thrown overboard" so he could "claim their insurance value as goods lost at sea" (192–193). Lady Montague even prepared a packet of newspaper stories for him, each with its own version of the "Thistlewood affair," which left Lord Montague to wonder whether Thistlewood was "veritably mad" as a consequence of years of "witnessing the horrors of the trade," or whether the defense of insanity was an attempt to ward off prosecution.

By fictionally dramatizing the actual slave ship *Zong* massacre, Dabydeen once again illustrates that the "story" of the slave trade consists of diverse stories, which are dependent upon the perspective of the teller as well as the occasion of the telling. In 1783, Captain Luke Collingwood sailed from Africa to Jamaica with some 440 slaves. When the slaves became ill, Collingwood ordered his officers to throw the sickest ones overboard, telling them that if they are ever questioned to say that they had experienced unfavorable winds and the ship's water supply was running out. These murders would be accepted under the principle of "jettison" in maritime law. A captain had the right to throw some cargo—in this case, Africans—overboard to save the rest. In all, 133 slaves were "jettisoned." When the *Zong*'s owners later filed an insurance claim for the value of the dead slaves, the insurance company disputed it. On 18 March 1783, a letter to the editor appeared in the *Morning Chronicle and London Advertiser*, which caught Equiano's attention. He brought the case to the attention of Granville Sharpe, who tried and failed to get the *Zong*'s owners prosecuted for murder.

Dabydeen addresses such discrepancies in his novel by having Lord Montague read news articles that pose the following questions: Should Thistlewood be "tried for murder" because the slaves were of the "HUMAN SPECIES," or were the sick slaves a "necessary sacrifice" and part of a "calculated decision" to save the rest of the slaves and the crew? Will the ship's owners reward Thistlewood for "saving the vessel" and give him a few months rest before resuming his duties, or will he retire permanently from the Trade? Is he still alive, or was he indeed found hanged in his home? Was there no suicide note, or was there one in which he confessed to the "*wickedness of his deed*" and implored forgiveness? Lord Montague ultimately determines that there was no "simple and straightforward account of events," and that "each version was calculated to inflate or depress the value of shares. Truth itself was a commodity changing hands at a price" (199). In other words, the humanitarian "facts" of the event and court case were virtually irrelevant in lieu of the economic implications of event and court case.

As I mention above, by producing a narrative for Mungo in which origins, truths, and facts are totally inaccessible, and which is a parody of linear, sequential narratives, Dabydeen invites his readers to revisit Sancho's *Letters*. Sancho borrowed his "radical" form from his friend and correspondent Sterne, whose style would have appealed to Sancho because, according to C. L. Innes, he "in all ways desired to escape the rigid categories of a society which sought to constrict so radically the possibilities for black people and to confine them as slaves, manual worker, or at best, servants and exotica" (25). But like Mungo, and as Sandhu argues, Sancho "was no slavish parroter of the English language" (70). By emulating Sterne, Sancho conveys his agreement with Sterne's narrator in *Tristam Shandy* (1759), who draws a parallel between his own narrative methods and those of historiographers when he declares that, while it is technically plausible for historiographers to write in a straightforward, sequential style, it is, "morally speaking, impossible" (Sterne 1983, 32). According to Sandhu, Sterne's narrator's attempt to provide a "lucid account" of his life is, accordingly,

> constantly interrupted by digressions such as the importance of knots or long noses. The tale is studded with lists and inventories of diseases, philosophers and even literary devices. Marbled pages, blank spaces, and various squiggles and illustrative diagrams break up the flow of words. Even normal grammar is eschewed with dashes replacing full stops to lend the novel even more of a hustling, dizzying quality. (49)

Sancho's *Letters* are a "canny recapitulation" of Sterne's prose style, which is especially evident in his emulation of Sterne's characteristic use of the dash to "produce a hesitatingly fluid style" (Ellis 82). Moreover, just as Mungo refuses to give Pringle a straightforward narrative, Sancho's *Letters*, although printed in chronological order according to the dates they were written, do not reflect a chronological progress of his life but, rather, his creative ingenuity.

But a "straightforward, sequential style" was what such late eighteenth-century racial theorists such as Edward Long called for, because they equated linearity with being capable of rational thought. Among the "proofs" that Long offers in his *History of Jamaica* (1774) for his theory that "Negroes" and "Whites" were a separate species was the bogus "evidence" that black Africans had no culture, no arts or sciences, and were incapable of achieving European levels of literacy. Even more than authorship and authenticity, what was at stake in the production and dissemination of slave narratives was the writer's very humanity as a human being and black writing subject. However, although Sancho recognized he would never be considered equal to whites in British society, his *Letters* do not read as if he is trying to "prove" his intelligence and literary capabilities. In fact, as Innes points out, those who participated in the "community" created by Sancho's letter-writing would have seen him as a "man inventing himself, and doing so with particular flair, wit and compassion, at a particular moment in history" (34–35). In other words, Sancho exercised his literary agency and fundamental human right to create and/or represent himself via his writings, as opposed to writing a formulaic linear narrative for the purpose of contesting polygenetic theories. While his *Letters* may have a place in abolitionist literature, they are distinct from the slave narratives that were produced during the heyday of the abolitionist campaign for the purpose of providing evidence of black humanity.

Dabydeen reiterates his critique of linear narratives, or rather the political implications of such narratives, by naming the abolitionist who is taking Mungo's testimony "Pringle." Dabydeen is likely referring to Thomas Pringle, who became secretary of the Anti-Slavery Society in 1827, and who exerted textual control over *The History of Mary Prince* (1831).[20] As Sarah Salih argues in "*The History of Mary Prince*, the Black Subject, and the Black Canon," Prince's narrative is for the most part the "construction of critics and editors." Like Thomas Pringle, Dabydeen's Pringle plans to write Mungo's "portrait in the first person narrative. A book purporting to be a record of the Negro's own words (understandably corrected in terms of grammar, the erasure of indelicate or infelicitous expressions, and so forth" (2). Also like Thomas Pringle, Dabydeen's Pringle wishes to use the ex-slave's narrative in the Anti-Slavery Society's campaign against the slave trade. More specifically, he "wants sober testimony that will appeal to the Christian charity of an enlightened citizenry who will, upon perusing [Mungo's] tale of woe, campaign in the Houses of Parliament for [his] emancipation and that of millions of [his] brethren" (5).[21] Mungo refuses to accommodate Pringle because he believes that Pringle, like Hogarth, "will replicate Moll and me in lies, for he believes Mr Hogarth's prints and the dozen pirated versions of them" (276).

Indeed, Pringle imagines that Mungo was once a "celebrity of slum and mansion alike, his presence greeted with equal excitement in seedy bagnio or baroque gallery. Beggars and nobility were his equal friends, and they flocked to him as he made his entrance to whore-house or High Church." Pringle's only evidence for this "story" is Hogarth's portrait of Mungo as a servant to the harlot Moll. What Pringle needs, then, is "the who, the when, the what, the how, and why of this and that" (4). But Mungo's narrative defies linearity and consists of half-truths, wild tales, the fantastic, and can even be read as a parody of what has come to be known as the slave narrative formula. This formula, first identified by Henry Louis Gates, Jr., includes a series of such crucial moments as: the loss of homeland and family, becoming enslaved, the discovery of literacy and attempt to acquire it, depictions of brutality, conversion to Christianity, awareness of the hypocritical Christianity of slave traders and slave-owners, and the escape to (or purchase of) freedom. These formulaic narratives, perhaps most clearly exemplified by Equiano's *Interesting Narrative*, served to evoke sympathy and incite readers to campaign for the abolition of slavery. The fact that Dabydeen's Mungo is in ill health and in dire need of charity functions as additional evidence that Dabydeen's Pringle refers to Thomas Pringle, without actually being him. Mungo's illness is most likely due to his advanced years and the fact that he is poverty stricken, although according to Pringle he has not been seen for years, "being attic bound through severe arthritis (or melancholy?)" (4).[22] Like Prince's *History*, Mungo's narrative would be, in addition to a political tool, a potential source of income.[23]

However, while Dabydeen's Mungo is grateful for the Abolition Committee's charity and pity, he "will not return their benevolence with the gift of confession" (1). Why would Mungo intentionally compromise the Committee's agenda by refusing to accommodate Pringle's desire for "sober testimony" and a narrative with a "beginning, middle and end," despite his awareness that the publication of such a narrative would aid the abolitionist campaign? Unlike Prince's narrative, which was deliberately censored by the abolitionist committee so that no part of her story would offend the moral sensibilities of readers, Mungo exercises a great deal of self-censorship.[24] By having his protagonist censor himself, and thereby position himself as "master of the situation" (1), Dabydeen criticizes the tendency of abolitionists to exert textual control, a tendency that in and of itself suggests that even those who opposed the slave trade and the institution of slavery did not consider Africans capable of producing their own narratives; even those who were sympathetic to Africans did not believe they were intellectual and cultural equals.[25]

Mungo is thoroughly aware of Pringle's resolve to "colour and people a landscape out of his own imagination," and thereby endow Mungo with the "gift of mind and eloquence" (3). But despite his supposed humanitarian concerns, Pringle's attitude toward Mungo has evidently been informed by the racial myths that circulated in print and were represented and disseminated in the period's art. According to Mungo, Pringle "cannot believe me capable of speech as polished as my teeth once were. No, nigger does munch and crunch the English, nigger does jape and jackass with the language, for he is of low brow and ape resemblances" (5). By attempting to construct Mungo's narrative for him, and by assuming that he lacks intellect, literacy and the capacity to reason, Pringle upholds the myths regarding the African's inferiority and simian ancestry. But Mungo knows he is not "uncouth" and, like Equiano, he has "imbibed" many British "mannerisms of language." He too could turn to the King James Bible for expressions that would "set your soul aglow with the plight of the Negro" (5). However, unlike Equiano, he does not "believe that a single book will alter the course of history," or that even a "whole library testifying to the plight of the Negro would deflect the English from their common pursuit. Money, not ideas, is what holds the nation together, and as long as it is profitable to trade Negroes, slavery will thrive" (256).[26]

Dabydeen's Pringle assumes that Mungo is suffering from the early stages of dementia because he does not provide a picturesque description of his African village. But Mungo knows that Pringle wants to hear that Africa is an Edenic place. The story of a Noble Savage whose innocence was corrupted by white European slavers would be at once familiar and appealing to white readers compassionate to the plight of African slaves. By the mid-eighteenth century, there was already a considerable body of literature devoted to the idea of the Noble Savage and, as Dabydeen explains in "Black people in Hogarth's criticism of English culture," in such literature the "white man is accused of destroying the innocent native by enslaving him or by teaching him to lie, cheat, trade, fornicate, rob and kill" (48). But no matter how appealing a story of sin and redemption would be to sympathetic readers, this is *not* Mungo's story. By refusing to have his narrative constructed for him, Mungo exhibits the kind of agency that slaves such as Mary Prince were either denied or presumed not to possess.[27] Yet while Mungo seems to position himself alongside Equiano, whose *Interesting Narrative* was "written by himself" (frontispiece), he refuses to exercise his literary agency by constructing the kind of formulaic narrative that would appeal to white readers and serve the abolitionist campaign.

Also unlike Equiano, Mungo refuses to tell Pringle of the slave ship's horrors and by this means grant him, as Wallace argues, "a vicarious, sadistic pleasure in the scene of suffering" (244). While graphic accounts of abuses inflicted upon slaves were undoubtedly intended to provoke the reader to a sense of indignation, Mungo refuses to tell Pringle that "evil" Captain Thistlewood took him to his ship and "so molested him that [he] became a willing disciple to the ways of animals" (70). Instead, Mungo tells Pringle that he admires Thistlewood and even has compassion for him: " . . . his pain is great, more than my own" (69). Mungo's rationalization for the beatings and rapes he was forced to endure prompts the ghosts of his village to charge him with betraying them, of becoming "'the whiteman's wife'" (59). Mungo accuses them of being "'beggars and fools,'" but their "gaze" fills him with "shame" (62–63). Nonetheless, Mungo tells the reader not to "doubt that Captain Thistlewood, even after seasons of abuse—being a veteran of a dozen slave voyages—is capable of redemption" (73). He cites as an example Reverend John Newton, a reformed slaver who became an evangelical minister of the Anglican Church. Newton's *Thoughts Upon the African Trade* was published by the Committee for the Abolition of the Slave Trade in 1788, and, according to Peter J. Kitson, his "grim exposé of the brutalities of the trade was all the more effective because it originated from an actual participant," and is therefore "less easy to refute" (75).[28] Mungo acknowledges that Pringle will interpret his account "as subterfuge," as a desire to conceal the abuses that he endured because he is ashamed of "public confession of the deeds wrought on [his] body." Pringle's "story" is "untroubled": Thistlewood is "a demon and [Mungo] his catamite" (75).[29] Although Mungo seemingly absolves the slaver of his sins for Pringle, Dabydeen does not supplant the horrific violence of the trade, and Mungo offers the reader such graphic descriptions of the Middle Passage as: "When the ship pitched in sudden rough sea, the chains tightened and cracked their ankles, spines and elbow joints. Sometimes, arms and legs and heads were wrenched clean off" (48). Dabydeen's point seems to be that oppositions between good and evil, abuser and abused, are not as clear-cut as they are presented in such moralizing narratives as Prince's and Equiano's.

Dabydeen reiterates this point by having Pringle imagine that Lord Montague should only be represented as the epitome of selflessness, graciousness and humanitarianism, and portray him accordingly as a peace negotiator whose concern for what foreign trade and slavery are doing to the fabric of English society outweighs his desire for personal wealth and power. *This* Lord Montague would wish he had never seen the advertisement for Mungo, "which disturbed him with a sense of his own involvement in the scheme of sin" (190), and motivated him to "rescue the boy" from the "merchant whose true instinct was to return England to state of savagery" (191). *This* Lord Montague presents the boy to his wife "for instruction, for his mind was as yet unformed and she would imprint upon it, as much as his heathen constitution could bear, something of the learning and chaste qualities which defined England's historic character" (199). However, like the period's portraiture and perhaps unbeknownst to Pringle, such a depiction of the Montagues simultaneously suggests that Africans are inherently inferior, although they can perhaps be "domesticated."

Mungo maintains awareness that Pringle's version of the Montagues must exclude or ignore the fact that this household is in actuality a microcosm of England's "savagery." As with the black figures in Hogarth's engravings, whose gazes expose the savagery that lurks beneath apparent "civility," Mungo (Perseus) is the supposed "savage" whose gaze exposes what is beneath the surface of the allegedly pristine Montague household. Mungo confides in the reader that two "uncommonly sinful" servants, Lizzie and Jane, chain him to the bed each night, beat him, mock him, and sexually abuse him. Lady Montague, despite her sophisticated reputation and elaborate social performances, is utterly insane. This is not the story Mr. Pringle wishes to hear or tell, and Mungo tells the reader: "*Of none of this I can talk to Mr Pringle. He don't want no dirt of woman but Moll's kind so I cannot tell more of Lady Montague's madness . . . To him, a Lady is not ever improper, and if she is, it can never be in print. Life and print: two different things.*" (225–226). Lady Montague deteriorates quickly, and within just three months she "abandons all dignity" and exhibits behavior considered "most unbecoming of a lady of quality" (225). When Lord Montague returns home from France, he hears the gossip (or truth) that the Jew "unpick the padlock of the Lady's treasure-box and shower fool's gold in it," and that she is "too fond" of Perseus (245). To avoid being sold to a West Indian merchant, Mungo (Perseus) takes refuge with the Jew and his stable of dying prostitutes.

Dabydeen is likely engaging here with Hogarth prints in which illicit sexual relationships between white mistresses and their black servants are suggested. For example, in Plate IV of *Marriage á la Mode* the sexual transgression of the white figures in the scene is reiterated by the presence of an erotic French novel, Crébillon's *Le Sopha*, in which white ladies are "liberal of their Favours with Negroes." One lady sleeps with a "frightful, mishapen

Negro" who is "capable of giving way to all the Fury of Vigorous Desire." Another "'lay'd with all the Negroes of the Palace," and a third lady, known for her reputation for purity, desires her black slaves who, "in spite of the Baseness of their Employment, are yet capable of the most hidden mysteries of love." According to Dabydeen, Hogarth's reference to Crebillon's novel serves, among other things, to "indicate one of the roles of the black man in the household of the English aristocracy. He does more than serve chocolate—the aristocratic ladies call upon their male black slave to relieve them of the burdens of civilization, in the moments when they felt the urge to be purely and passionately savage" (79).[30] But at the same time, Hogarth's black figures laugh at the whites' sexual transgression "from all levels—from on high, from the horizontal, and from below" (79). A smiling black boy on the floor points to Actaeon's horns (emblems of cuckoldry) and thereby illuminates the conversation behind him, in which the Countess's lover points to a screen showing a masquerade (an event notorious for illicit sexual encounters) and invites the Countess to accompany him. A black servant laughs as he serves a cup of chocolate to the opera singer swooning over a castrato. Similarly, in Plate 2 of *A Harlot's Progress*, Hogarth's black slave-boy has a look of surprise on his face as he walks into the scene, and as Uglow argues, his "gaze directs our gaze across the room to the monkey (a sign of exotic and deviant sexuality) and the upset tea table" (36), which is supposed to distract the Jew from noticing that Moll's young lover, whom she met at a masquerade the night before, is sneaking out of the room. But while Hogarth's black figures observe and draw attention to the degeneracy of white society, as foreigners or "exotics" they are simultaneously associated with illicit sexual activity and moral decay. As Sander Gilman argues, in the eighteenth century the black, both male and female, became "an icon for deviant sexuality in general, almost always, however, paired with a white figure of the opposite sex" (81).[31]

At the same time as Mungo withholds "factual" information about his abuse aboard the slave ship and in the Montague household so as not to alienate his readership, he also makes up stories to accommodate Pringle's (and his readers') expectations. For example, when Pringle insists that Mungo describe his journey from the Montague's home to the Jew's stable, Mungo confesses to the reader that he remembers little but can certainly "invent familiar perils and comforting ideologies" and make himself an "exemplary and heroic Negro" (248). He then offers Pringle an hour-by-hour account of his journey, chock-full of encounters with thieves, beggars and rogues reminiscent of a Fielding novel. But when the ghost of Ellar asks him why he describes her as beautiful as opposed to telling the truth, which is that she "was covered in [her] own shit" and raped by sailors even after she died from one too many lashes, Mungo (Perseus) is "stilled by her outrage." Ellar declares that he should "curse them outright as white devils, tell the story as it is and not bother with the consequences. . . . 'What more can they do to you worse than slavery?'" Mungo (Perseus) responds to her chastisement by saying, "'They can refuse to buy my book, and I'll starve.'" He "will not repel his readers by calling them necrophiles" (257).

It is also conceivable, as Charles P. Sarvan proposes in his review of *A Harlot's Progress*, that Mungo is "unwilling to tell his story partly because it is impossible to make his experiences real, and, were he to succeed, he would not be believed, so incredible are the experiences he and others like him were forced to undergo" (795). In other words, no generic form or mode of representation has the capacity to fully and completely replicate the reality of his (or any slave's) actual experiences and, if it were possible to do so, it would seem to any reader with any sensibility like a work of fiction.

***

The advertisement for Mungo's sale appears alongside advertisements for "new plays, miracle cures and Mr Hogarth's latest prints," but when Mungo reads that he is supposed to answer to the name Noah the "pleasure of seeing himself in print is disrupted." He asks Betty who gave him this name, and she responds that she knows him only as Mungo, nor does she know what his name was before she came to him. Mungo says, "'But I thought 'Mungo' was what whitepeople called our folk, like 'Negur' and 'Blackamoor' and 'Boy' and other words the sailors used on us'" (164). Mungo is absolutely correct that "Mungo" is not really a name and, by naming his narrator Mungo, Dabydeen comments on the fact that Mungo (like Sambo) was a common or generic name used for an African in the eighteenth century. In Frances Burney's play *A Busy Day* (1801), the rich heiress Eliza has a black servant named "Mongo," who never appears on stage. The name "Mongo" implies that the servant is African, but apparently he has been recently imported from Calcutta. According to Tobin, this "Mongo" seems to be both Indian and African, but it does not matter whether he is from Africa or India, for "a Black's but a Black," as Eliza's English servant says. Significantly, the fact that "Mongo" never appears on stage does not lessen the power of his presence. He is the "object of Britain's imperial might and imperial magnanimity; Mongo exists in the mind's eye of the audience, put there by such artists as Hogarth" (55).

But Africans named Mongo/Mungo who contested the stereotypical identity that this name signifies also appeared on stage during the period. With his portrayal of Mungo, Dabydeen may be engaging with Isaac Bickerstaff's dramatic portrayal of a "Negro servant called Mungo" in his comic opera *The Padlock*. Bickerstaff (1733–1808) grew up in Dublin, arrived in London in 1755 and, according to Peter A. Tasch, was the "playwright responsible for the initial triumph of comic opera" (x). In addition to his four major comic operas, Bickerstaff wrote seven short musical pieces, five of them with Charles Didbin. The plot of Bickerstaff's *The Padlock* is based on Cervantes's "The Jealous Husband," but the opera tells the story of sixteen-year-old Leonora, who is literally locked up in the house of her much older and wealthy suitor, Don Diego. According to the agreement he made with her parents, after three months Don Diego could either return her to her parents "spotless" and keep half her dowry, or make her his wife in exchange for the entire amount. Leonora knows that it is her duty to marry him and does not wish to seem ungrateful, but she has no desire to marry him. Leander, the young scholar who falls in love with her, dresses up as a cripple and befriends Mungo in order to acquire information. Bickerstaff's Mungo seems at first to be a self-deprecating fool, an Uncle Tom figure, because he responds to Don Diego's physical and verbal abuse with such statements as: "you very good massa" (I. vi). But, when Diego asks him if he has observed any mischief in the house, Mungo articulates his suffering even though he knows it will incur punishment: " . . . you lick me every day with your rattan; I'm sure Massa, that's mischief enough for poor Neger man" (I. vi.).

Bickerstaff's Mungo is at once a stereotypical comic black servant and a victim of oppression who conveys his humanity with a song in Act I, scene vi:

> Dear heart, what a terrible life am I led,
> A dog has a better, that's shelter'd and fed:
> Night and day 'tis de same,
> My pain is dere game:
> Me wish to de Lord me was dead.
> Whate'er's to be done,
> Poor black must run;
> Mungo here, Mungo dere,
> Mungo every where;
> Above and below,
> Sirrah come, Sirrah go;
> Do so, and do so.
> Oh! Oh!
> Me wish to de Lord me was dead.

By having his Mungo make such claims as, " . . . even though I am a nigger . . . susceptible, because of what I am by nature, to hysteria, befuddlement and exaggeration" (73), and lapse into dialect as part of his performance for Mr. Pringle, Dabydeen alludes to the fact that such stereotypical dramatic representations of Africans as Bickerstaff's were, as Tasch argues, "played for laughs, not abolition." Even Mungo's song (above) was remembered "not for its pathos" but for the lines: "Mungo here, Mungo there, Mungo every where." Whether Mungo's speech is West Indian, as Didbin claimed, or African, Mungo "is no Oroonoko." In 1942, Wylie Sypher wrote in *Guinea's Captive Kings* that Bickerstaff "discards the language of the noble Negro; [Mungo] speaks a mongrel English that has its dramatic effect" (35). The original Mungo was supposed to have been played by John Moody, who had been to the West Indies and supposedly "knew the dialect of the negroes." But Moody's inability to perform the role became increasingly more apparent, and Didbin eventually took the part "with reluctance and secret indignation" (*Life*, I. 70). According to Tasch, Didbin (in blackface) "proved to be a brilliant Mungo" (154).[32] While there had been servants who hated their masters on stage before, the "addition of the color and dialect made the part new" (157). Mungo was so popular that his lines, "Mungo here, Mungo there, Mungo everywhere," were "soon heard here, there and everywhere" (157–158), and political cartoons with Mungo's image appeared all over town.

Mungo's extraordinary popularity can be attributed to the fact that he did, indeed, get laughs, which made him memorable. For example, when Don Diego goes "abroad" for a night, he puts a padlock on the house and orders Mungo to watch over the house and not "sleep a wink." But Leander, because he has already gained Mungo's sympathy, and by endearing himself to Don Diego's maid Ursula, manages to gain admittance. While Leander and Leonora are declaring their love for each other, the jealous Don Diego unexpectedly returns home and finds, first, an intoxicated Mungo. In the exchange that takes place between them, Mungo seems to be (more than anywhere else in the play) what Jeffrey N. Cox refers to as "the butt of the farce" (xv). Between hiccups, Mungo tells Don Diego not to make any noise because there is a gentleman with the young lady; "he plays guitar, and she like him better dan she like you. Fal, lal, lal" (II. vi). When Don Diego tells him to "lie down" in his "stye and sleep," Mungo responds: "Sleep you self, you drunk—ha! ha! ha! look a Padlock, you put a padlock on a door again, will you? Ha! ha! ha!" (II. vi).

Mungo's intoxication, dialect, and audacity in the face of his "master" is what, for eighteenth-century audiences, would have made him not only hilarious but genuinely likeable. Yet Dabydeen's Mungo's refusal to play a comic or farcical part designed to amuse white audiences or readers draws attention to how these performances, although funny and entertaining, served to reinforce racial myths and stereotypes. In fact, as Cox points out, in slave-holding Jamaica, where audiences were slave-owning planters and their families, the popularity of *The Padlock* suggests that a "comic portrayal of the enslaved Mungo reassured British West Indians about their treatment of African slaves" (xv). Yet as Cox also notes, eighteenth-century dramas featuring Africans reflect "the strange mix . . . of anti-slavery sentiments and racist attitudes" (xviii), and *The Padlock* could be considered "the first blackface comic figure on the London stage to use something approaching an accurate dialect—as a voice of resistance" (xv). However, according to Cox, while *The Padlock* could have been played for tears as well as laughs, most likely neither mode of performance would have influenced the institution of slavery.

The direction which a farce takes is dependent upon who plays the role on stage, and how. In her introduction to *Farce*, Jessica Milner Davis explains that, while farce is like other forms of comedy in its ready use of burlesque, slapstick and improbable coincidences, the characteristic which distinguishes it from other comic styles is that "it does so without seeking to point any particular lesson for its audiences . . . No airs and pretences . . . no preaching for a revolution" (3). Frequently the violence that is omnipresent in the genre is directed toward "unwitting third parties," and these "targets of aggression" are usually presented as "responsible for inviting their own fate . . . and always they lack self-consciousness" (4). Yet they must not be totally unbelievable or unsympathetic, or audiences would have no interest in the performance. While laughter is evoked because the victim brings punishment upon himself by his or her "rigidities and stupidities," and by "seeking to interfere with the course of nature," the audience can also enjoy themselves because these stock characters are "less than fully human." However, when "an element of empathy, or of moral comment" enters into the domain of farce, then an "unease creeps into the audience's laughter," as their attention is diverted from just having fun "toward the need for reform and change, either in society or in human nature itself" (14).

Bickerstaff's comic black servant only really became a symbol of anti-slavery when the black actor Ira Aldridge played the part of Mungo in London, as an afterpiece to his *Othello*, in the nineteenth century. According to Tasch, Aldridge's Mungo "became more than merely comic as actor and audience invested him with social and even tragic significance. Without lecturing or moralizing, Mungo became a conscience to his white audiences."[33] While one can only speculate on Bickerstaff's intentions, the dramatic work evidently provided the material for Aldridge to transform the "silly black servant into a human being more courageous than Uncle Tom, who is too humble to have a temper, or Oroonoko, who is too proud to use it" (162). By having his Mungo perform for Pringle and rebel against stereotypical representations of Africans, Dabydeen exposes the possibility that Bickerstaff's Mungo already was, or could be (by the actor), endowed with an agency that is often absent or displaced from eighteenth-century visual and dramatic representations of Africans. For example, Bickerstaff's Mungo curses Don Diego behind his back (I. iv) and, while intoxicated, ridicules him (II. vi). In the final scene, Mungo directly (and soberly) confronts Don Diego after he relinquishes Leonora (and her dowry) to Leander, and dismisses Ursula from her duties but generously gives her five hundred crowns, by asking if he is to receive nothing. Don Diego says, "Yes, the bastinadoes for your drunkenness and infidelity . . . Oh man! Man! How short is your foresight, how ineffectual your prudence, while the very means you use are destructive of your ends" (II. Scene The Last).

As opposed to passively accepting this verbal abuse, Mungo retaliates in the final song, which begins with Diego singing of the "manoeuvres" men must make to "hold a woman." Ursula follows by accusing "masters" of being quite "absurd" for attempting to "rule our sex," and suggests that gentleness, not force, will make a woman yield to a man. She then refers to a "fable," which teaches the lesson of how "the sun's warm and melting rays" more readily bring about "what wind and rain, / with all their fuss, attempt in vain." Mungo, similarly, communicates his opinion by referring to a fable. He sings: "An owl once took it in his head / Wid some pretty young bird to wed; But when his worship came to woo, / He could get none but de cuckoo." Thus Mungo grounds these lessons in actual material conditions by addressing Don Diego directly, as opposed to addressing a theoretical man and woman. He alludes to the fact that Don Diego has been cuckolded, and then announces that Don Diego is left with only a "cuckoo." To whom is he referring? Given that Mungo remains enslaved by Don Diego at the end of the play, it seems as though Mungo is referring to himself. But, although Don Diego considers Mungo a fool, Mungo is more aware than anyone in the play of how he is viewed. He even begins his verse by asking his "Massa" not to be angry at a "Neger man," and thus performing the "Uncle Tom" stock slave. But like Dabydeen's Mungo, he rebels against this identity construction by speaking his mind at the risk of being punished, and thus he exercises his autonomy. Bickerstaff's Mungo, like Dabydeen's, is not only self-aware or self-conscious; he is potentially the "master of the situation." Moreover, by contesting Don Diego's accusation that he *deserves* his victimization, Bickerstaff's Mungo even calls the genre of farce itself into question.

Dabydeen's portrayal of Mungo also enables a reinterpretation of a little-known pantomime, Mr. W. Bates's *Harlequin Mungo; Or, A Peep into the Tower*, which may have been performed as early as 1750 in London, and which was published in 1788. Unlike Bickerstaff's Mungo, who remains enslaved despite his agency at the conclusion of *The Padlock*, *Harlequin Mungo* is, much like Friday in Sheridan's pantomime of Robinson Crusoe, liberated through the transformation scene. Act I of *Harlequin Mungo* takes place in the West Indies, and the first scene in particular is notable for its portrayal of a slave market. The captain of a newly-arrived slave ship calls the planters to market, and a woman, an old man, and a Justice each in turn purchase a slave. Eventually, all the slaves are sold, except Mungo, who is repeatedly offered and refused by potential buyers. When Pantaloon enters, accompanied by his daughter Columbine and the Clown, he buys Mungo, whose price is reduced because he is the only slave left. Scene iii, which takes place at Pantaloon's "Plantation," opens with the Clown (a whip in his hand) showing Mungo his work amongst the slaves and threatening to beat him if he does not work fast. Columbine, however, reprimands the Clown for his severity. Unable to adapt to life as a slave, Mungo decides to commit suicide. He removes his waistcloth, puts it around his neck, and ascends a tree with the intention of hanging himself. But the branch gives way and he falls, and from the trunk of the tree a Wizard appears who criticizes Mungo for attempting to end his life. The Wizard waves a hand and transforms him into Harlequin.

In the meantime, Pantaloon is in the process of arranging his daughter's engagement to a Chinese man. But when the Wizard and Harlequin Mungo visit the house, the Wizard encourages Harlequin to transform himself into the Chinese man. After doing so, he signs the marriage contract and receives Columbine with her father's blessing. Harlequin secretly reveals his "identity" to Columbine before leading her off. When the real Chinese man reappears, he, an amazed Pantaloon, and eventually the Clown, begin their pursuit of the couple, who along with the Wizard board the ship now setting sail for England. Act II opens with Harlequin and Columbine landing in England, where Pantaloon, the Chinese man and their servants soon arrive. Each time Harlequin and Columbine are about to be discovered, Harlequin waves his wand and changes the scene. Pantaloon eventually captures Columbine and imprisons her, leaving the distressed Harlequin at a loss regarding how to recover her. But the Wizard reappears, waves his Wand, and transforms the scene to a country house, where Harlequin and Columbine are reunited. Pantaloon, *et al*, appear there too, but the Wizard traps them until Pantaloon agrees to forgive Harlequin and Columbine. In the end, the Chinese man resigns his pretensions to Columbine, the Wizard presents Harlequin (as his son), and Pantaloon joins his hand to Columbine's. The last scene, like traditional pantomimes of the era, is a grand ballet.

The fact that *Harlequin Mungo* was written and performed in the mid-eighteenth-century, a few decades before the abolitionist movement really gained momentum, suggests that the form of pantomime itself enabled anti-slavery sentiment to be presented quite some time before it was popular. Bates not only portrays Mungo sentimentally and, perhaps, sympathetically via the slave market and attempted suicide scenes, the audience is invited to cheer him on as he, in the form of Harlequin, dupes the white characters and pursues an interracial marriage that is ultimately sanctioned at the conclusion of the play. As with Walcott's *Pantomime* and Sheridan's *Harlequin Friday*, there is no evidence in Dabydeen's novel that he is engaging with *Harlequin Mungo*. But the fact that Dabydeen's Mungo is at once a compilation of eighteenth-century visual and textual representations of "blacks," who liberates himself from these constructed identities by taking control of his narrative and exerting his agency, enables a reinterpretation of Bates's Mungo as a dramatic figure who is endowed (with the help of the Wizard) with agency.

***

For Dabydeen's Mungo, it is not enough to simply be aware that he symbolizes conflicting stories, myths and ideals. In order to understand why a simple man like himself was "deemed to be the undoing of England . . . infecting and strangling and poisoning and blighting England's heritage," he turns to yet another generic form that contributed to maintaining or reinforcing identity constructions—journalistic accounts—for "confirmation or denial of his characteristics." He collects clippings from *The Craftsman*, *The Monthly Intelligencer*, *The Spectator* and *The Daily Journal*, as well as from Grub Street broadsheets and penny-ballads, and from these clippings he creates an "archive" of his "own morals and manners."[34] Mungo learns that he has participated in "'Slave Revolts,' 'Mutinies,' 'Runaways,' 'Suicides,' 'Infanticides,' 'Executions . . . by Hanging . . . Burning . . . Gunshot,'" and that in the "faraway plantations of the West Indies, in the barracoons of the African Coast," he has rebelled, stabbed, poisoned, raped, and sought escape by killing himself and his offspring. In return, he has been "strangled, flogged to death, roasted alive, blown away and lynched." He has "made havoc in the hearts and minds of whitepeople [*sic*]," and "compromised their civility, sharpening their Christian principles to breaking-point" (244). Mungo concludes that, as a collection of newspaper items, as a collection of images, he is a "false parcel and counterfeit story" that will "pass hands as easily as a forged banknote" (243). While he hesitates out of "honour, or perhaps shame" to "capitalize" himself by selling the archive, others, such as Hogarth, perpetuate lies about him for profit. He tells the reader: "Centuries from now, when your descendants think of a Negro, they will think of a pimp, pickpocket, purveyor of filth. Mr Hogarth's pictures sold uncommonly well, spreading the message of me throughout the realm" (273).

For Dabydeen, these "descendants" are the racist Britons he encountered upon migrating to England in the mid-twentieth century, which is why he identifies with the black figures in Hogarth's prints, who are likewise objects of racial prejudice and oppression. But at the same time, Dabydeen identifies with Hogarth because, with his satirical critiques of British society, he conveys compassion for the marginalized and dispossessed and endows them with narratives and subjectivities. As Uglow explains, Hogarth's criticisms spread beyond London to Europe and outward to the colonies, built on slavery and convict labour. "All the arguments of his time run through his work: the nature of liberty, the dangers of mercantilism and luxury, the duty of the rich to the poor" (xi). The great "imaginary heroes" in the Age of Hogarth are "not epic figures. They are often outsiders, castaways, servants, rogues or wanderers, orphans and illegitimate children, whose comic trials criticize their society and query the nature of the self" (xv). These "heroes" include Defoe's Crusoe, Swift's Gulliver, Gay's Polly and Macheath, Sterne's Tristam Shandy—and Hogarth's Harlot. For Dabydeen, Hogarth's "blacks" are also among these "imaginary heroes."

Moreover, Dabydeen identifies with the form of Hogarth's pictorial stories. Hogarth was a "literary artist" and his works require a particular "kind of reading." Like a novelist, he manipulates our point of view by offering multiple, oftentimes conflicting yet always somehow intersecting, points of entry into each plate or image. Dabydeen's Mungo, similarly, had "many beginnings." In addition, Hogarth believed that every picture "may *suggest* a story but it is the viewer who *tells* the tale, frames the narrative and fills the gaps" (xv-xvi). Hogarth implicates the viewer, who is free to peruse the images and glean meaning in accordance with his or her own background and orientation. Similarly, via Mungo's narrative, Dabydeen implicates the reader, who is free to wade through the many stories and choose which, if any, contain remnants of factual truths. By revisiting Hogarth's prints through Dabydeen's parody of the linear form of eighteenth- and nineteenth-century slave narratives, the fact that Hogarth's *A Harlot's Progress* is a parody of a straightforward moral tale becomes all the more apparent. While Hogarth drew on the familiar Bunyanesque spiritual journey from sin to grace, he reversed this formula by depicting the "progress" of this innocent country girl as a decline into prostitution, imprisonment, venereal disease and death. In addition, as Uglow argues, the story can be read several different ways, as the "ruin of the innocent by the guilty and the weak by the powerful," or as a tale of "mercantile self-interest, of the harlot as a business-like predator who lures men off the streets and robs them of wealth and health. The question of who is exploiting who is far from clear" (197–198).

Similarly, as Wallace contends, in Dabydeen's novel it is difficult to determine which is the more brutal place, "Mungo's birthplace, where petty jealousies, rumors, and innuendoes lead to the horrific murder of an innocent man and his family, or Lord Montague's apparently pacific estate, where servants nightly torture animals and slave boys behind thick, closed doors" (244). Thus for Mungo to give Pringle the story he wants to hear "entails perpetuating a false distinction between the two cultures" (244). If there is any factual truth at all, it is that tyranny, unequal power relations, and human suffering exist everywhere. In addition to the brutality of the slave trade and plantation slavery, and the cruel treatment of women in Mungo's African village, in England the domestic imprisonment of women like Lady Montagu leads to despair and madness. Just as Hogarth seems to implicate everyone equally in his depiction of capitalist greed and social degradation, in his version of *A Harlot's Progress* Dabydeen implicates everyone equally in the brutality and exploitation that comprised the slave trade.

However, by parodying the slave narrative formula to make his point that "savagery" and "tyranny" exist in all regions of the globe and within all social classes, and to illustrate that Hogarth and even abolitionists upheld stereotypes and myths about Africans, Dabydeen fails to acknowledge the crucial role the slave narrative genre played in the campaign for abolition. While eighteenth-century art, dramatic works, and journalistic accounts indeed served to reinforce racist imagery and attitudes for the period's readers and viewers, slave narratives—whether classified as historical documents or literary creations—contested this imagery, responded to these attitudes, and contributed to bringing about the end of the slave trade. Nonetheless, there is a strength to be located in Dabydeen's novel which is that, by drawing on and reworking so many cultural forms, Dabydeen exposes that genres can only represent (or contest) stories and identity constructions; they can never fully capture individual and actual experiences.

Chapter Five

Literary Impersonations

Beryl Gilroy's *Stedman and Joanna: A Love in Bondage* and John Gabriel Stedman's *Journal* and *Narrative*

Life in Stedman's Surinam in the mid-eighteenth century was worlds away from such idealized colonial landscapes as Inkle and Yarico's cave or Crusoe's island. As Richard Price and Sally Price explain, when Stedman arrived in Surinam in 1773 to help quell the most recent maroon uprisings he found that "heavy speculation, planter absenteeism, and rapid changes in plantations ownership were posing a serious threat to the colony's viability." Approximately "three thousand European whites, who must have sensed their world was coming unglued," were living in "grotesque luxury off the labor force of some fifty thousand brutally exploited African slaves" (xii). When Stedman published his *Narrative* in 1796, abolitionists latched on to its detailed reports of planter cruelty and slave suffering as evidence of an abolitionist stance and immediately put his text into the service of the movement. In actuality, Stedman occupied a middle-of-the-road position with regard to slavery. But according to Price and Price, it is "[p]recisely because he was no abolitionist" that his accounts of the slave owners' "decadence" and the slaves' "dignity" take on "special authority" (xiii).

By transforming Stedman's diaries pertaining to his early life and his *Narrative* into a novel, Gilroy conveys her interest in the psychological roots of Stedman's humanitarian concerns. For example, by dramatizing entries from Stedman's *Journal*, Gilroy proposes that the physical and emotional abuse he endured at the hands of his mother, uncle, and tutor likely fueled his sympathetic portrayal of the Surinam slaves in the *Narrative*. In addition, Gilroy offers a purely fictionalized account of the historical Stedman's visit to London prior to embarking for Surinam, in which she imagines that he attends a lecture by abolitionist Granville Sharpe, hears the ex-slave James Albert Ukawsaw Gronniosaw recount his story, and learns about the Mansfield decision. These encounters cause the fictional Stedman to begin recognizing the humanity of Africans and influence the role he plays in Gilroy's novel as the voice of morality amidst moral corruption in Surinam, which serves to highlight the fact that the historical Stedman presents himself as the voice of morality amidst moral corruption in his *Narrative*.

At the same time, by reading Stedman's *Narrative* through the lens of Gilroy's novel and in tandem with his much less moralizing *Journal*, it is virtually impossible to ignore the extent to which the historical Stedman situates his writings within such literary traditions as the realist novel, captivity narrative, picaresque romance, and sentimental domestic fiction. For example, he aligns both his diaries of his early life and his *Narrative* with Behn and Defoe's realist prose narratives by pleading for the authenticity of his text: " However insignificant, and like the style of romance, this relation may appear to some, it is nevertheless a genuine fact, which I flatter myself may not be uninteresting to many others."[1] Stedman aligns his diaries of his early life with Tobias Smollett and Henry Fielding's novels by retrospectively envisioning his younger self as a hero of picaresque romance. He aligns his *Narrative* with the authors of captivity narratives by presenting himself as a national hero who survived the brutal ordeal of fighting slave rebels in the colony and lived to share his experiences with the British reading public. He also aligns his *Narrative* with such descendents of the captivity narrative as Samuel Richardson's epistolary novels by endowing his mulatto "wife" Joanna virtuous language and behavior reminiscent of *Pamela*, and by portraying himself as a rake transformed by Joanna's virtue.[2] By situating his writings at what Aravamudan refers to as the "culmination of a national culture" (235), Stedman ultimately reassures his readers that the British empire's global power remains secure despite such challenges as slave rebellions in the colonies and the impending revolution in France.

Gilroy's novel also exposes that, while Stedman's sentimental depiction of his relationship with Joanna may have made his sexual activities in Surinam acceptable to an eighteenth-century readership, it disregards what David Richards refers to as the "essential determinants of power, violence and money which conditioned all relationships between white men and black women in the colony" (102). Thus by romanticizing his relationship with Joanna, Stedman diminishes the brutal realities of sexual exploitation in the colonies. Nonetheless, Gilroy is evidently content to believe that Stedman loved Joanna and to forgive his portrayal of their affair as, at first, a drawing-room romance, and then, a tragic love story. In fact, Gilroy herself adopts the sentimental mode to illuminate the historical Stedman's insistence that their relationship is a reversal of *Inkle and Yarico*. As the opposite of Inkle, Stedman not only represents Gilroy's belief that true love can transcend racial barriers, but also her hope that racism will eventually give way to egalitarianism.

***

Stedman was born in 1744 to a prominent Scottish family dating back to the sixteenth century. His father was an officer in the Scots Brigade, a regiment of mercenary troops established in 1570 to protect the Protestant Netherlands. Stedman's mother, Antoinette Christian van Ceulen, was Dutch. At the age of sixteen, in debt and feuding with his family, Stedman followed in his father's footsteps and joined the Scots Brigade, serving first as an ensign and then at the rank of lieutenant. At the age of twenty-eight, Stedman was finally able to appease his wanderlust by responding to a call for volunteers to serve in the West Indies, specifically to assist local troops fighting against the maroons in the eastern regions of Surinam. Stedman was promoted to the rank of captain and, under the command of General Henry Louis Fourgeoud, he left Holland in December of 1772 and arrived in Surinam in February of 1773. While in Surinam, Stedman "married" the beautiful mulatto slave Joanna, who nursed him when he was ill and bore him a son, Johnny. Joanna was the daughter of a rich Dutch planter named Kruythoff and an African mother named Cery, very well educated, and a favorite amongst the Dutch settlers despite her slave status. Historians and literary critics generally agree that, although Stedman's "marriage" to Joanna was essentially formal concubinage, he loved her. However, when Stedman returned to Holland in 1777 neither Joanna nor Johnny accompanied him.

Early in 1782, Stedman married Miss Adriana Wierts Van Coehorn, and in November of that year news arrived from Surinam that Joanna was dead, presumably poisoned. Their son Johnny was then sent to live with his father and his new wife, who bore her husband two daughters and three sons.[3] Also in November of 1782, the Scots Brigade came to an end when the States General adopted a resolution that all officers had to swear an oath of fidelity to the States of Holland and renounce their allegiance to the British Crown, or forfeit their commissions and quit the service of the Dutch Republic. In January 1783, Stedman and several other officers resigned their Dutch commissions and moved to England, settling in Devonshire. Johnny was educated as a son in the Stedman household, and then enlisted as a midshipman in the British Navy. He drowned off the coast of Jamaica at the age of nineteen. After Johnny's death, Stedman's health declined rapidly, most likely because of the tropical ailments he endured while in Surinam. Despite his poor health, Stedman managed to produce extensive autobiographical manuscripts. The most famous is the *Narrative*, sumptuously published in 1796 in two volumes with eighty engravings, including sixteen by William Blake. Stedman also wrote what Price and Price describe as a "rollicking account of the first twenty-eight years of his life (until his departure for

Surinam)"(xiv). These writings are essentially a series of "retrospective diary entries—in effect, an autobiography covering the period 1744–72" (lxviii). In these diaries, Stedman claims to have written them "'principally . . . to amuse myself,' but also for 'my friends during my life[time]' and then afterwards, perhaps, 'for all people to read.'"[4] Such claims not only indicate that Stedman intended his retrospective diaries to be read by his friends and, after his death, the general public, but also that they are much more than a record of his daily activities before and after his sojourn in Surinam, or the source material for his more stylistically polished *Narrative*; they are self-conscious literary creations.

Stedman died on 1 March 1797 at the age of 52 and, in the "Afterword" to *Stedman and Joanna*, Gilroy writes that, because neither Joanna nor Johnny appear on the Stedman genealogical table, it "was as if this true story never occurred" (181). It seems, then, that with *Stedman and Joanna* Gilroy endeavors to resurrect this "true story" from oblivion. While historians and literary critics have come to see Stedman as an unreliable narrator for reasons I will discuss throughout this chapter, Gilroy evidently believes that Stedman should be remembered as a humanitarian whose eyewitness accounts of the abuses inflicted upon slaves in Surinam served the abolitionist campaign. Toward the end of her novel she invites her readers to (re)read Stedman's *Narrative* through the lens her revision as an antislavery treatise by having her Stedman—distraught over the death of Joanna—announce: "I vowed to do my bit to disclose the horrors of slavery that I had witnessed with my eyes and with my heart . . . I felt compelled to stand up for the injustice [Joanna] had experienced" (165). Indeed, Stedman's vivid and impassioned reports of the brutal treatment of slaves serve as evidence that he was very concerned with planter brutality and the mistreatment of slaves in the colonies. However, by claiming in her "Afterword" that the 1796 *Narrative* was "watered down for home consumption" (181), Gilroy suggests that Stedman's original manuscript served as a call to end the institution of slavery, not just a critique of its pervasive corruption.

Gilroy is correct that Stedman's manuscript was edited for publication in such a way as to give it a more pro-slavery slant than his original. According to Anne Rubenstein and Camilla Townsend, Stedman sent his manuscript for the *Narrative* in February 1791 to Joseph Johnson of London, a "notorious free thinker" who published the works of William Godwin and Mary Wollstonecraft. When he received it, Johnson divided up the pages to send them to various illustrators, and in 1794 he turned the entire manuscript over to an editor named William Thomson. Stedman saw his book at various points during the process, and disliked the way it was being handled.

According to Price and Price, Thomson had taken it upon himself to make the *Narrative* "less radical (and more proslavery)" (lx). Thomson not only slanted Stedman's "'moderate' opinions . . . in the direction of a rigid pro-slavery ideology," he deleted many of Stedman's "observations that suggested the common humanity of Africans and Europeans" (lviii), and deleted or muted many of Stedman's "blunt general remarks about the pervasiveness of misconduct and debauchery among European planters" (lix). Only after Stedman saw the printed pages in 1795 and complained would Johnson have realized the extent of Thomson's changes. But in all likelihood, he probably thought the "overall message of the book had not really been changed at all." Johnson "understood that the *Narrative* (with its numerous chilling eyewitness accounts of barbaric tortures of slaves and its graphic accompanying illustrations) would, even in its edited form, stand as one of the strongest indictments ever to appear against plantation slavery" (lxi). Sure enough, a reviewer for the *Analytical Review* wrote:

> It will be impossible to peruse the numerous relations of shocking cruelties and barbarities contained in these volumes without a degree of painful sympathy, which will often rise into horror. Many of the facts are indeed so dreadful, that nothing could justify the writer in narrating them, but the hope of inciting in the breasts of his readers a degree of indignation, which will stimulate vigorous and effectual exertions for the speedy termination of the execrable traffic in human flesh, which, to the disgrace of civilized society, is still suffered to exist and is, even in Christian countries, sanctioned by law.[5]

A reviewer for *The Critical Review* similarly observed, "we have never opened any work which is admirably calculated to excite the most heart-felt abhorrence and detestation of that grossest insult on human nature—domestic slavery."[6]

Rubenstein and Townsend propose that the conflict between Stedman and Johnson can be explained by placing it in the context of events in the 1790s, especially the Haitian Revolution. Stedman submitted his manuscript in the year (1791) that revolution began on the French island of Saint-Domingue. "By the time the book was in press, Britain had 60,000 troops committed to the war against the ex-slaves and mulattoes. Everyone in Johnson's circle would have been discussing events avidly; to them, Stedman's faith in the possibility of slavery being made workable with kinder and firmer treatment for the slaves must have appeared naïve" (286). In addition to the Haitian Revolution, the British had also just faced serious rebellions in

Jamaica, Grenada, and St. Vincent. While the debate regarding slavery had raged for over a decade in print and through speech in England, when the slaves entered into the debate with their violent actions they made it difficult for Europeans to see them as "either passive victims of evil slave-masters or as inherently suited to a benevolent system of slavery" (278).[7] In fact, as David Brion Davis explains, slave rebellions "reinforced the conviction (of slaveholders especially) that slave emancipation in any form would lead to economic disaster as well as the slaughter of whites" (159). The Preface to Stedman's 1796 *Narrative* reflects this pro-slavery fear of revolt:

> As to the shocking cruelties that here are so frequently exposed, let it suffice to say that to deter others from similar inhuman practices, and teach them virtue, was my sole and only motive; while, on the other hand, it must be observed that LIBERTY, nay even too much lenity, when *suddenly* granted to illiterate and unprincipled men, must be to *all* parties dangers, if not *pernicious*. Witness the *Owca* and *Sarameca* Negroes in Surinam—the *Maroons* of Jamaica, the *Caribs* of St. Vincent, &c."[8]

Thus as much as the author abhorred the practice of torturing slaves and hoped his writings would influence planters in the direction of treating their slaves more humanely, he was clearly against abolition and emancipation.

Stedman's middle-of-the-road, or what seems today to be a contradictory position with regard to slavery, is particularly apparent in chapter nine of the *Narrative*, in which he endeavors to relate some of his own "unbiased sentiments upon the slave trade" (88). He begins by claiming that he has read the abolitionist Thomas Clarkson's essays "with pleasure," as well as the "debates and newspaper controversies," but has concluded that most of the "learned gentlemen . . . have erred . . . some by misinformation and prejudice, and others by stubbornness and passion." On the one hand, he asserts, it is "idle, from a principle of humanity alone, to persist in supporting such arguments as are confutable by common sense," while on the other hand it is "equally absurd, for the sake of drinking rum and eating sugar, to persevere in the most unjust and diabolical barbarity" (88). Stedman then claims that the number of Africans transported annually to the West Indies is small in comparison to the millions that die in Europe each year "under the name of Liberty, loaded with the pangs of want and disease and crushed under the galling chains of oppression." Thus the trade in African slaves "is not so bad a thing as some try to support." What is a problem, he argues, is that the "too-helpless" African slaves are treated so poorly and, if properly looked after, they might be made happier than "our sailors or soldiers." Stedman also thinks it would be "ungenerous" to "deprive the West Indian planters of their property" when they "have no other method of procuring a subsistence for their families" (92). If Britain really wishes to keep its remaining West Indian colonies, it must be with awareness that they "can never be cultivated but by Negroes alone, neither the fair European nor the American Indian being adequate to the task" (93). In answer to the "grand question" of whether Africans should remain enslaved or set free, Stedman answers "without hesitation" that the institution of slavery must be preserved to maintain social order. Although Stedman has come to "love the African Negroes," he wishes from the "bottom of [his] heart" that the British Parliament would *not* rule in favor of abolition. If they do, he prophesies, "thousands and thousands shall repent it, and may be ruined by the rash proceeding."[9] However, while Stedman does not support emancipation, he prays and pleads for what he describes as the "abolition of a trade" that is "carried on with unbounded barbarity and usurpation" (94).

In *Stedman and Joanna*, Gilroy endeavors to offer some psychological insight into this historical figure whose mind was divided and whose attitudes regarding slavery were at odds. Gilroy's Stedman begins his narrative as follows:

> I, John Gabriel Stedman, was born in 1744 and from my youth have had the adventures of one many times my age. All through my intrepid youth, and indeed, far into my manhood, there have been inside me feelings tightly held by powers beyond my understanding, powers that led me sometimes to acts of the greatest generosity and concern and at other times to feats of recklessness" (3).

Rather than condemn Stedman, or serve him up (like Inkle) for her readers to criticize, Gilroy proposes that his inconsistent behavior can be attributed, at least in part, to his abusive childhood. For example, Stedman had a troubled relationship with mother, who favored his younger, weaker brother, William George, and vacillated between neglecting Stedman and treating him with unsympathetic cruelty. In the novel, Gilroy's Stedman announces, "it was my resentment and frustrations with my mother that caused me to express myself in dueling and fighting" (4). In addition to being the object of his mother's unruly temperament, the young Stedman experienced severe treatment at the hands of his uncle in Holland and a particularly malevolent schoolmaster. In the *Journal*, Stedman writes that at the age of seven or eight, a schoolmaster "almost tore one of my ears from my head."[10] At the age of eleven, a servant "us'd me so d-mnably roughly, that . . . I run away from him." Hunger forced him to return to the "*tyrant*," who beat him and locked him in a garret without a bed or food (10). This same servant eventually delivers Stedman to his uncle in Scotland, who subjects him to both physical abuse and cruel neglect. Stedman admits that if it not been for the few kind friends who sympathized with his situation, "I would have lost my senses" (14). Life did not improve much for Stedman when he returned home to Holland, as his mother frequently had him beaten, and he often acted out by participating in duels and street fights. He writes: "I was not only bold and strong, but quarrelsome, and had the greatest pleasure in dealing to the Dutch boys those blows, with interest, which I had so often received in Scotland" (21). From this moment onward, Stedman's *Journal* is filled with anecdote after anecdote of drunken brawls, street fights and duels, as well as stories about his excessive drinking, gambling, and sexual encounters with women in all social positions.

However, for Gilroy, Stedman's tendency toward reckless behavior is overshadowed by his extreme sensitivity and capacity for empathy, which she draws attention to when she has her Stedman weep "copiously" after learning of the death of his best friend, George Cunninghame.[11] When George's dog, MyLord, came scratching, whimpering and howling at his door, Stedman again "sobbed . . . [and] from that moment he could not be separated from me" (6).[12] Gilroy also points to Stedman's sensitivity by dramatizing his devastation over the loss of his father. In the novel Stedman writes, "sadness, like a great mantle, enveloped me" (12).[13] In Gilroy's vision, the death of his father in 1771 prompts Stedman to evaluate his life. As he has no immediate plans for a career or marriage, he decides to auction some of the books his father had left him to raise money for a trip to London.

One of these books is a collection of Hogarth's prints. According to the fictional Stedman, his father had loved Hogarth's works and, as if to warn his son against "acting hastily," had shown him pictures in which Hogarth used marginalized figures to "parody the pompous adults of the time" and also to "question the established order" (14). As I discuss in Chapter Four, Hogarth's position with regard to Africans in general and the institution of slavery was ambivalent. In works such as *A Harlot's Progress*, Hogarth uses the exotically-dressed African slave boy in Plate 2 to symbolize Moll's enslavement and also expose the moral corruption of the white merchant, who uses the money he made from colonial trade to indulge in excessive materiality and encourage prostitution. The pregnant black woman in Plate 4 serves to emphasize Moll's fallen social position and loss of freedom, and she also represents the sexual and economic exploitation of African women in the colonies. In another of

Hogarth's satirical series, *The Four Times of the Day*, Hogarth puts a fashionably dressed white woman whose austere countenance suggests her elevated sense of morality at the center of Plate I, "Morning." However, although on her way to church, she ignores the outstretched hand of a black beggar woman. While the conversion of "savages" was a rationalization for slavery, this supposedly pious woman is unwilling to assist the poverty-stricken African woman, and thus Hogarth uses this black figure to expose the hypocrisy of a Christian society that allowed the establishment of slavery. While there is no question that Hogarth utilized racial stereotypes for his depictions of Africans, he also humanizes his black figures in ways that invoke the viewer's compassion. Gilroy's readers cannot help but wonder, then, why she has her Stedman distance himself from Hogarth's social satire by selling the book of Hogarth's prints he so admires. One possibility is that, because the historical Stedman engaged in all kinds of debauchery while in Europe and, while in Surinam, participated in the sexual exploitation of female slaves, he reflects the moral corruption with which Hogarth was concerned; he is the white European toward which Hogarth's criticism, via his black figures, is directed.

Rather than Hogarth, Gilroy opts to align Stedman with Jean-Jacques Rousseau, specifically his philosophy of education, by having the fictional Stedman decide to keep in his possession a copy of *Émile: Or, On Education* (1762). According to Rousseau, a child cannot put himself in the place of others, particularly those who are suffering, but once they have reached adolescence they are capable of being loving and feeling beings with such complex human capacities as sympathy:

> Groans and cries will begin to stir his compassion, he will turn away his eyes at the sight of blood; the convulsions of a dying animal will cause him I know not what anguish . . . So pity is born . . . To become sensitive and pitiful, the child must know that he has fellow-creatures who suffer as he has suffered, who feel the pains he has felt, and others which he can form some idea of, being capable of feeling them himself. Indeed, how can we let ourselves be stirred by pity unless we go beyond ourselves, and identify ourselves with the suffering animal, by leaving, so to speak, our own nature and taking his. (220)

Gilroy illustrates that her Stedman has reached this stage of his education by having him recall and analyze just such an experience:

> I had once kept a tumbler of water with a fish in it and, the weather being deuced cold, everything had become frozen, the fish so stiff that

by mere press of the hand would have broken into two. But feeling pity, I had placed it near the fire, the water melting, and it recovered its life and swam once more, showing me how firm was the life in the body of living things. Were its sensations those that I now felt, I pondered long and well. What did it feel? That poor fish! (13–14)

Gilroy's Stedman, like Rousseau's student, is "stirred by pity" and even identifies with the suffering fish. Gilroy thus once again draws attention to the fact that throughout his diaries Stedman expresses his empathy for both animals and people and describes his attempts to alleviate suffering wherever he saw it. In the *Narrative*, Stedman frequently writes of how, while visiting planters' homes, he intervened to prevent the punishment of slaves.

The other book that Gilroy's Stedman decides to keep is one of Blake's poetry. Gilroy does not provide a title, but she hints at which of Blake's works she deems relevant by having her Stedman reflect upon a few lines from "a song" that his father had written as an inscription:

> And when the night comes I'll go
> To places fit for Woe.
> Walking along the darkened valley
> With silent melancholy. (ll. 13–16)

These lines are from Blake's "Song: Memory, hither come," which Blake allegedly wrote at the age of fourteen and which was first published in *Poetical Sketches*, printed by private subscription in 1783, the same year the actual Stedman was working on his retrospective diaries in London. The speaker of this poem, like Rousseau's pupil, faces the sorrowful aspects of life head on and experiences the suffering of others as his own, just as Gilroy believes the historical Stedman did in Surinam.

Of course, the more obvious reason that Gilroy aligns Stedman with Blake is, as I mention above, that Blake engraved sixteen (out of eighty) plates for the 1796 edition of the *Narrative*. According to Rubenstein and Townsend, the tendency to read the *Narrative* as an anti-slavery document was "shaped not only by editorial changes but much more by its illustrations, particularly those done by Blake" (288). In her novel, Gilroy references the Blake engraving known as "Flagellation of a Female Samboe Slave," as well as Stedman's observations of this scene:

> The first object of my compassion . . . was a beautiful African tied
> up by both arms to a tree. She was as naked as the day she came into

the world and lacerated in such a shocking manner by the whips of two drivers that she was from the neck to her ankles dyed in blood. Her crime? She had firmly refused the embraces of her detestable tormentors. (86)

Here, as in the *Narrative*, Stedman is at the center of the tale.[14] In the *Narrative*, Stedman adds: "It was after receiving two hundred lashes that I perceived her with her head hanging downwards, a most miserable spectacle." Subsequently, he takes action by imploring the overseer to untie her. But the overseer, wishing to "prevent all strangers from interfering with his government," had made it an "unalterable rule" that such interferences would result in doubling the slave's punishment, which he immediately executed. Stedman claims: "I tried to stop him but in vain, he declaring the delay should not alter his determination but make him take vengeance with interest upon interest." Stedman then explains that he was left with no choice but to leave the "detestable rascal, like a beast of prey, to enjoy his bloody feast" (145). Interestingly, as Rubenstein and Townsend observe, the tortured, naked woman does not move or make a sound or even look at anyone, and thus she is the smallest part in this scene. However, in his engraving, Blake tells the story differently by making three crucial changes. "First, the woman is at the center while the men are small and marginal, not even clearly identifiable. Second, the woman is clothed in more than her own blood and does not seem sexually alluring. Third, she looks up, not down. This woman does not ask for pity from those who watch her as she raises her eyes skyward instead of looking toward the men, or at us" (290). Thus unlike Stedman, Blake makes the slave the central figure in the story and thereby demonstrates his deep concern for slavery.

Gilroy also alludes to a similar Blake engraving, known as "A Negro Hung Alive by the Ribs," when her Stedman, after voicing his objection to the execution of an African who committed the same crime as a European, is approached by a man who tells him the following story:

'The other day, sir, I saw with my own eyes an African suspended alive from the gallows by the ribs, between which an incision had been made to accommodate the hook. He hung alive for three whole days, sipping only water that ran down his face from the merciful rain, which alone saved him from dire thirst and from the taunts of passersby who loathed the wet weather. He never groaned or shed a tear, but said that no evil of the European was strong enough to make him weep.' (55)[15]

The major difference between this scene and "Flagellation of a Female Samboe Slave" is that here the tortured slave is male and hung by a hook through his ribs rather than a rope around his wrists. As Rubenstein and Townsend observe, in Blake's engraving the man "looks out of the page with a blank expression. Like the female slave, he does not seem to ask us for mercy, only to require our witness." Unlike Stedman's descriptions, in which the woman's "offense was specifically sexual and her posture alluring," and the man's "lingering death was marked by his admirably masculine stoicism," Blake makes them both "completely individual and almost outside racial or sexual categories" (291). In the years following the publication of the *Narrative*, abolitionists frequently adopted Blake's powerful images for their pamphlets, and anyone who saw them could not forget them.

With the money he earns from auctioning his father's books, Stedman sets off to see Hogarth and Blake's London for himself, a city chock full of smells, crime, decay, poverty, blood, alehouses and ruffians. As in the *Journal*, Gilroy's Stedman sails in the disguise of a common sailor, but in the novel he behaves like a civilized and pious gentleman, keeping to himself, reading his Bible and the *Songs of Mr. Blake*. In London, Stedman comes out of his disguise and dresses as an ensign, as an ensign in a foreign army would be regarded with more respect than a common sailor. Determined to see more than the docks and haunted by memories of his beloved father, Stedman seeks peace at St. Martin's Church, where he hears a sermon by the abolitionist Granville Sharp, one of the foremost British campaigners against slavery. By having her Stedman meet Sharp in 1771 or 1772, Gilroy drops him right in the middle of the beginning of the abolitionist campaign.

In the late 1760s, just before Gilroy's Stedman visits London, Sharp was engrossed in conducting research on the legal arguments against slavery and actively seeking a definitive ruling on the question of whether a slave, once in England, could be forced to leave the country. In 1769, he published *A Representation of the injustice and dangerous tendency of admitting the least claim of private property in the persons of men, in England, etc.*, the first major antislavery work by a British author. Sharp worked on gathering information about slaves and former slaves who had been kidnapped and put aboard ships bound for the colonies. By far the most well known and influential of these cases was the case of an African slave, James Somerset, who was brought to England in 1769 as the property of Charles Stewart, but who escaped in 1771. When he was recaptured and imprisoned on a ship bound for Jamaica, Sharp intervened and the captain of the ship was forced to bring Somerset before the court of King's Bench. The judge, Lord Chief Justice Mansfield, ordered a hearing, although the case was not actually heard until February of

1772. In June of 1772, Mansfield ruled that Somerset's "master" could not force him to return to the colonies. In fact, he ruled that no master was ever allowed to take a slave by force to be sold abroad because he deserted from his service or for any other reason. However, while Somerset's supporters celebrated the ruling as a great victory, Mansfield had not ruled that slavery was illegal in England. Nonetheless, as Debbie Lee explains, the "case was interpreted in the popular imagination to mean that slavery was abolished on British soil. It gained a huge following and took on a mythological status after it was settled" (11). Sharp continued campaigning against slavery, and in 1787 he and his friend Thomas Clarkson formed the Society for Effecting the Abolition of the African Slave Trade.

After hearing Sharp's sermon, Gilroy's Stedman joins a group, "consisting of some Negroes, gathered to tell their stories and pay their respects at the graveside of one Thomas Smith, a Christian slave who had died from years of ill usage." The first to tell their story is Patrasso, a "one-armed giant." His "mistress" had his hand amputated after he jumped in the river to save his drowning "master" but failed because the current was too strong (23). After Petrasso, an African by the name of Gronniosaw told his story, for which Gilroy draws directly from *A Narrative of the Most Remarkable Particulars in the Life of James Albert Ukawsaw Gronniosaw, an African Prince*, which was the first slave narrative in the English language. Published in 1772, Gronniosaw's narrative is a detailed account of his life from the moment he is captured in Africa, to his experiences as a slave in the West Indies, to a life of extreme poverty and heartbreaking suffering England. On his last night in London, Gilroy's Stedman (like the historical Stedman) attends a christening, but in Gilroy's novel it is a christening party for Harold, "a freed black who was much admired for his knowledge of mathematics and music" (29). By recounting their stories and excelling in "western" forms of knowledge, Petrasso, Gronniosaw, and Harold serve to refute eighteenth-century claims that black Africans were devoid of humanity, and that Africans were either a primitive version of "western" societies and culture or had no collective history at all. Similarly, in the *Narrative*, Stedman recognizes that Africans are "not divested of a good ear, and even of poetical genius," if they have the "advantage of education." He asks his readers to "witness among others a black girl called Phyllis Wheatley," who was a slave in Boston and learned Latin. Wheatley wrote "thirty-eight pieces of poetry on different subjects," which were published in 1773. Stedman also mentions Ignatius Sancho, "whose sublime letters and sound philosophy would even add luster to the brightest European genius of the age," and Thomas Fuller, known for his "amazing mental faculties," particularly his "memory and calculation" (262).

In *Ghosts of Slavery*, Jenny Sharpe explains that Gilroy's depiction of Stedman's London visit is a "literary invention, as there is no reason to believe that he was familiar with its free black population of around 1,200 people, most of whom lived on the margins of society" (89). However, the trip marks the beginning of the fictional Stedman's "journey toward recognizing the evils of slavery" (90). Indeed, while Gilroy's Stedman is in this frame of mind—troubled by the suffering of the poor and the punishments inflicted upon the powerless in London—he hears about the slave revolts in Surinam and learns that the Dutch Nation "was reputed to be the most barbarous in its suppression of slaves" (37). In fact, Gilroy implicates Stedman's own family by having his mother, who traveled to Surinam prior to her marriage, recount the following anecdote: "'My Aunt Hilde did not spare her slaves. Why, she drowned a baby for crying too loudly. And if the slaves had too many brats, she threw them into the river after picking out the sturdiest. She was the devil's daughter, my Aunt Hilde!'" (37). With this anecdote, Gilroy alludes to Stedman's description of a mistress whose inhumanity exceeded that of her male counterparts. The historical Stedman reports that a Mrs. Stolker, who was traveling to her estate in a tent-barge, ordered a Negro mother to hand over her crying infant. Then, "in the presence of the distracted parent, she thrust it out one of the tilt-windows and held it underwater till it *was drowned*." When the mother leapt overboard and tried to end her own life, her mistress ordered that she be punished for her "unnatural temerity with three or four hundred lashes" (148).

When Gilroy's Stedman arrives in Surinam, he witnesses firsthand the planters' sadistic treatment of their slaves: "Their children and their women could be taken at will, and they must submit to tortures such as flagellations and live burnings . . . Throughout the colony, one-legged and one-armed men were common. Legs were lost for running away from persecution and hands for raising them against whites, however sore and unjust the provocation" (109). Over the years, with the help of Joanna and her family, he develops his compassion for the African slaves, and in his narrative Gilroy's Stedman writes, "I had learned to love the black people. I had come to know their kindness, their loyalty, and their humanity and could not understand why they were treated in such an unchristian way by those who claimed an enlightened life as their heritage" (130). Gilroy thus draws attention to the historical Stedman's remarks on the Africans' humanity in the unedited *Narrative*. Stedman writes, "all Negroes believe firmly in a God whose goodness they trust more than many whining Christians," and "no Negro ever breaks an oath, "to the shame and infamy of those Europeans who break it daily, and treat with contempt this race of people more religious than themselves"

(262–263). He also notes that the African slaves "need not be told to love their brethren as themselves, since the poorest negro among them, having but an egg scorns to eat it alone, but were twelve present and every one of them a stranger, he would cut or break it into as many shares" (264).

According to Sharpe, "in choosing to tell the story of Stedman's growing recognition of the humanity of slaves, Gilroy projects onto an eighteenth-century male authored travel narrative a perspective on slavery that was developed by nineteenth-century women abolitionists." More specifically, her novel reflects the "anti-slavery position that emerged after 1824, when the British abolitionist and Quaker Elizabeth Heyrick called for the immediate emancipation of slaves in the British colonies in her pamphlet *Immediate not Gradual Abolition*" (95). Heyrick's "radical" anti-slavery position was further developed in the United States by Boston abolitionist Lydia Maria Child. According to Sharpe, Child distinguished herself as an abolitionist by making a case for slave revolts as "acts of self defense" and celebrating the achievements of Jamaican maroon leaders, Juan de Boas and Cudjoe, as well as Toussaint L'Ouverture, leader of the San Domingue rebellion. In addition, Child defends the "intelligence and moral character of the Negro race" by giving examples of the "literary talents of educated black men and women, as does Stedman" (95). Interestingly, Child herself produced one of the first engagements with Stedman's *Narrative* when she published "Joanna" in the Boston antislavery collection *The Oasis*. While much of "Joanna" was excerpted from Stedman's *Narrative*, Child endeavors to put Stedman's text into the service of the abolitionist movement by adding her own commentary in several places. For example, with regard to Stedman's attitude toward slavery and the slave trade, she writes: "Captain Stedman appears to have been extremely kindhearted, and strongly prepossessed in favor of the African character. He was often made ill and wretched by the cruelties he witnessed;—(cruelties which the imagination of the most fanatical Abolitionist could never have conceived)" (104). The implication, then, is that by 1834—the year emancipation went into effect in the British colonies, but long before emancipation in America—Stedman's text was no longer a strong enough indictment of slavery to be in and of itself useful to abolitionists.

According to Werner Sollers, Child "attempts to put Stedman to abolitionist use, precisely because he wasn't one" (192). But as much as Child "mistrusted" Stedman's account, she "was not suspicious enough. For as we can now safely assert in hindsight," with the help of Price and Price's critical editions of Stedman's manuscripts, "even the skeptical reader Child fell for a good part of Stedman's sentimentalized self-representation; she probably would have been surprised by the extent to which the historical figure . . . invented himself as a romantic character" (201). Today, by reading

Stedman's *Journal* and *Narrative* through the lens of Gilroy's revision, the extent to which Stedman invented himself as a romantic character becomes strikingly apparent.

***

At the beginning of her novel, Gilroy engages directly with Stedman's diaries pertaining to his early life, most likely the published version entitled *The Journal of John Gabriel Stedman: 1744–1797 Soldier and Author* (1962), edited by Stanbury Thompson, as this text would have been more readily available to her than Stedman's manuscripts, which are in the James Ford Bell Library at the University of Minnesota.[16] Gilroy's Stedman begins by announcing that in his youth he had been a handsome young man "of Scot and Dutch extraction" with exceptional promise: "I was well-built in stature, and I cut an elegant dash in my uniform" (4). Like Gilroy's Inkle, the fictional Stedman presents himself as a heroic figure, even a national hero, who at a young age developed a passionate desire to see the New World: "I had longed for adventure ever since reading of the colonizations of the intrepid James Cook in the Pacific, not only of his conquests over the minds of natives, but also of his securing fresh lands for civilization to occupy" (5). In the eighteenth century, scientific surveys and such expeditions as Cook's contributed to the body of knowledge that mapped and classified the world from a Eurocentric perspective. Moreover, the narratives of Cook's three voyages are mainly concerned with furthering English trade interests and territories abroad, and thus reveal direct imperialist ambition.[17] By introducing her Stedman as having been influenced by Cook's narratives, Gilroy suggests that the historical Stedman retrospectively viewed his younger self as an agent of colonial conquest and hand of the British empire.

When he enlists in the Scots Brigade, Gilroy's Stedman does so with the hope that he will someday be sent to sea, which is undoubtedly an allusion to Stedman's claim in the *Journal* that "a military life without either money or interest was my antipathy, especially in times of peace, when I must lie inactive, without the smallest hopes of honour, or preferment. Thus I propose that I may be sent to sea, to which indeed I have always had the greatest inclination" (21). By highlighting the actual Stedman's desire for overseas adventure, Gilroy proposes that in his *Journal* Stedman aligns himself with the protagonists of such early eighteenth-century fictional travelogues as Defoe's *Robinson Crusoe*. Crusoe similarly declares at the beginning of his narrative, "I would be satisfied with nothing but going to Sea" (4), and "my Thoughts were . . . entirely bent upon seeing the World" (6). As I discuss in Chapter Two, Defoe's "realist" *Robinson Crusoe* ultimately became a prototype for imperialist narratives, its hero being representative of such empire-building activities as global trade and colonialism. By aligning himself with Crusoe, Stedman resurrects for his late eighteenth-century readers images of the early eighteenth-century British empire's glory days, when the British led the world in colonial acquisitions and slave trading, and when the notion of a culturally-superior British identity still remained, as far as the British were concerned, unchallenged.

These images were also particularly apropos for the latter part of the eighteenth century. After the Seven Years' War (1750s- 1763), Britons began to think in terms of a single, monolithic British empire that included England, Scotland, Ireland, and all of Great Britain's overseas territories. The war had not only ended France's power, both in the Americas (where it lost many of its colonial possessions) and in continental Europe until the time of the French revolution, but Great Britain emerged as the dominant colonial power in the world. The Seven Years' War ended with the acquisition of Canada, the Floridas, and additional West Indian islands. While the American Revolution caused what P.J. Marshall refers to as a "temporary dislocation," after Britain conceded American independence in 1783 there was a "new phase of growth," which was sustained well into the nineteenth century as the British empire expanded eastward into Asia and Africa (20). British dominance was not confined to the acquisition of, and authority over, overseas territories. This was a commercial empire, whose economic growth and strength was assured by the Navigation Acts, which required that all colonial trade be carried in English ships, and that all European goods bound for the colonies be shipped through England, where they would be unloaded, inspected, taxed and reloaded. The British empire's economic security was also dependent upon the cultivation of raw materials and maintenance of slave labor in the West Indian colonies. According to Michael Craton, despite "threats of slave rebellions and attacks from the French and Spanish (especially during the Seven Years' War and American War of Independence), Jamaica by 1775 boasted seven hundred sugar plantations . . . Until the end of slavery, this single island produced half the total tonnage of British West Indian sugar, from the labor of half of all British West Indian slaves" (320). Because of sugar, Adam Hochschild writes, the "value of British imports from Jamaica alone was five times that of the thirteen mainland colonies" (54). In England, almost everyone benefited in some way or another from the sugar industry and the slave trade.

However, as Craton also points out, the "power of Jamaica and the pretensions of its planters did not go unchallenged." Despite the opposition of the Jamaica lobby, the British acquired four new plantation colonies in the Windward Islands at the Treaty of Paris, which ended the Seven Years' War in 1763: Dominica, Saint Vincent, Grenada, and Tobago. While these islands were regarded as a "potential extension of the sugar frontier," progress was slowed, "not just by opposition from the older colonies, but the islands' mountainous terrain" and the "resistance of the Caribs and maroons in Saint Vincent and Dominica." While the "dominance of the Anglophone planters seemed assured after 1783, when Stedman settled in England and was working on his manuscripts, it was "once more threatened by the internal and external upheavals of the French Revolution," and later, the Napoleonic Wars.[18] It was therefore essential, at this moment in history, to bolster the confidence of Britons at home by producing texts which served to counter or alleviate what Kathleen Wilson describes in "The Sense of the People" as the "widespread fears of the emasculation and degeneracy of the British body politic" (185), and to portray "empire—its attainment, acquisition, settlement and preservation"—as the "bulwark and proving ground of the true national character, of national (and middle class) potency, identity and virtue" (189). Not surprisingly, the figure or idea of Robinson Crusoe in its many manifestations continued to be both popular and relevant.

But Crusoe is not the only literary figure with which Stedman identifies. By lifting examples of his raucous antics from the *Journal* almost word for word for her novel, Gilroy illustrates that—in addition to the hero of an imperialist travelogue—the historical Stedman retrospectively envisioned his younger self as the hero of an eighteenth-century picaresque romance. While the historical Stedman insists in the *Journal* that his readers are "not reading a romance embellished with all the fruitfulness of imagination, but a genuine history kept by a man of character, and only wrote [*sic*] for his own gratification, and that of his best friends" (43), he also readily admits that his writings are imitative:

> And throwing aside Plutarch's *Lives, Flavius Josephus, Spectator,* &c., I read romance, setting out with *Joseph Andrews, Tom Jones, Roderick Random,* which heroes I resolved to take for my models from this date. *Roderick Random* I liked best, and in imitation of he, immediately fell in love at the dancing assembly with a Miss Diana Bennet, whom I shall call *Narcissa* [the heroine of Smollett's *Roderick Random*]. (*Journal* 53–55)

It makes sense that Stedman liked Smollett best, as they had much in common. As Paul-Gabriel Boucé notes, Smollett was (like Stedman) a "notoriously fiery-tempered Scotsman" who (also like Stedman) belonged to a good family but "had no personal fortune at his disposal" (ix). When Stedman first encountered Smollett through his writings he would have admired him for living—despite his limited means—the kind of adventurous life that Stedman fantasized about, and for producing a successful novel based loosely on that life. While critics warn that *The Adventures of Roderick Random* should not be viewed as an autobiography, there is no question that Smollett's first novel reflects the author's lived experiences, such as his departure from Scotland, his discovery of what Boucé describes as a "fascinating kaleidoscope of glittering life in the metropolis," his experiences in the Navy during an expedition to the West Indies, and his "wooing and winning of a Jamaican beauty and heiress" (x).

Stedman also admired Smollett's protagonist, although after receiving his ensign commission he writes in the *Journal* that he thinks his "misfortunes superior to [Roderick Random's], he being his own master" (72). Roderick "Rory" Random was born to a nobleman and a lower-class mother, and consequently shunned by his father's family. When his mother dies shortly after his birth, his father goes mad with grief. At first Roderick's grandfather reluctantly pays for his education, but he casts him out when Roderick's abusive tutor submits negative reports about his progress. Roderick eventually receives guidance and some financial support from his maternal uncle, Tom Bowling, a naval lieutenant. After attending the University of Glasgow, Roderick briefly serves as an apprentice to a surgeon, and then sets off on the road to London, where he is press-ganged into the Navy. When a shipwreck enables him to return to England, he serves as a footman to the aunt of Narcissa, with whom he falls hopelessly in love. When Roderick saves Narcissa from being raped by a neighbor, he runs away and is captured by smugglers and taken to France. After a series of escapades and coincidental reunions in France and back in England, Roderick takes a position as a surgeon on a slave ship commanded by his uncle. They sail to Guinea and Angola and then cross the Atlantic with their cargo of slaves. In Buenos Aires, Roderick meets a Scottish gentleman who turns out to be his long-lost father. Together they return to London where Roderick, because his aristocratic social status has been restored, is able to marry Narcissa and purchase the family estate in Scotland from its bankrupt owner. Thus as Anna Neill points out, it "is not, then, the impenetrable innocence and steady virtue of the hero but rather the artifices of romance that bring about a happy and morally comfortable resolution to his story" (130).

In her novel, Gilroy exposes the similarities between Stedman (or his literary persona) and the hero of *Roderick Random*. Like Roderick, Stedman experienced extensive personal abuse as a young child at the hands of relatives and a tutor. Like Roderick, Stedman left Scotland with very little money and traveled to London, where he witnessed the conspicuous consumption and pervasive corruption that were the result of London's role in the mid-eighteenth century as the center of a rapidly expanding British empire. Like Roderick, Stedman traveled to the New World and witnessed first-hand the effects of colonialism and slavery on Europeans and Africans alike. However, Stedman is distinctly *unlike* Random because he cannot ignore the suffering of the slaves, whereas Roderick is seemingly indifferent to the lives of the African captors on board his ship between Guinea and New Spain.[19] Nonetheless, by portraying himself as a picaro and aligning his *Narrative* with Smollett's novel, Stedman endows his *Narrative* with two, seemingly at odds, political functions. On the one hand, whereas Smollett critiques what Neill describes as the "corruption of a metropolitan culture under the influence of global commerce and imperial aggression" (122), Stedman critiques the corruption of European settlers in the colony by depicting Surinam as what Richards describes as a "cesspit of perverse sexual practices" where the "pursuit of sexual gratification is enmeshed with slave ownership and violence" (92). On the other hand, whereas Smollett "sees the protection of British colonies as essential to both the economic and (less directly) the moral infrastructure of their mother country" (128), Stedman sees the protection of the British colonies as essential for preserving social order and assuring the empire's commercial prosperity. Thus by forging an alliance with Smollett, Stedman's text implicitly promotes the political and economic goals of the empire.

In addition to Smollett's *Roderick Random*, Stedman draws on Fielding's picaresque novels of the road: *Joseph Andrews* (1742) and *Tom Jones* (1749). Gilroy reveals that Stedman draws directly from *Joseph Andrews* when her Stedman narrowly averts the sexual advances of his landlord's wife but then engages in a tryst with her maid Maria. With this scene, Gilroy points to the moment in the *Journal* when Stedman writes: "Jan Slootmaker, the Zeeland-er's wife, treats me with drams. Pays me frequent visits in my bedroom. I treat her like Joseph did Potiphar's wife, and prefer her maid, Maria Bymans" (57). At the beginning of *Joseph Andrews*—the "authentic History" (16) of the brother of Pamela, the virtuous heroine of Richardson's *Pamela, or Virtue Rewarded* (1740)—Joseph's recently widowed employer, Lady Booby, and her servant, Mrs. Slipslop—comic equivalents, respectively, of Richardson's Mr. B. and his housekeeper Mrs. Jewkes—make attempts on Joseph's virtue. Fielding's Joseph not only emulates his virtuous sister Pamela but also, by refusing Lady Booby's sexual advances, lives up to his given name: the Old Testament Joseph who resisted Potiphar's wife. At the age of seventeen, the biblical Joseph was sold to a caravan of Ishmaelites en route to Egypt. In

Egypt, the Ishmaelites sold Joseph to Potiphar, an officer of Pharaoh. Joseph prospered in Potiphar's service and became an overseer of all he possessed. Potiphar trusted Joseph completely, and Joseph is described in Genesis as "goodly" and "well favoured" (Gen. 39:6). When Potiphar's wife became infatuated with Joseph, he refused her sexual advances, but she was not dissuaded and continued to pursue him until one day, when he fled her grasp, she left a piece of her garment in his hand. She then screamed, gathered witnesses, and accused him of rape (Gen. 39:14). Potiphar had no choice but to send Joseph to prison, although this would have been a fairly lenient punishment in an era when death was usually the sentence for attempting to rape the wife of high-ranking government official.[20]

Yet unlike Joseph, whose virtue is exemplary, Stedman's literary persona in the *Journal*, "Desperate Jack" is less than a stellar example of virtue, and subsequently his accounts of excessive debauchery (drinking, gambling and promiscuity) more closely resembles those of the hero of *Tom Jones*. In Gilroy's novel, the fictional Stedman recalls: "Pretending to be Tom Jones, I had sung in the alehouses songs of my own making, mentioning all the names of the maidens I loved while throwing my lace ruffles amongst those who had come to bid us farewell as we left that post" (13). Here, Gilroy points to the following claim in Stedman's *Journal*: "The Pleasure I had in humouring my father, and mortifying my mother who construed everything for the worst was excessive, while my getting drunk was entirely owing to my being over-joy'd at my brother's recovery, something like *Tom Jones* for his friend, *Mr. Allworthy*" (89). In Fielding's novel, Mr. Allworthy is Tom's kind and generous benefactor. Stedman is alluding here to the scene in Book V when Tom, having been summoned home from Squire Western's neighboring estate, finds Mr. Allworthy so ill that he reads his will aloud. Later, when the doctor assures Tom that Mr. Allworthy is out of danger, Tom celebrates: "This account so pleased *Jones*, and threw him into such immoderate Excess of Rapture, that he might be truly said to be drunk with Joy. An Intoxication which greatly forwards the Effects of Wine; and as he was very free too with the Bottle on this Occasion, (for he drank many Bumpers to the Doctor's Health, as well as to other Toasts) he became very soon literally drunk" (252). By comparing his drinking to Tom's, Stedman invites his readers to view his drunkenness as celebratory rather than irresponsible, and good-natured rather than malicious. In other words, in addition to romanticizing his youth, Stedman encourages his readers to view him as having noble intentions.

Similarly, by comparing his tendency to indulge his romantic passions with Tom's, Stedman encourages his readers to view his behavior with regard

to women as romantic rather than licentious. In the novel, Gilroy's Stedman falls "most desperately in love with fair Cornelia" (5). After her father
catches him kissing Cornelia and beats him mercilessly, he falls into a "fitful
sleep" and dreams about "another beautiful but sensible girl, Heligonda van
Calker, who often looked with smiles and pleasures in [his direction]" (6).
In the *Journal*, Stedman writes: "Fall most desperately in love with Cornelia
Cornel, a skipper's young daughter, whose breath was like violets, and forget
poor *Narcissa*. I never could marry Cornelia. I abominated to debauch her,
yet could never be happy without seeing her, which was only sometimes by
stealth. I fight a bull-dog in her presence, to give her proof of my courage,
and actually beat him" (54). In Book IV of *Tom Jones*, the reader learns that
Tom is infatuated with Molly Seagrim, the daughter of Black George, Squire
Western's gamekeeper. When Molly becomes pregnant, and tries to hide
her condition by wearing a dress to church that was given to her by Sophia
Western, the envious village women attack her. Fortunately, Tom comes to
her rescue, vowing the "utmost Vengeance on all who had been concerned,"
wrapping her in his coat, and "wiping the Blood from her Face as well as
he could with his Handkerchief," before making arrangements to carry her
"safely home" (183–184). Just a few days later, while hunting with Squire
Western, Sophia Western is thrown from her horse. Tom catches her "in his
Arms," breaking an arm in the process. (200). While Sophia is recovering,
her maid reports that she had found Tom kissing her hand warmer a few
days earlier, a sign that he is in love with Sophia even though he is having an
affair with Molly.[21] While Tom certainly seems to the reader be fickle, one
cannot ignore that his actions are chivalrous rather than utterly roguish.

Gilroy reiterates her view that Stedman should be remembered as a
man whose chivalry and noble intentions match the period's popular literary
picaros, and who took action whenever he witnessed suffering, by including
in her novel a scene in which Stedman notices a woman in labor in a pigsty
and sets about helping the "poor woman" (7). The onlookers chide him,
refusing to believe that he is not the father, and the grateful mother—seeing
him as "an angel come from heaven"—names her child after him (8). In the
Journal, Stedman writes: "I find a woman *in labour* in a pig-sty. I get her
relieved by the parish, give her some money and linen &c., beg for her to my
landlady, aunti slootmaker, who declares I was the father; to my great shame,
since I never saw this poor wretch before now. The miserable woman calls
me *an angel* sent from heaven, to save her life. The child was christen'd by
my name, and I publickly derided" (57). Yet as much as this anecdote seems
to testify to Stedman's good character it is also drawn from *Roderick Random*
and/or *Tom Jones*, each of which includes a case of mistaken or possibly

misdirected paternity, and thus serves to undermine that good character. In *Roderick Random*, the surgeon to whom Roderick is apprenticed saves his reputation by letting everyone think that Roderick is responsible for his maidservant's pregnancy. In *Tom Jones*. Tom confesses to Allworthy that he is Molly's lover and could be the father of her child. But when he brings her money, he discovers her other lover, Square, hiding in her closet, and later learns that she has had yet another lover, who is just as likely as Tom or Square to be the father.

By aligning his writings with Smollett and Fielding's picaresque romances, Stedman endows his writings with the same function as the period's novels, which, according to Patricia Meyer Stacks, "came to fulfill a traditional epic function by articulating the nation's values and its complicated sense of itself in a period of dramatic change" (4). Yet interestingly, as Richards argues, the literary identity that Stedman created for his *Journal* out of the picaresque romance—which in the eighteenth century was the "adventures of the rakish dashing blade let loose on a tempestuous world of sinful urban pleasures" (89)—gave way in his *Narrative* to other types of narrations that could "effectively validate and structure the experience" (95). For example, as Gilroy exposes, Stedman situated his *Narrative* within a tradition of captivity narratives and sentimental fiction that can be traced back to Mary Rowlandson's 1682 narrative of her captivity by Algonquin Indians in the New England wilderness. According to Michelle Burnham, by showing that she was "moved to tears" by her experiences, Rowlandson encouraged a community of readers on both sides of the Atlantic to care about an "unimportant Englishwoman and her suffering" (51). Gilroy's Stedman, similarly, invites his readers to sympathize with his suffering: "I was weary of a life always so close to death, such a restless unsettled life, and I fell upon my naked knees invoking heaven to lead me away from the service to which I was fettered by conventions and loyalties" (128). Gilroy thus points to the fact that, like the authors of captivity narratives, the historical Stedman utilized sentimental tropes to encourage sympathetic identification with his literary persona.

While Stedman was not a captive in the New World, his experiences in the jungles of Surinam attempting to quell the maroon rebellions were as demoralizing and challenging to his sense of a supposedly superior European identity as the subjugation experienced by white captives of American Indians. In her novel, Gilroy conveys just how powerful and dangerous the maroons in Surinam were by having her Stedman learn prior to leaving Holland that, from the early days of slavery, escaped slaves "set up settlements and returned in the dead of night to plunder, hack their tormentors to death, and set the torch to their former owners' possessions." In the "wake of destruction and failed enterprise," whites "fled their plantations."[22] The maroons in Surinam were organized in a number of small groups under the leadership of three men, Boni, Joli Coeur and Baron, all of which were encamped around the Cottica River. The government called in the Scots Brigade in hopes of solving the problem and eliminating the rebel leaders. Gilroy's Stedman writes: "I was not going to a conventional war but to guerrilla warfare in the jungles of Surinam, chasing rebels from site to site in an effort to corrode their resistance" (37).

When he arrived in Surinam, Stedman was sent in a gunboat up the Cottica and, although they made contact with Boni's rebels, most of them escaped further into the forests. The jungle warfare practiced by the Scots Brigade was poorly organized and for the most part ineffective against the maroons. [23] Moreover, lying in wait of the maroons effectively made Fourgeoud's troops vulnerable to tropical diseases. Gilroy's Stedman writes that the "men were dying of life in the bush, where we were exposed to ringworm, looseness, and bellyjack, to creatures such as bats that twice bled my toes as well as rats, spiders, bush worms, ants, ticks, wood lice and scorpions" (62). Stedman and the troops were not only "prone to sickness" but also to what Richards describes as the "taunts of the rebels" (94). Indeed, in the *Narrative* Stedman reports that, when General Fourgeoud offered the rebels "life, liberty, victuals, drink, and all they wanted," they "replied, with a loud laugh, that they wanted nothing from him . . . They told us, that we were to be pitied more than they; that we were *white slaves*, hired to be shot at and starved for fourpence a day; that they scorned to expend much more of their powder upon such scarecrows" (283). Thus Stedman and the troops were humiliated and emasculated in their encounter with the maroons. To make matters worse, Fourgeoud's troops were dying rapidly and, while they eventually managed to drive out the rebel leader Boni and his people, who settled in French Guiana, the cost was enormous loss of life amongst the Europeans.

Like the white captives of American Indians who managed to escape, return home and produce a narrative of their captivity, Stedman survived brutal and distressing encounters with African slave rebels and tropical diseases in the Surinam wilderness, returned home and produced an account of his "heroic" adventures restoring order in the colony. In doing so he attempts to restore, as I discuss in Chapter One, what Snader refers to as the cultural imbalance—the violation of the imagined hierarchy that placed western above non-western cultures—that he experienced in Surinam and assures his English readers that their cultural and political dominance remains intact during a moment in history when slave rebellions were threatening "western" hegemony.[24] Stedman's allegedly "heroic" experiences would have been particularly interesting to Britons at home. As Colley explains in *Captives*, once troops from Britain and their families began crossing the Atlantic in substantial numbers, after the outbreak of the Seven Years War in 1756, the metropolitan market for tales of captivity and other information about the New World skyrocketed. With large numbers of "their own kind" traveling to overseas territories, "not to settle, but to fight and hopefully live to conquer and return," the New World and all its "complex dangers came to seem to Britons at home infinitely more real and absorbing" (161). It is no wonder that Stedman's *Narrative* was so successful, going through more than twenty-five editions in six languages.[25]

Stedman's experiences would also have been appealing to Britons at home because he utilized imagery to represent the New World and its peoples with which his readers would have been familiar. For example, as Gilroy exposes, Stedman's depiction of the slave Joanna is informed by the images of "noble savagery" that emerged with Behn's *Oroonoko* and continued to be prevalent throughout the eighteenth century in both colonial and abolitionist texts. When Gilroy has a character in her novel explain that Joanna is the "daughter of a respectable gentleman named Kruythoff, a man of culture and learning," and Cery, an African woman," she alludes to the following description of Joanna in Stedman's *Narrative*: "Joanna was by birth a gentleman's daughter from Holland; and her mother's family were [sic] the most distinguished people on the coast of Africa" (267). Stedman thereby presents Joanna as a conflation of European aristocracy and African royalty. Just as Yarico's "beautiful shells, bugles and bredes" indicate that she is a person of distinction, Joanna's gold chains, rings, amulets, and medals, all presents from her father, indicate that she is socially superior to the average slave. As Aravamudan explains, the "cliché of the royal black captive recurs incessantly in British literary representations from *Oroonoko* to *Rasselas*" and "Africans in British literary discourse were oftentimes blue blooded." Gronniosaw's mother was eldest daughter of the reigning king. Ottobah Cugoano's father was a "chief" and Equiano's father was one of "those elders or chiefs." Aravamudan adds that Sancho showed a desire for aristocratic connections, wishing to play the noble African parts of Othello and Oroonoko on stage (252).

Although Joanna's status as an African royal would have made her, like Oroonoko and Yarico, an appealing and sympathetic figure to a white, western readership, it would not have been enough to make Stedman's affair with her entirely palatable. By drawing almost directly from Stedman's description of Joanna in the *Narrative*, Gilroy invites her readers to see that Stedman goes even further by either denying the key physical markers of Joanna's racial identity or representing them as imitations of European models of beauty:

> She was taller than middle size and elegantly shaped. She moved her well-formed limbs with more than common gracefulness. Her face was full of the modesty of her people, and her black eyes were large and full of expression. In spite of her dark skin, her cheeks showed a vermilion tinge. Her nose was well formed and small, and when she spoke she showed two rows of regular and wonderfully white teeth. Her hair was dark brown with lighter streaks and formed a crest of ringlets in which she worked flowers and gold spangles. (44)

In the *Narrative*, Stedman writes:

> Rather more than middle-sized, she was perfectly straight with the most elegant shapes that can be viewed in nature, moving her well-formed limbs as when a goddess walked. Her face was full of native modesty and the most distinguished sweetness. Her eyes, black as ebony, were large and full of expression, bespeaking the goodness of her heart. With cheeks through which glowed (in spite of her olive complexion) a beautiful tinge of vermillion when gazed upon, her nose was perfectly well-formed and rather small, her lips a little prominent which, when she spoke, discovered two regular rows of pearls as white as mountain snow. Her hair was dark brown, next to black, forming a beauteous globe of small ringlets, ornamented with flowers and gold spangles. Round her neck, her arms, and her ankles she wore gold chains, rings and medals . . . (41).

Here, as Richards observes, Joanna's color is "euphemized by Stedman, as Oroonoko's "ebony" skin was euphemized by Behn, into "vermillion." Moreover, her nose is small, her teeth are white, and—contrary to the racial stereotype of African women as promiscuous—she is both modest and virtuous.

Gilroy also illustrates how extensively Stedman drew on the sentimental mode for his depiction of Joanna by having her Stedman declare: "And one day it all changed . . . a young mixed-race girl, no more than fifteen, entered the room . . . The girl's perfection of face and form startled me. There was music and all the light and shade of poetry in her movements. My eyes followed her around the room with the utmost compulsion" (42). Gilroy's Stedman cannot stop thinking about Joanna, who he claims "became torture" to his "heart." When Joanna asks him what he wants of her, he responds: "To love you, Joanna. Deeply. Truly. In your presence my feelings become sublime and I believe in virtue and commitment and even in the existence of angels. I want to purchase you, and keep you always with me" (45). According to Lynn Festa, the sentimental mode "held sway over the British and literary imagination at a time when Europeans were fanning out across the globe in search of commercial and colonial dominion." In the latter part of the eighteenth century, when Stedman was working on his retrospective manuscripts, sentimentality had attained a "dazzling popularity" and become the "mode of choice for writing about colonized populations, about slaves, about the disenfranchised, and the eighteenth-century poor" (2). The sentimental mode was particularly popular amongst abolitionists, who used sentimental figures in their poetry and prose to rouse the sympathies of their readers and help them imagine relations to distant peoples. Thus as Tassie Gwilliam observes, Stedman's relationship with Joanna is "produced as a spectacle controlled by literary precursors and by his audience" (662).

As I have already mentioned, Gilroy is content to believe that Stedman loved Joanna. However, while she prefers the edited and overly sentimentalized 1796 *Narrative* version of their relationship, one cannot ignore that Stedman's *Journal* entries serve as evidence that Stedman entered into what Gwilliam describes as the "quintessentially colonial economic/sexual agreement of formal concubinage with Joanna" (654).[26] Moreover, one cannot ignore that Stedman himself, in his 1790 manuscript for the *Narrative*, self-consciously transforms Surinam into what Price and Price describe as "an example of pure and faithful love" by drawing on the "then-current European sentimental ideals," which "effectively captivated European audiences" (xxxiv).[27] In doing so, Stedman not only attempts to sanitize his affair with an African slave for European consumption but he also situates his text within the tradition of the period's extraordinarily popular epistolary novels, which would certainly have served to boost the *Narrative*'s popularity. By lifting Joanna's speech from the *Narrative*, Gilroy draws attention to the fact that Stedman endowed his mulatto lover with the same sentimental language Richardson gave to his virtuous heroine in *Pamela*:

> 'I am born a low contemptible slave. Were you to treat me with too much attention, you must degrade yourself with all your friends and relations; while the purchase of my freedom you will find expensive, difficult, and apparently impossible. Yet though a slave, I have a soul, I hope, not inferior to that of an European; and blush not to avow the regard I retain for you, who have distinguished me so much above all

others of my unhappy birth. You have, Sir, pitied me; and now, independent of every other thought, I shall have pride in throwing myself
at your feet, till fate shall part us, or my conduct become such as to
give you cause to banish me from your presence.' This she uttered with
a down-cast look, and tears dropping on her heaving bosom, while she
held her companion by the hand. (45–46) [28]

Gilroy's Stedman (like the historical Stedman) pulls out the whole arsenal of
sentimental tropes, from modesty to blushes to tears, and thereby draws attention to the fact that the historical Stedman enforces a sentimental reading of
Joanna's speech by referring to it as a "humble declaration" (48), and describ-
ing Joanna as delivering it with "downcast looks and tears dropping upon her
heaving bosom" (49). Evidently, Gilroy's Joanna transforms the rakish Stedman with her beauty and virtue, as shortly thereafter he writes: "For the first
time I wanted to be tethered to a wife, a home, and perhaps a family, with a
woman who was both lovely and virtuous" (47). Thus in the process of portraying Joanna as comparable to Richardson's Pamela, Stedman portrays himself as comparable to Richardson's Mr. B.

Richardson's *Pamela* is the story of a young servant girl who is relentlessly
pursued by a wealthy landowner, Mr. B., in his country house in Lincolnshire.
Although she is abused, held hostage and almost a victim of rape, she eventually marries Mr. B. out of love, having maintained her virtue and impressed
Mr. B. with her resolve. As Armstrong asserts, Pamela's displays of resistance
"miraculously convert the libertine, who metamorphoses on the spot from vil-
lain to hero and agrees to marry on her terms" (374). Like Mr. B., Gilroy's
Stedman insists that his intentions are legitimate: "'How can I persuade you
to believe in my sincerity? You do not have to be my slave—simply my lover,
my wife!'"[29] Similarly, in the *Narrative*, the historical Stedman stresses that he
had intended to make Joanna his legal Christian wife and bring her back to
Europe with him. As Sharpe explains, the fictional Stedman "follows his historical counterpart in representing himself as different from other European
men in the high regard he has for Joanna, declaring his intentions to marry her,
and resenting it when his friends treat her as a slave" (98). [30]

When the Fauconberg estate is sold, so too is Joanna. According to
Richards, this event "throws the lovers into a flurry of Richardsonian propor-
tions and accomplishes the transformation of Joanna into the textual form of
eighteenth-century sentimentalism" (102). In the *Narrative*, Stedman writes:
"Good God!—I flew to the spot in search of poor Joanna: I found her bathed
in tears.—She gave me such a look—ah! Such a look!—From that moment I
determined to be her protector against every insult, and persevered, as shall be

seen in my sequel; yet assuredly my feelings will be forgiven me—by those few only excepted—who delight in the *prudent* conduct of Mr. *Incle* [*sic*] to the hapless and much-injured *Yarico* at Barbadoes" (59). This statement not only serves as evidence that Stedman relied heavily on the sentimental mode for his portrayal of his relationship with Joanna in the *Narrative* but also that he intended his *Narrative* to be an engagement with, and reversal of, the story of *Inkle and Yarico*. In fact, Sollers goes so far as to argue that Stedman's narrative can be said to "*subvert* the *Spectator*'s: Instead of acting as a mercantile traitor to his beloved, the hero and narrator casts himself as human being who—against the prejudices of his peers—wants nothing more than to see his beloved (and, later, their son) free and together with him" (197). Indeed, whereas Inkle sells the pregnant Yarico into slavery to make back the money he lost while spending time with her, Stedman "marries" Yarico and, prior to leaving Surinam, makes arrangements for their son's manumission and his economic security.

However, Stedman's version of an interracial love affair is not as different from Steele's as he would like to think. As Mary Louise Pratt argued in 1992, Stedman may be the opposite of Inkle because he loves Joanna and does not wish to abandon her, and Joanna may be the opposite of Yarico because she refuses to follow her lover to Europe, but the "bottom line is the same in both stories." Joanna and Yarico both "end up husbandless and enslaved in the colonies, while Inkle and Stedman end up back in England." In both stories, the "vision of cultural harmony through romance is not fulfilled," and the "allegory of an integrated postslavery society never completes itself" (100). Moreover, while the sentimental mode enables both Steele and Stedman to portray the "other" as appealing and deserving of a European readership's sympathies, it also contributes to keeping the "other" at a distance. According to Lynn Festa, as much as "sentimental tropes furnish tools for imagining collective relations during this period" by creating the *semblance* of likeness," they also uphold forms of national, cultural, and economic difference." It is here, then, that "sentimentality is useful to the nation. The sentimental allows us to see things *as if* they were like, *as if* they belonged to the same body" (51). The point is that, while sentimentality incites feelings for the plight of other people, such as Yarico in Steele's *Spectator No. 11*, Joanna in Stedman's *Narrative* and African slaves in abolitionist poetry, these sentimental objects never become subjects and, subsequently, are never fully absorbed into the imagined community or nation. In short, they are always the "other." The sentimental mode thus "allows for the provisional acknowledgement of the humanity of others while upholding differences between communities" (55).

Gilroy illustrates this point by lifting Stedman's description of his final moments with Joanna, which is dripping with sentimentality, directly from the

Journal: "Joanna now shut her beauteous eyes. Her lips turned the color of death. She bowed her head and motionless sank into her chair" (147). In the manuscript for his *Narrative*, Stedman modifies this description only slightly: "Here the beauteous Joanna, now but nineteen years of age, shut her tear-bedewed eyes; the color of her lips became the color of death, she bowed her head and motionless sank into her chair" (313). No matter how effective the sentimental mode was for Stedman in making his love affair with a mulatto slave acceptable to an English readership, it cannot enable Stedman or Joanna to overcome the realities of life in the late eighteenth-century British empire; Stedman and Joanna can never be together as equals. As Pratt observes, the "lovers are separated, the European is reabsorbed by Europe," and almost too conveniently, the "non-European dies an early death" (97).[31] At the same time, by drawing on the sentimental mode for her engagement with Stedman's *Journal* and *Narrative*, Gilroy is able to convey her belief that, although Stedman and Joanna could not be together in the late eighteenth-century, a transracial love such as theirs can transcend racial and political boundaries. It lives on in Stedman's memories of her, and in their son, Johnny, who Gilroy's Stedman describes as the "child of that time when my heart and soul were stirred by love's most tender sentiments" (171). Thus whereas Sharpe describes Gilroy's novel as a "utopian vision of what could have been rather than a literary intervention into what was" (104), it is also the case that *Stedman and Joanna* is a utopian vision of what could be in the twentieth and twenty-first centuries, rather than what is.

***

Throughout the nineteenth century, the love story between Stedman and Joanna generated what Pratt refers to as a "romantic literary progeny" that includes a German play by Franz Krattle titled *Die Sklavin in Surinam* (1804), a story titled "Joanna or the Female Slave" published in London (1824), Eugène Sue's novel *Adventures d'Hercule Hardi* published in Paris (1840), and the Dutch novels *Een levensteeken op een dodenveld* by Herman J. de Ridder (1857), and *Boni* by Johan Edwin Hokstam (1893). For Gilroy, who published *Stedman and Joanna* in 1991, this transracial love story continues to be pertinent today because—at least in her revision—it represents hope for the future of our world, which has been devastated by racism and violence. Gilroy's Stedman's attitudes toward race relations are not only wholly transformed by his experiences in the New World and encounter with African slaves but, after returning to Europe, he vows to work toward creating a "new environment in which [his son] would learn new functions and view new horizons. For him life would never be a series of moments as uncertain and frightening as nightmares from hell" (156). Gilroy even imagines that Stedman reprimands his Dutch wife for her "barbarity," the "harshness of her blood," and her "inbred brutality" when she fails to treat his son with Joanna, Johnny, with kindness (174).

Gilroy's novel is also hopeful in that, as with the other retrospections in this project, it challenges the notion of a distinctly "western" or English literary history. More specifically, Gilroy's engagement with Stedman's *Journal* and *Narrative* demonstrates not only that Stedman took great strides to situate his writings within various literary traditions, but that these antecedents came into being *as a consequence of* encounters with non-Europeans in the New World. For example, Stedman employs sentimental rhetoric to incite his readers' sympathy for his experiences in the New World that stretches back to Mary Rowlandson's 1640 captivity narrative. For his depiction of Joanna, Stedman utilizes the noble-savage imagery introduced by Behn in *Oroonoko* in 1688 as a means to represent West African slaves and plantation culture in the New World, and later used in slave narratives and abolitionist poetry. By engaging with and ostensibly reversing the story of *Inkle and Yarico*, Stedman engages in a dialogue with Steele's *Spectator No. 11* (1711) and reminds his readers that this interracial love story—which periodical essayists and dramatists adopted for the purpose of transforming the manners and morals of the British reading public—originated in the New World. By utilizing realist narrative tactics and portraying himself as a Crusoe-esque figure, Stedman aligns his writings with such imperialist travelogues as Defoe's *Robinson Crusoe*. By retrospectively envisioning himself as a picaro, Stedman alludes to the fact that Smollett and Fielding's picaresque romances of the road can be considered descendents of the imperialist travelogue. Similarly, by portraying Joanna as comparable to Richardson's virtuous heroine, Stedman alludes to the relationship between captivity narratives and sentimental domestic fiction. According to Armstrong, English readers consumed captivity narratives "almost as avidly as they did sentimental fiction, and they consequently knew exactly what kind of story would ensue once they recognized it as the testimony of a captive woman" (373).

Gilroy's engagement with Stedman's autobiographical manuscripts exposes that Stedman was not simply influenced by these various literary antecedents; he self-consciously positioned his text at the pinnacle of a series of cultural developments. While many of these developments—captivity narrative, periodical essay, realist novel, romance, picaresque, sentimental domestic fiction—came to serve nationalist and/or empire-building agendas throughout the eighteenth century, their origins can be located in the New World. Perhaps more than any other engagement with an eighteenth-century cultural artifact, Gilroy's engagement with Stedman's *Journal* and *Narrative* brings to the forefront that literary history can be implicated in the early processes of globalization.

Epilogue
Global Retrospections

Early studies of postcolonization writings sought to analyze the methods with which writers from once-colonized regions of the globe respond to, resist, and disrupt imperial ideologies and racial hierarchies by "writing back" to western culture, and how these writings reflect efforts to recover and promote local cultures and histories. Today, scholars acknowledge the impossibility of locating and representing *authentic* identities and cultures. As Kwame Anthony Appiah notes in "Language, Race and the Legacies," if there is a "lesson in the broad shape of the circulation of cultures, it is surely that we are all already contaminated by each other" (405). Appiah's reference to the "circulation of cultures" serves as a reminder that the issues at stake in analyses of postcolonization writings are far more complex than paradigms pitting "the West's" assertion of dominance against local celebrations of allegedly pure cultures. In addition, by claiming, "we are all already contaminated with each other," Appiah acknowledges that the circulation, or globalization, of culture has a long history.

While I have addressed in this study how transatlantic retrospections engage with a sampling of the realist cultural forms that emerged during increases in global trade and the trafficking of slaves, more work needs to be done on how transatlantic retrospections engage with non-fiction that impersonates fiction. For example, Caryl Phillips, who was born on St. Kitts, self-consciously engages with such eighteenth-century writings as Equiano's *Interesting Narrative,* and such nineteenth-century writings as the travel diaries of Lady Nugent and Mrs. Carmichael, in his historical novel *Cambridge* (1991).[1] In doing so, he draws attention to how these texts have functioned historically as both historical documents and self-conscious literary productions serving nationalist and empire-building agendas. As with Dabydeen in *A Harlot's Progress*, Phillips alludes to the critical debates regarding the historical facts of Equiano's slave narrative, which propose that this abolitionist text was at once popular and effective *because* Equiano may have suppressed historical facts and utilized his creative agency by adapting or imitating forms, conventions, and imagery already popularized in England. As Aravamudan has already shown, Equiano situates himself within a long tradition of historical narratives and literary genres serving the agendas of imperialism, colonialism and British nationalism. While Equiano writes "from Friday's subject position," he also "implicitly recognizes the preceding literary production rationalizing the nation" (261, 235).[2] Phillips's engagement with the *Interesting Narrative* enables contemporary readers to further appreciate Equiano's acute awareness of how such first-person fictional narratives as *Robinson Crusoe* served to mediate global events and shape the global vision of British readers, and of his own participation in this tradition.

While revisiting allegedly non-fictional and so-called realist works through transatlantic retrospections enables readers to see how literary texts operate as responses to global encounters and contribute to the construction of both Britishness and "otherness," Soyinka's retrospections of the Scriblerians' satiric works invite reinterpretations of an entirely different side of eighteenth-century English culture within a global context. According to Clement Hawes, Soyinka's engagements with the Scriblerians facilitate appreciation for "the true significance of the challenge" posed by Swift and Gay to the British national identity that emerged in conjunction with imperial expansion (139). Rather than indulge in "mere artistic eclecticism," Soyinka identifies with the Scriblerians' use of satire as a vehicle to critique global exploitation and conquest, the oppression of non-European peoples both in and outside of England, the vices of contemporary London society, and the corruption of Robert Walpole's government. While I discuss in Chapter Three how Soyinka engages with *Gulliver's Travels*, his "Gulliver" is also an implicit engagement with the satiric opera *Polly*, in which Gay condemns the British planter, the British soldier, the slave trade, the transportation of British criminals, the imperial appropriation of lands and commodities, and the enslavement of peoples on the borders of the British empire. According to Hawes, whereas Soyinka portrays the neocolonial government as "glorified piracy," Gay dramatizes colonialism and slavery as "glorified piracy" (146).

Moreover, just as the Federal Military Government of Nigeria removed the political activist Soyinka from circulation, Gay encountered government censorship when *Polly* was banned in 1728. Thus Soyinka's engagement with the Scriblerians' satires and articulation of socio-political critique from behind the mask of Gulliver reminds us that his cultural forbears similarly faced an oppressive totalitarian regime that ruled by fear, which is likely the reason they often disseminated their "vision" anonymously or from behind the shield of such fictional personas as Martinus Scriblerus, Isaac Bickerstaff and Mr. Spectator. While I propose in Chapter One that the form of the early eighteenth-century periodical essay was prompted by global activities, more work needs to be done on the utilization of fictional personas within a global context.

Along these same lines, Soyinka's *Opera Wonyosi* (first performed in 1977), invites further consideration of how Gay's *The Beggar's Opera* (1728) was shaped by and participates in the processes of globalization. When Soyinka adapted and transformed *The Beggar's Opera*, in which Gay lashes out at Walpole's corrupt administration and British colonial forces, he added a new dimension to his repertoire of satirical attacks on the ruling military government by incorporating direct references to actual Nigerian people and situations. Soyinka thereby points to how the form of these eighteenth-century satires, like fictional personas, enabled writers to simultaneously mask and reveal global realities to the British public.

By reading and teaching transatlantic retrospections alongside each other as well as those produced by their western cultural forbears, the boundaries of national literatures, literary periods, and generic forms become increasingly blurred, and linear trajectories of literary histories and exclusive models of cultural forms become outmoded. Thus transatlantic retrospections serve as additional evidence for Michael Valdez Moses's claim in *The Novel and the Globalization of Culture* that the "very existence of a single and hegemonic Eurocentric conception of literature" can be "rendered obsolete, insofar as Western literature itself becomes part of a larger body of work that is truly global, hybrid and cosmopolitan" (xiii). The postcolonization writings through which I revisit eighteenth-century cultural artifacts expose that the local, regional, and global are all implicated in eighteenth-century British culture. By utilizing transatlantic retrospections as tools for critical analysis, readers can better grasp the complex ways genres cut across historical periods and political and cultural systems, and also the historical role cultural forms have played in global systems of exchange.

Thus rather than, or perhaps in addition to, "transatlantic" or "postcolonial" retrospections, these contemporary African and Caribbean writings are "global" retrospections. As opposed to invoking contradiction, the term "global" indicates that these writings propose a more comprehensive historical and material approach to the eighteenth-century British texts they look back on and transform. While theories of globalization do not generally acknowledge the concerns of postcolonialism, transatlantic and postcolonial studies are inherently concerned with the implications of globalization. Transatlantic retrospections acknowledge that the histories of globalization and postcolonialism are interconnected by (re)appropriating the cultural forms that were being adapted and transformed in England during an era of burgeoning global mercantilism, colonialism, migration, forced transportation, increased transnational exchange and intercultural contact; in other words, during the dawn of globalization.

Notes

NOTES TO THE INTRODUCTION

1. For many years it was virtually impossible to find a critical study with "post-colonial" anywhere in the title or introduction that did not include a lengthy explanation of how and why the author was using the term. While I have no intention of rehashing the numerous and varied critiques of the term, I follow Neloufer de Mel's caution that the term "postcolonial" (and any variations) be "used advisedly, in awareness that despite the end of direct political imperialism, new forms of economic, military, and cultural colonialism continue to marginalize the former colonies, forcing them to be ever dependent on the econo-political centers of the world. The postness of coloniality continues therefore to be a site of contention" (142). Srinivas Aravamudan similarly warns that to "consider we are beyond colonialism in any way is to misrecognize—dangerously—the world's current realities" (16). In this project, I use the term "postcolonial" to refer to academic scholars and ideas, and thus to signify a theoretical project, and I use the term "postcolonization" to refer to post-independence writers and writings.

2. In *The Black Atlantic: Modernity and Double Consciousness*, Beryl Gilroy's son Paul Gilroy focuses on culture and identity, rather than on commerce or politics, and his study can be understood as an alternative to the "white Atlantic" model. According to Paul Gilroy, "the idea of the black Atlantic can be used to show that there are other claims to it which can be based on the structure of the African diaspora into the western hemisphere." More specifically, the "fractal patterns of cultural and political exchange and transformation that we try and specify through manifestly inadequate theoretical terms like creolisation and syncreticism indicate how both ethnicities and political cultures have been made anew in ways that are significant not simply for the people of the Caribbean but for Europe, for Africa, especially Liberia and Sierra Leone, and of course, for Black America" (15).

3. Joseph Roach coined the term "circum-Atlantic" for his study of performance as a medium of cultural exchange, *Cities of the Dead: Circum-Atlantic*

Performance (1996), in which he argues that "the circum-Atlantic world as it emerged from the revolutionized economies of the late seventeenth century . . . resembled a vortex in which commodities and cultural practices changed hands many times." Accordingly, the concept of a *circum*-Atlantic world (as opposed to a transatlantic one) insists on the "centrality of the diasporic and genocidal histories of Africa and the Americas, North and South, in the creation of the culture of modernity" (4–5). However, according to Armitage, while *circum*-Atlantic history is "*trans*national," it is "not *inter*national" (18). *Cis*-Atlantic history is the "history of any particular place—a nation, a state, a region, even a specific institution—relation to the wider Atlantic world. While *cis*-Atlantic studies are comparable to *circum*-Atlantic studies, the approach differs in the sense that the focus is "not on the ocean itself but rather on the way specific regions were defined in their relation to that ocean" (Armitage 22).

4. The three concepts that Armitage outlines are not exclusive but, rather, reinforce each other. "Taken together, they offer the possibility of a three-dimensional history of the Atlantic world. A *circum*-Atlantic history would draw upon the fruits of various *cis*-Atlantic histories and generate comparisons between them. *Trans*-Atlantic history can link those *cis*-Atlantic histories because of the existence of a *circum*-Atlantic system. *Cis*-Atlantic history in turn feeds *trans*-Atlantic comparisons" (Armitage 20).

5. In *Discours sur le colonialisme* (1950; *Discourse on Colonialism*, 1972) Césaire argues that the circulation of colonial ideology, which is an ideology of racial and cultural hierarchy, is as essential to colonial rule as a police force and forced labor. In *Peau Noire, Masques Blancs* (1952; *Black Skin, White Masks*, 1967), Césaire's student Franz Fanon attempts to offer a "psychological and philosophical explanation of the *state of being* a Negro" (13). Like Césaire, he deplores the implications of French psychologist Dominique O. Mannoni's *Psychologie de la colonization* (1950; *Prospero and Caliban: The Psychology of Colonization*, 1964). In his investigation of colonial relations in Madagascar, Mannoni had proposed that Europeans mask their own feelings of inferiority (the Prospero complex) by asserting dominance over the natives, who in turn are wholly dependent (the Caliban complex) upon the colonizer. A glaring flaw in Mannoni's theory is his insistence that the achievements of the colonized are indebted to, and even dependent upon, Prospero's gift of language. For Fanon and Césaire, Caliban should be specifically associated with the oppressed. By imposing European language and culture upon him, Prospero obliterated Caliban's cultural identity, just as European colonization destroyed Caribbean, American and African identities. Tunisian Jew Albert Memmi's declaration in *Portrait du Colonisé* (1957; *The Colonizer and the Colonized*, 1967) that "the most serious blow suffered by the colonized is being removed from history" (91) is comparable to Fanon's claim in his second book, *Les damnés de la terre* (1961; *The Wretched*

of the Earth, 1963), that colonialism is a "systematic negation of the other person" (200).

6. In *Orientalism* (1978) Edward Said argued that by viewing orientalism "as a discourse" it is possible to "understand the enormously systematic discipline by which European culture was able to manage—even produce—the Orient politically, sociologically, militarily, ideologically, scientifically, and imaginatively during the post-Enlightenment period." Orientalism is a "Western style for dominating, restructuring, and having authority over the Orient"(3). In *Culture and Imperialism* (1993), Said further develops his analysis of the "general worldwide pattern of imperial culture" that develops both to justify and reinforce the establishment and exploitation of the empire, and the counterbalance to this, which is "the historical experience of resistance against the empire"(xii). Abdul R. JanMohamed, who was profoundly influenced by Fanon, similarly argues in *Manichean Aesthetics: The Politics of Literature in Colonial Africa* (1983), that colonialist fiction is "generated predominantly by the ideological machinery of the Manichean allegory" and that colonialist fiction "obsessively" portrays the "supposed inferiority and barbarity of the racial Other, thereby insisting on the profound moral difference between self and Other." JanMohamed sees the Third World's "literary dialogue" with western cultures as consisting of two "broad characteristics: its attempt to negate the prior European negation of colonized cultures and its adoption and creative modification of Western languages and artistic forms in conjunction with indigenous languages and forms" (22–23).

7. Ashcroft, Griffiths and Tiffin borrow their title from Salman Rushdie, who coined the phrase for his article in *The Times* of London (3 July 1980), "The Empire Writes Back to the Centre," in which he attacks "collaborators" among the colonized who migrated to the West. Thus they too ironically allude to the American film in which the Empire attempts to crush the rebellion that would end the Empire's domination of the universe.

8. Nor was Englishness a fixed identity position "in relation to its own territory either." In fact, "it was only by dint of excluding or absorbing all the differences that constituted Englishness, the multitude of different regions, peoples, classes, genders that composed the people gathered together in the Act of Union, that Englishness could stand for everybody in the British isles. It always had to absorb all the differences of class, of region, of gender, in order to present itself as a homogenous entity" (22).

9. For Srinivas Aravamudan, even the recognition of cultural hybridity is not enough to thoroughly grasp what is *in* each individual eighteenth-century text and work of art. In *Tropicopolitans*, Aravamudan argues that the "messy legacies of empire do not always afford such clear-cut choices" as "hybridity and authenticity, or collaboration and opposition." Aravamudan proposes that in analyses of cultural and historical texts it is the "act of reading" that

"makes available the differing mechanisms of agency that traverse texts, contexts and writers themselves" (4). For example, while Swift is "notoriously misogynistic and racially prejudiced" in his writings, he is nonetheless an early anticolonial voice. Another significant example is the manumitted slave Olaudah Equiano, who "went along with various colonialist projects for the resettlement of the black poor as a productive labor force." Aravamudan's fundamental point is that these and other historical figures cannot be "readily characterized as colonialist villains or anticolonial heroes" (14). Transatlantic retrospections both reflect and invite the kind of *reading* practices to which Aravamudan refers because the postcolonization writers who produce transatlantic retrospections are themselves readers, and they are as engaged in the act of reading the works of their cultural forbears as they are in revising them. By revisiting eighteenth-century cultural artifacts through the lens of transatlantic retrospections, which are at once identifications *and* assertions of difference, at once investigations of the past *and* examples of using the past to represent the present, readers can likewise detect the kinds of ambiguities and contradictions that Aravamudan points out.

10. Jay borrows this phrase from Susan Stanford Friedman, who uses "multidirectional flows" in reference to "power" in *Mappings: Feminism and the Cultural Geographies of Encounters* (Princeton: Princeton University Press, 1998).

11. Quoted in: Michael McKeon, *The Origins of the English Novel: 1600–1740* (Baltimore: The Johns Hopkins University Press, 1887), 121.

12. Linda Colley, *Captives: the story of Britain's pursuit of empire and how its soldiers and civilians were held captive by the dream of global supremacy, 1600–1850* (New York: Pantheon, 2002).

13. As Winston James explains in "The Black Experience in Twentieth-Century Britain," the lives of black Britons have been "persistently blighted by racial prejudice and discrimination" and, while some progress has been made, it has "come slowly, unevenly, and at a heavy price" (348).

14. For Walcott, the West Indian occupies a position comparable to that of Crusoe in the fictional world created by Defoe. In "The Figure of Crusoe," he explains that while the homes of West Indians are elsewhere (England, Africa, India) their words, "when written, are as fresh, as truly textured, as when Crusoe set them down in the first West Indian novel." Walcott is also extremely critical of the "Marxist-evolved method" of analyzing figures from literature as if "they were guilty." Although he considers some to be "brilliant re-creations," he views others as far too reductive for simply representing Prospero as the "white imperialist" and Caliban as the "ugly savage" (34–36).

NOTES TO CHAPTER ONE

1. According to Catherine E. Moore, in *The Spectator* version of Inkle and Yarico gender conflict overshadows racial conflict. The faithlessness of

women is the issue under debate, not the faithlessness of Europeans toward other races (27).

2. In his influential *The Rise of the Novel* (1957), Ian Watt argues that early eighteenth-century novelists broke from tradition by "naming their characters in such a way as to suggest that they were to be regarded as particular individuals in the contemporary social environment" (19). Moreover, the technical characteristics that comprise Watt's notion of "formal realism" contribute to "furthering an aim which the novelist shares with the philosopher—the production of what purports to be an authentic account of the actual experiences of individuals" (27).

3. According to Azim, the "discourse of the novel is based on the notion of a sovereign subject." The novel is an "imperialist project" because the "central subject who weaves the narrative" deliberately ignores other subject-positions and/or invokes "the Other" only to forcefully eradicate or obliterate "the Other" (37). Gilroy's Inkle, accordingly, can only understand his identity in relation to, or within a confrontation with Yarico, her tribe, and (later) his African slaves, all of whom threaten his sense of sovereignty as a white British male and must therefore be dismissed or somehow eliminated in the end.

4. Whereas Watt argued in 1957 for an analogy between the rise of the novel and the rise of the middle class, Michael McKeon proposes in *The Origins of the English Novel: 1640–1740* (1987) that the analogy "lies not outside the novel, between literary and social formations, but within in it . . . the emerging novel internalizes the emergence of the middle class and the concerns that it exists to mediate." For McKeon the genre of the novel "can be understood comprehensively as an early modern cultural instrument designed to confront, on the level of narrative form and content, both intellectual and social crises simultaneously" (22). In both cases, however, it is assumed that that the novel is a distinctly western, or English, invention. For critical studies of English literary history that also adhere to the notion that eighteenth-century print culture was for the most part dependent on social conditions *within* England, see, for example: Benedict Anderson, *Imagined Communities* (London: Verso, 1982); Terry Eagleton, *The Function of Criticism: From the Spectator to Post-Structuralism* (London: Verso, 1984); John Brewer, *The Pleasures of the Imagination: English Culture in the Eighteenth Century* (Chicago: U of Chicago P, 1989). Jürgen Habermas, *The Structural Transformation of the Public Sphere* (Cambridge, Mass." MIT P, repr. 1991).

5. In "The Pamphleteers Protestant Champion: Viewing Cromwell Through the Media of his Day," Kevin A. Creed writes: "The Irish rebellion which broke out in October 1641 initially was directed against Protestant English settlers and landholders, large numbers of whom were murdered and abused. The reporting in England of the massacres brought the normal disdain for

the 'uncivilized' Irish to a fever pitch of hatred. Streams of pamphlets, some highly fictionalized, concerning the revolt poured forth and it is obvious many people accepted them as truth" (4).

6. Jeffrey N. Cox points out that Mrs. Weddell, who wrote her *Inkle and Yarico* in 1742, is likely the first person to dramatize the popular story of Inkle and Yarico, and also the first to link the story "firmly to the issue of the African slave trade" by making Inkle a slave trader and Yarico an African, or 'negro virgin'" (2). George Colman the Younger's *Inkle and Yarico; an Opera, in Three Acts* was certainly topical when it appeared in 1787, although any antislavery sentiment is compromised by the fact that the real atrocities of the slave trade are ignored in favor of sentimentalizing the story, as in Steele's essay.

7. Hill Collins writes: "Rape and other acts of overt violence that Black women have experienced, such as physical assault during slavery, domestic abuse, incest and sexual extortion, accompany Black women's subordination in a system of race, class and gender oppression. These violent acts are the visible dimensions of a more generalized, routinized system of oppression. Violence against Black women tends to be legitimized and therefore condoned while the same acts visited on other groups remain non-legitimated and non-excusable" (177).

8. According to Felsenstein, it is the "ineptitude of the colonizing English in differentiating one racial group from another, the simultaneous tendency, conscious or otherwise, to barbarize the native," that are the "targets" of George Colman the Younger's three-act comic opera, *Inkle and Yarico*, first performed at the Theatre Royal in the Haymarket, London, August 4, 1787. One of the Englishmen in Colman's lighthearted satire, Medium, fears being "eat[en] up by the black devils" (205) or being cut up and "ate raw by an inky commoner" (178).

9. Gilroy is perhaps playing on Swift's "yahoos" here.

10. Joseph Addison and Richard Steele, et al. *The British Classics*. Vol. 1: 29–33.

11. Armstrong points specifically to Mary Rowlandson's well-known account of her abduction and captivity in Indian Territory, first published in 1682 and in its fifth edition in England by 1720.

12. Defoe expressed from the outset his dislike for writing the "Advice" column, but apparently he considered it necessary. In the Preface to Volume I he writes that to offset the "Difficulty" that the "World would never Read" a "thing very Historical" and "very Long," he needed to include "some form of Entertainment, or Amusement at the end of every Paper upon the immediate Subject, then on the Tongues of the Town."

13. Joseph Addison and Richard Steele, et. al. *The British Classics*. Vol. 5: iii-vi.

14. In *The Tatler No. 1*, Bickerstaff announces: "I am at a very great Charge for proper Materials for this World, as well as that before I resolv'd upon it, I had settled a Correspondence in all parts of the Known and Knowing World. And forasmuch as this Globe is not trodden upon by mere Drudges

of Business only, but that Men of Spirit and Genius are justly to be esteem'd as considerable Agents in it, we shall not upon a Dearth of News present you with Foreign Edicts or dull proclamations, but shall divide our Relations of the Passages which occur in Action or Discourse throughout this Town, as well as elsewhere, under such Dates and Places as may prepare you for the Matter you are to expect." *The British Classics*, Vol. 1:1–11.

15. Joseph Addison and Richard Steele. *The British Classics*. Vol. 1:48–52.

16. Arietta is referring to the following anecdote: Yarico "chanc'd be with child, by a Christian servant, and lodged in the *Indian*-house, amongst other women of her own country . . . This *Indian* dwelling near the sea-coast, upon the Main, an *English* ship put in to a bay, and sent some of her men ashore, to try what victuals or water they could find, for in some distress they were: But the *Indians* perceiving them to be up so far into the country, as they were sure they could not make safe retreat, intercepted them in their return and fell upon them, chasing them into a wood, and being dispersed there, some were taken, and some kill'd: but a young man amongst them straggling from the rest, was met by this *Indian* maid, who upon the first sight fell in love with him, and hid him close from her countrymen (the *Indians*) in a cave, and there fed him, till they could go safely down to the shore, where the ship lay at anchor, expecting the return of their friends. But at last, seeing them upon the shore, sent the long-boat for them, took them aboard, and brought them away. But the youth, when he came ashore in the Barbadoes, forgot the kindness of the poor maid, who had ventured her life for his safety, and sold her for a slave who was as free born as he: And so poor *Yarico* for her love, lost her liberty." See Ligon, *A True and Exact History of the Island of Barbadoes*, second edition (1673), 43–59, 65; reprinted in Felsenstein.

17. According to Brown, Ligon's fascination with these (free) women because of their physical beauty is in stark contrast to his subsequent portraits of enslaved women working in the cane fields in Barbados, whom he apparently does not find attractive. Ligon's depictions of African women subsequently beg the question, was slavery the result of racial prejudice, or did racial prejudice arise after slavery was chosen as a labor system? See Brown, "Beyond the Great Debates: Gender and Race in Early America." *Reviews in American History* 26.1 (1988), 96–123.

18. Reprinted in Felsenstein, 43–59, 65.

19. According to Felsenstein, Steele's "interest in Barbados was certainly more than academic, for in 1706, on the death of his first wife, he had inherited the freehold of a considerable plantation there." Although the property had been sold by the time Steele produced *The Spectator*, "it is most likely that his attention would have been drawn to Richard Ligon as a result of his inheritance" (13).

20. According to Hulme, this is "quite an achievement for somebody earlier described as 'Naked American.' As a person of distinction Yarico can, like

the princely Oroonoko and the noble Pocahontas, evoke aristocratic sympathy" (Colonial Encounters 238).

21. In *Leaves in the Wind* Gilroy contends that, "by setting and resetting the
    angle of vision," European "explorers, missionaries, travelers, and truth-
    gatherers . . . created attitudes and evidence that distorted reality and
    invented stereotypes" (79).

22. According to Azim, the eighteenth century "constructed the concept of the
    sovereignty of the human individual in opposition to other subject-posi-
    tions, which it had either dominated or annihilated in the process" (36).

23. Although the English left the Garifuna with food supplies, utensils, fishing
    cords and seeds for planting, it was difficult to prepare the terrain before the
    rainy season. The Garifuna asked the Spanish to take them to the Hondu-
    ran coast, which the Spanish agreed to because this gave them control of the
    Bay Islands and an additional labor force. The French captured St. Vincent
    from the English in 1779.

24. The subtitle of Gilroy's novel is "Being the narrative of Thomas Inkle con-
    cerning his shipwreck and long sojourn among the Caribs and his marriage
    to Yarico, a Carib woman." By referring to Inkle's captivity in the New
    World as a "sojourn," Gilroy reiterates that, in her version of Inkle and
    Yarico, Inkle is "the Other." In this sense, then, her novel exemplifies post-
    colonial theories regarding "writing back" to the empire.

25. Gilroy also became the first black headmistress in Britain, at Beckford pri-
    mary school. The 1991 reprinting of her autobiographical *Black Teacher*
    (1976) testifies to the continuing relevance of her work on the British school
    system.

NOTES TO CHAPTER TWO

1. Crusoe's self-interestedness can also be understood to reflect the commercial ideals promoted by Defoe, who as a merchant considered colonialism
   and slavery essential for British prosperity.

2. Catherine E. Moore, "Robinson and Xury and Inkle and Yarico," *Modern
   Language Notes* 19.1 (1981): 24–29.

3. John Thieme, *Derek Walcott*. (Manchester: Manchester UP, 1999), 7.

4. Walcott's plays examining the postcolonial condition, such as *Dream on
   Monkey Mountain*, owe much to folk and Creole tradition and history.
   They combine storytelling, singing, dancing, and the rhythms of calypso
   with rich metaphorical language, both in English and West Indian dialect. His most well known play is *Dream on Monkey Mountain*, which was
   originally commissioned by the Royal Shakespeare Company in the late
   1960s.

5. See: "The Passions of Derek Walcott," *Boston Globe*, Sunday April 25,
   1993. Arts and Film section, B25. The phrase "mulatto of styles" is from

his essay "What the Twilight Says" (1972). Walcott's influences are as diverse as Homer, Wordsworth, Joyce, T.S. Eliot, Gauguin, Cezanne, Baudelaire, Césaire and Jean Rhys, and his poetry and prose recognize the combination of European and African heritages that have influenced the formation of cultural identities in the Caribbean.

6. Walcott's attitudes toward "history" are comparable to those of Edouard Glissant, born on Martinique, who believes the search for origins is based on an illusion, as the past can never be recovered. In *Caribbean Discourses* Glissant writes: "History (with a capital *H*) ends where histories of those people once reputed to be without history come together. History is a highly functional fantasy of the West, originating at precisely that time when it alone 'made' the history of the world" (64). Glissant rejects History (with a capital H) as a totalizing project in Western (colonial, imperial) discourse, which constructs a universal narrative that sets Europe at the center of humanity and thrusts the people without writing to the margins, and he advocates putting emphasis on the "lived reality" of the Caribbean world. Wilson Harris, born in Guyana, similarly contends that history as a linear continuum has no place in his search for "the life of the imagination" ("Continuity and Discontinuity," *Selected Essays* 177). Harris has a cyclic sense of time that sets no barriers between people and epochs in the fluid and ongoing history of the Caribbean world" ("Tradition and the West Indian Novel," *Selected Essays* 141).

7. Samad presented this paper at the PostColonialismS/PoliticalCorrectnesS conference in Casablanca (12–14 April 2000).

8. For a thorough discussion of the history of literary developments in the West Indies, see: Laurence A. Breiner, *An Introduction to West Indian Poetry* (Cambridge: Cambridge University Press, 1998).

9. Walcott reiterates this point in his Nobel Prize lecture of 1992: " . . . this process of renaming, of finding new metaphors, is the same process that the poet faces every morning of his working day, making his own tools like Crusoe, assembling nouns from necessity" (262).

10. See Bruce King, *Derek Walcott: A Caribbean Life* (Oxford: Oxford UP, 2000).

11. Walcott compares the figure of Crusoe to "Christofer," which means "Christ-bearer," who was a third-century Christian martyr. Christofer was a young man of extraordinary strength, who accepted the task of carrying people across a raging stream. One day he was carrying a child who continually grew heavier, so that it seemed to him as if he had the whole world on his shoulders. When Christofer asked, the child claimed to be the Creator and Redeemer of the world. To prove his statement, he ordered Christofer to put his staff in the ground. The next morning it had grown into a palm-tree bearing fruit. Apparently, this miracle converted many to Christianity.

12. See, for example: Lloyd King, "Derek Walcott: The Literary Humanist in the Caribbean" *Caribbean Quarterly* 16.4 (1970).

13. Interestingly, by this time Crusoe has used up his ink, and thus he is no longer writing his journal, or what for Walcott is the first West Indian novel.

14. King's story of how Walcott came to produce *Pantomime* is drawn from interviews with Brenda Hughes (Port of Spain, 1990) and Author Jacobs (St. Lucia, 1990).

15. *In Rime of the Ancient Mariner*, the mariner tells the wedding-guest: "Alone, alone, all all alone, / Alone on a wide wide sea" (ll. 232–233). Harry's loneliness is also comparable to that of Defoe's Crusoe.

16. English pantomimes are subsequently comparable to Addison and Steele's periodical essays, which likewise held up mirrors to the readers. The first pantomime performed in London as an afterpiece is generally thought to be *The Loves of Mars and Venus* (1717), which was composed by dancing-master and performer John Weaver, a close friend of Addison and Steele's. That same year John Rich, son of Christopher Rich, former patentee of Drury Lane Theatre, advertised his "Italian Mimic Scenes," or Pantomimes, in the "Daily Courant," of December 20. Rich's productions consisted of two parts, one serious, the other comic. Between the acts, he interwove a comic fable, consisting chiefly of the courtship of Harlequin and Columbine.

17. All scene descriptions are from *A Short Account*, unless otherwise noted.

18. The editor of *Sheridania: or Anecdotes of the Life of Richard Brinsley Sheridan; His Table-Talk, and Bon Mots* (London: Henry Colburn, 1826), reports: "An instance of [Sheridan's] readiness and rapidity when he chose to exert himself" occurred while his pantomime of Robinson Crusoe was under production at the Drury Lane theatre, of which he was the proprietor. "He happened to call at the Theatre one day, while the pantomime was in rehearsal, and found them in the greatest confusion, not knowing what to introduce to give time for the setting of a scene. It was suggested that a song would afford sufficient opportunity for the carpenters for their preparation; accordingly he sat down at the prompter's table, on the stage, and wrote on the back of a play-bill the beautiful ballad of The Midnight Watch, which was set to music by his father-in law, Mr. Linley, in a style which has established its reputation as one of the most beautiful specimens of pure English melody" (83).

19. *The Universal Magazine* vol. 68 (February 1781): 60–61.

20. *The Morning Herald* (30 January 1781).

21. The two sections of O'Brien's book are separated by this unnumbered chapter, entitled "Entr'acte: 'Why is Harlequin's Face Black?'" O'Brien uses the term *entr'acte* to signal both the section's place at the midpoint of the book and its "speculative key" (120).

22. Cited in David Dabydeen, *Hogarth's Blacks: Images of Blacks in Eighteenth Century British Art* (Athens: U of Georgia P, 1987), 17.

23. These two myths are reflected in Isaac Bickerstaff's *The Padlock*, which I discuss in relation to Dabydeen's *A Harlot's Progress* in chapter four.

24. See David Garrick, *Harlequin's Invasion*, in *The Plays of David Garrick*. Ed. Harry William Pedicord and Frederick Louis Bermann, 2 vols. (Carbondale: Southern Illinois UP, 1980), I:213, 223.

25. McVeagh sites G.A. Nettleton's review of the 1791 version, in which he describes an affecting farewell scene between Crusoe and Friday, which may or may not have been in the 1781 version. See Nettleton's essay in *TLS*, 30 June 1945, p. 312.

26. *The Gazetter and New Daily Advertiser*, 30 June 1781.

27. This suggests dialogue, but none is mentioned in either *A Short Account* or the reviews.

28. McVeigh explains that Sheridan modeled this scene after a well-known satirical print called "Provision for a Convent" (145). This print still exists and can be seen in volume three of F.G. Stephens's *Catalogue of Political and Personal Satires*. It represents (in Stephens's summary) "a friar, with a huge crucifix hanging around his neck, walking to the gate of a monastery, and bearing on his back a sheaf of corn, in which the head of a girl appears. He also carries a basket" on which is written "PROVISION" (145).

29. *The Ladies Magazine*, February 1781; *The London Convent*, 31 January 1781. In the late nineteenth century, Robinson Crusoe pantomimes were even more elaborate. The 1881 production of *Robinson Crusoe*, for example, had an orchestra of thirty, one-hundred-and-fifty dancers, and two-hundred-and-sixty children and extras. The figure of "Man Friday" was played in blackface, and African and Indian cultures were freely mixed in this performance. The tribe of "cannibals" from whom Friday is rescued, for example, danced an East Indian ballet. A transformation scene introduced the Harlequinade, in which the Clown, Harlequin and Pantaloon were all firmly established in a desert island environment. As in Sheridan's production, as opposed to the characters from the main plot transforming into pantomime characters, the characters from the main plot reappeared in the Harlequinade sequence to rescue the Clown, Harlequin and Pantaloon, who were kidnapped by cannibals. This production reflects both Britain's colonization of India and the influence of Indian culture on Britain.

NOTES TO CHAPTER THREE

1. Amnesty International uses the term "prisoner of conscience" to refer to anyone who is imprisoned or otherwise physically detained because of their political or religious beliefs, or because of their ethnic origin, sex, color, or language, and who has not used or advocated violence.

2. For a more detailed chronology of the important events in the Nigerian Civil War, see: John J. Stremlau, *The International Politics of the Nigerian Civil War, 1967–1970* (Princeton: Princeton UP, 1977).

3. For a comprehensive analysis of Soyinka's journalistic writings prior to his arrest, see: James Gibbs, "Tear the Painted Masks. Join the Poison Stains: A Preliminary Study of Wole Soyinka's Writings for the Nigerian Press," in *Research on Wole Soyinka*, Eds. James Gibbs and Bernth Lindfors (Trenton, N.J.: Africa World Press, Inc. 1993), 225–264.

4. *The Sunday Post* 29 October 1967 reported that: "Police investigations have shown that Soyinka was in Enugu on August 6 with arch-rebel Odumegwu-Ojukwu. Mr. Soyinka was also said to have admitted in a statement that he came to an arrangement with Mr. Ojukwu to assist in the purchase of a jet aircraft to be used by the rebel Air Force" (reprinted in *The Man Died*, 72).

5. Ogunyemi suggests that the image of the caged bird operates in conjunction with the idea of "being buried alive in a crypt. The prisoner shuttles back and forth from life to death, tormented by the fear of imminent death and the knowledge that his fellow prisoners were dying slowly, unheeded by the authorities" (78). Thomson similarly proposes that Soyinka's "poetic eye witnesses the atrocities of his prison," and through the shuttle he "attempts to transcend their confines" (94).

6. While in solitary confinement Soyinka managed to produce the fragments that would later become *The Man Died* (1972), his play *Madmen and Specialists* (1970), his novel *Season of Anomy* (1973), and his collection of prison poems, *A Shuttle in the Crypt*. Wright calls these writings Soyinka's "quartet of civil war writings" (134), and Jeyifo similarly refers to them as Soyinka's "tetralogy on the Nigerian civil war" (178).

7. Soyinka adds: "For fear of providing clues which would lead to a reconstruction of the circumstances and the certain persecution of probably innocent officers, I cannot even provide the titles of these books much less indicate at which periods of my imprisonment they were smuggled in to me one by one."

8. According to Osundare, Joseph is "the colorful dreamer, the straight one in a crooked world; pilloried for his dreams, bouncing back eventually, triumphant." Yet Soyinka's Joseph is no "cursed martyr," and he understands there is "danger in delay." Soyinka's Hamlet, conversely, is "disabled by a failure of will, withdrawing into graveyard musings" and "gallery of abstractions." Thus Soyinka's Hamlet "becomes a trope for those trapped into inaction by fear of error. At a more immediate level he becomes a symbol for those dithering, prevaricating, procrastinating 'intellectuals' . . . ever too ready to intellectualize and justify rank manifestations of the 'state's disease.'" Soyinka's Gulliver, however, is "anything but gullible." This poem is, consequently, one of Soyinka's most "caustic exoriations of the contemporary tin-gods, especially of the African variety, those baffling throw-ups of history who scheme to reduce

humanity to their puny stature." Finally, Soyinka's "Ulysses" is the lone wanderer" who takes "time out to interrogate the purpose of the quest" (195).

9. In his memoirs Soyinka explains that, as a consequence of his isolation, his
    mind began to unravel. "A few months reliving a few months past means a
    few months obliterated in an empty future. It will, I slowly acknowledge,
    become the pattern of existence. Only, control it Kronos! Control the debris
    or memory in the waters of Lethe" (131). Soyinka summons Kronos (Cro-
    nus), the Greek god of time, for assistance as he becomes increasingly more
    aware that, as a consequence of the repetition of thoughts and memories, he
    is losing a grasp on time. In addition, because it was prophesied in Greek
    mythology that one of his children would dethrone him, Kronos (King of the
    Titans) swallowed each of his children immediately after they were born. The
    implication, then, is that Kronos fed off himself, which is exactly what Soy-
    inka was forced to do while in solitary confinement, and feeding off one's own
    mind can drive human beings insane. Soyinka is thus praying for some con-
    trol over his mind. Interestingly, the Romans adopted Kronos as their God of
    Agriculture, Saturn, when he fled to Italy. There he brought about the Golden
    Age, which was a time of peace and happiness. Even after his reign, a celebra-
    tion was held every winter remembering the Golden Age. The theme of the
    party was equality and that no human being is better than another. While the
    celebration was going on, prisoners and slaves were released and war was post-
    poned, which is yet another reason Soyinka may have invoked Kronos.

10. See: J. Bentham, *Works*. Ed. Bowring (London, 1843), IV: 60–64.

11. Soyinka's encounter with this physical "thing" that dehumanizes him is
    fraught with contradiction, for "in the experience of the physical thing the
    individual does not stand alone, most especially a black man." He supposes
    that his "non-acceptance of such treatment bordered . . . on racial mem-
    ory" (39). Thus his individual experience of being enchained ignites within
    him a collective memory of slavery.

12. According to David Oakleaf, with this scene in which Gulliver extinguishes
    the palace fire by urinating on the flames Swift "recapitulates his position as
    a bumbling servant punished for his unclean expedients: when Gulliver puts
    out a palace fire by urinating on it, he wins not the gratitude but the Queen
    of Lilliput's anger." This may be Swift's most ironic comment on his brilliant
    career as a government propagandist. Oakleaf adds that, in the dying days of
    the Tory Ministry, Swift was rewarded with the deanery of St. Patrick's, but
    many felt, as Swift did, they he deserved more recognition. Unfortunately, *A
    Tale of the Tub's* "apparent irreverence" and *The Windsor Prophecy's* "attack on
    one of her intimates apparently determined Queen Anne never to prefer the
    ambitious champion of the Irish church who coveted English deaneries in her
    gift" (35).

13. Gibbs adds: Soyinka "must have realized" that the effect of his words "would
    be like pouring paraffin on smoldering embers. Inevitably the strong words

with which the article closed distracted attention from the plea that the title of the article summarized and the proposal with which he began. Tempers flared" (242).

14. Swift's depiction of the "Big-Endians"(Catholics) and Little-Endians (Anglicans) is a satire of the Catholic-Anglican controversy that dates back to Henry VIII's reign. According to Johae, Soyinka's allusions connote ethnic and racial, as well as political, conflicts. He argues that the repeated capitalization of the "U" in "Us" has a "spurious elevating function similar to the Lilliputians' dismissal of Little-Endian dogma in *Gulliver's Travels.*" Moreover, "at the structural level of signifiers the color leitmotif appears as complementary ('Lillywhite' and "albinos of the Albumen"), semantically they function in opposition: 'Lilliwhite King Lillipuss appears like an arch claim by the king of the Lilliputians ('Lillipuss') to innocence and purity of intention (Lilliwhite'), while the uncomplimentary "Albinos of the Albumen' reads like the same king's curse on his enemies; for Africans lack[ing] black skin pigmentation is both exceptional and unwelcome because it offers no protection from the sun. In "Gulliver," because the "Sun" functions as a metaphor for the King, the inference here is that the "Sun" is going to "show no mercy" to the Albinos," as General Gowen showed no mercy to the Igbos of Biafra. In other words, the "Sun" will "burn the 'Albinos' off the face of the earth, i.e. commit genocide" (33).

15. This scene is generally considered a commentary on the devious methods of interrogation and coercion practiced by the Whigs after Queen Anne died in 1714. The Whigs started a virtual witch-hunt against their Tory predecessors, setting up a Committee of Secrecy to investigate their conduct over the peace.

16. It is well known that the Lilliputian Emperor can be viewed as an ironic depiction of King George I, and Swift's early eighteenth-century readers would have been amused by the Emperor, whose physical features—his handsomeness, his youth, his athletic agility—were in marked contrast to the sluggish and boorish King George. The Emperor's love of military display and pageantry, however, does bear a direct resemblance to those features in King George's character.

17. According to J. Paul Hunter, "[s]eeing and perceiving are crucial issues throughout *Gulliver's Travels*, especially when sight and insight fail its hero-reporter, the safety of whose eyes and spectacles obsess him wherever he goes. Because he has at his disposal both long and short views, Swift can readily offer a 'perspective' on the magnitude of England's national ambitions and international relations." (230).

18. The debates on how to dispose of Gulliver's body have been interpreted as Swift's satiric commentary on the Whig debates regarding how to punish Bolingbroke and Oxford, whom they had charged with treason.

19. In Swift's text, Gulliver's decision not to stand trial is likely a commentary on, and perhaps even a defense of, Bolingbroke's decision not to stand trial and flee to France.

20. For thorough discussions of Part III as an essential component of the narrative's thematic and generic structures, see: Douglas Lane Patey, "Swift's Satire on 'Science' and the Structure of *Gulliver's Travels*, and Jenny Mezciems, "The Unity of Swift's 'Voyage to Laputa,'" in *Jonathan Swift: A Collection of Critical Essays*, Ed. Claude Rawson. (Upper Saddle River: Prentice Hall, 1995), 216–240 and 241–263.

21. Nigeria was granted its independence from Britain on 1 October 1960 and, as in other newly independent colonies, the Federal Military Government was virtually a replication of colonial rule. Whether Soyinka is alluding here to the continuing influence of Britain, particularly during the Nigerian Civil War, is open to interpretation.

22. A Canadian journalist who witnessed the May 1966 massacres, reported: "Many thousands of Igbos were slaughtered in towns and villages across the North, and hundreds of thousands of others were blinded, crippled or maimed, or simply left destitute as they attempted to flee to the Igbo homeland in the Eastern Region" (quoted in Jacobs, 21).

23. See, for example: No. XIII (2 November 1710), No. XV (16 November 1710), No. XVI (13 November 1710), No. XVII, (30 November 1710), No. XX (21 December 1710), No. XXIII (11 January 1710–1711), and especially, No. XXVIII (8 February 1710–1711) and No. XXIX (22 February 1710).

24. Swift ultimately imputes the "continuance of the war to natural indulgence between our general and allies, wherein they both so well found their accounts; to the fears of the money changers, lest their tables should be overthrown; to the designs of the Whigs, who apprehend the loss of their credit and employments in a peace; and to those at home, who held their immoderate engrossments of power and favour by no other tenure, than their presumption upon the necessity of the affairs" (*SW* iv. 352).

25. For an in-depth discussion of Swift's writings of the 1720s as they relate to both the injustices of England's economic policies toward Ireland and international mercantilism, see Charlotte Sussman, "From Curiosity to Commodity," *Consuming Anxieties: Consumer Protest, Gender & British Slavery, 1713–1833* (Stanford: Stanford UP, 2000), 49–80.

26. Lindalino is the second city of the Kingdom and its name is generally thought to be an anagram for Dublin. In this episode, "the Inhabitants who had often complained of great Oppressions, shut the Town Gates, seized on the Governor, and with incredible Speed and Labour erected four larger Towers, one at each Corner of the City" (162–163). At the top of each of these towers they placed a great Loadstone. It took eight months for the Laputian king to realize that the Lindalinians were rebelling, at which time he "hovered over them for several Days to deprive them of the Sun and the Rain." He then "commanded all the Inhabitants of the Island to cast great Stones" onto the town. Finally, the king ordered that the "Island should

descend gently" upon it. To the Lilliputians' surprise, they could not keep the Island "in a firm position, but found it inclining to fall" (163). Eventually they discovered that the island was "violently attracted" to the Top of the Towers, and the king was forced to "give the Town their own Conditions" (164). The account of the Lindalino rebellion was removed from the first edition and published for the first time in 1896.

27. Another passage that apparently gave great offense reads: "I, M. B. Drapier . . . am so far from depending upon the people of England, that if they should ever rebel against my sovereign (which god forbid!) I would be ready, at the first command from his Majesty, to take arms against them, as some of my countrymen did against theirs at Preston. And if such a rebellion should prove successful as to fix the Pretender on the throne of England, I would venture to transgress that statute so far, as to lose every drop of my blood to hinder him from being King of Ireland" (*SW* vi. 446).

28. Bogel adds that, if "some of the satiric texts of this period seem to display a fascination with the disruptive and the anarchic, or a distrust of established orders and common forms, they do so in an exemplary or ironic way and in order, ultimately, to reaffirm a commitment to stability, the very security of which is demonstrated by the extravagance of such licensed deviation" (16).

NOTES TO CHAPTER FOUR

1. David Dabydeen, *Slave Song* (Mundelstrup, Denmark: Dangaroo, 1984); Mark McWatt, "His True-True Face: Masking and Revelation in David Dabydeen's *Slave Song*," *The Art of David Dabydeen*, ed. Kevin Grant (Leeds: Peepal Tree, 1997). In his second collection of poems, *Coolie Odyssey* (1988), Dabydeen illustrates the relationship between white colonialists and indigenous South Americans.

2. In *The Counting House* (1996), Dabydeen similarly combines his academic, artistic and personal interests. This novel tells the story of an Indian couple whose hopes of a new life in colonial Guyana (at the end of the nineteenth century) end in tragedy. The story represents the historical tensions between indentured Indian workers and Guyanese of African descent, tensions that continued to exist, and which Dabydeen witnessed as a child, in the mid-twentieth century.

3. *Hogarth's Blacks* was first published in 1985 by Dangaroo Press. All references, however, are from the 1987 edition, published by The University of Georgia Press.

4. Michael D. Harris similarly acknowledges in *Colored Pictures: Race & Visual Representation*, that images of blacks in British and European art most often "iterated limited or derogatory perceptions held by most whites and helped to create a visual iconography for black representation. Usually they naturalized a social order with black subjects on the periphery doing menial

tasks or exhibiting stereotypical behavior so as to emphasize their social and political inferiority" (40).

5. In *Picturing Imperial Power: Colonial Subjects in Eighteenth-Century British Painting*, Beth Fowkes Tobin points out that images of Africans were included in portraits of aristocratic men and women as a way "to indicate the colonial connections of these wealthy and powerful people," and thus the black servant in domestic portraiture is "emblematic of overseas trade and colonialism" (28). According to Tobin, such "paintings, as is the case with all cultural production, are not merely reflections of larger social and economic forces; they participate in the production of meaning, in the dynamic construction of identities and in the structuring within discursive fields of particular positionalities" (1).

6. In *Hogarth, Walpole and Commercial Britain* (1987), Dabydeen focuses on Hogarth's treatment of the "working" classes. Like Hogarth's black figures, his prostitutes and beggars also constitute the marginalized and the dispossessed.

7. *The Analysis of Beauty* (ed. Joseph Burke, Oxford, 1955), 189. Quoted in Dabydeen, *Hogarth's Blacks*, 41.

8. Sabor adds that *Hogarth's Blacks* has some "major shortcomings." For example, Dabydeen is "less than just in declaring that Ronald Paulson, the doyen of Hogarth scholars, has wholly neglected the subject of Hogarth's blacks. A passage in *Book and Painting* (Knoxville: Tennessee, 1982), pp. 80–82, which predates *Hogarth's Blacks* by three years, reads like a summary of the later book." Paulson acknowledges in a footnote (p. 161, n. 18) that Dabydeen is dealing with the subject of Hogarth's representations of blacks in a forthcoming book, and points out that whenever a black boy appears in one of Hogarth's pictures he is "both peripheral and subversive, a sharp comment on the grown-up English whites" (80). While Hogarth's blacks are portrayed in such conventional poses as serving tea or coffee, they may also have a "sharp twinkle" in their eye, such as in *The Wallaston Family*, or, as in *Marriage à la Mode*, they "look and laugh." By following the gaze of the "*supposed* savage, the African black who serves these civilized people," the viewer would see the target of Hogarth's satire, which is "apparent civilization concealing savagery" (81). Thus for Paulson, as Dabydeen later argued in *Hogarth's Blacks*, Hogarth employs images of blacks to "express a critique of society in the mid-eighteenth century" (82).

9. Ogude's critique of Dabydeen stems from his determination that Hogarth's prints do not "in any way" differ from the blacks in portraits by European and English painters in that they are "not the focus of the paintings" but merely an "aspect of the social culture of the aristocratic class" (246).

10. According to Dabydeen, Charteris was not only a notorious rake; he was an "unscrupulous and extremely wealthy businessman who squeezed and robbed the defenseless" (*Hogarth, Walpole and Commercial Britain*, 93).

11. Although Hogarth was critical of commercialism, he was an active partici-
    pant. According to Bindman, the method of marketing *A Harlot's Progress*
    was "new and ingenious." The series of painted versions was also available
    for viewing at his studio in Covent Garden and each day, according to rival
    engraver George Vertue, "persons of fashion and Artists came to see these
    pictures." Apparently, Hogarth wanted to make his studio part of the urban
    spectacle. Contributions for the engravings were initially raised by means
    of an engraved subscription ticket, as a way to get half the payment in
    advance. Hogarth also allowed a cheaper set of copies of *A Harlot's Progress*
    to be produced, which, according to Bindman, suggests that he already had
    a potential audience in mind for his Modern Moral Subjects beyond those
    who came to his studio or heard of *A Harlot's Progress* by word of mouth.

12. According to Eli Faber, the fact that Jews participated in the slave trade—
    by investing in companies that engaged in it, as owners of slave ships, and
    as slave owners when they settled in the Americas—has long been known
    from a substantial body of work produced by Jewish historians. Faber adds
    that the book published by the Historical Relationship Department of the
    Nation of Islam, *The Secret Relationship Between Blacks and Jews* (1991),
    "charged that Jews had financed and dominated the slave trade, owned slaves
    in excess of any other group, and inflicted cruelty with abandon on slaves"
    (6). In "Black Demagogues and Pseudo-Scholars," Henry Louis Gates, Jr.
    characterizes this book as the "bible of the new anti-Semitism."

13. According to Reyahn King, one of the most well known paintings of a black
    figure is an unfinished work by Reynolds (1770), now in the Menil Foun-
    dation. In the mid-nineteenth century the figure was identified as Francis
    Barber, Dr. Johnson's servant. Barber was much beloved by Johnson, who
    supervised his education and bequeathed to him his entire inheritance. But
    apparently the figure was incorrectly catalogued as "Barber, Frank, Servant
    of Sir Joshua Reynolds" in 1861 at the British Institution. The difference
    is crucial given that, unlike Johnson, Reynolds seems to have had a low
    opinion of his servant. According to King, when his servant was robbed,
    Reynolds "was appalled to find the apprehended criminal under threat of
    execution and made his servant provide the convict with food from his own
    table." This was not, however, because Reynolds was opposed to the death
    penalty. In fact, he was "publicly criticized for attending the execution of
    another servant personally known to him" (34).

14. For the first biography of Sancho, see Jekyll's *Life of Sancho*, which prefaced
    every edition of *The Letters of the Late Ignatius Sancho*. In 1782 Jekyll was
    a friend of Sancho's but not well known publicly. According to Brycchan
    Carey, this is likely the reason the biography is not attributed to him in early
    editions. Jekyll later became a well-known Whig politician and lawyer, and
    his authorship of the biography is subsequently acknowledged in the 1803
    edition. The 1803 edition also includes a long footnote to this biography by

Sancho's son, William, which is reprinted in Paul Edwards and Polly Rewt's 1994 edition.

15. Caretta notes that Sancho's attempt at a stage career playing Othello and Oroonoko failed because of his speech impediment (xi).

16. Sancho writes: "I am sure you will applaud me for beseeching you to give one half-hour's attention to slavery, as it is at this day practiced in the West Indies.—That subject, handled in your striking manner, would ease the yoke (perhaps) of many—but if only of one—Gracious God!—what a feast to a benevolent heart!—and, sure I am, you are an epicurean in acts of charity.—You, who are universally read, and as universally admired—you could not fail—Dear Sir, think in me you behold the uplifted hands of thousands of my brother Moors.—Grief (you pathetically observe) is eloquent;—figure to yourself their attitudes;—hear their supplicating addresses!—alas!—you cannot refuse.—Humanity must comply—in which hope I beg permission to subscribe myself" (Edwards and Rewt, Letter 36, pp. 85–86). Edwards and Rewt also note that Crewe incorrectly dates Sancho's letter as 1776, which they date as 1766. Ellis dates it as 1765.

17. For example, S.E. Ogude sees Sancho as a "divided-self," and writer Caryl Phillips views him as "doubly-conscious." According to Philips, the "personal anxieties of such negotiations resulted in the development of a 'double consciousness' along the lines which the great American philosopher and writer, W. E. B. Du Bois would later identify in the United States" (13). Du Bois identified "double consciousness" in his essay "The Strivings of the Negro" (1895) as the "sense of looking at one's self through the eyes of others, of measuring one's soul by the tape of a world that looks on in amused contempt and pity" (194).

18. Brycchan Carey argues that Sancho wished to see his letters in print, and perhaps revised them for publication, in "'The Hellish Means of Killing and Kidnapping': Ignatius Sancho and the Campaign against the 'Abominable Traffic for Slaves," *Discourses of Slavery and Abolition*. Eds. Brycchan Carey, Markman Ellis and Sara Salih (London: Palgrave Macmillan, 2004), 81–95.

19. In "Through a Looking Glass," David Richardson writes: "The enslaved who died in the Atlantic crossing were largely victims of respiratory, intestinal or epidemic diseases. Some of these diseases were the product of conditions experienced by the enslaved before boarding ship, but shipboard conditions undoubtedly exacerbated such disorders and proved a breeding ground for additional ones. While disease was the principal killer of slaves," a significant number of shipboard deaths were caused by "white action." Slaves were cruelly abused and relentless beaten, "notwithstanding instructions by owners of ships banning such behaviour. Typically motivated by sex and overwhelmingly directed against female slaves, such abuse sometimes resulted in the premature death of those who sought to resist the unwanted advances of

ruthless and sadistic masters or other crew. For women, therefore, to the risk of death from disease was added rape and murder" (74–75).

20. Thomas Pringle (1789–1834), a Scottish poet, went to South Africa in 1820, where he edited a newspaper and a magazine. Pringle returned to England in 1826. He published *African Sketches*, a book of verse and prose in 1834; his autobiographical *Narrative of a Residence in South Africa* was published in 1835.

21. According to Salih, Prince's *History* is a 'piece of propaganda." Unlike Gronniosaw and Equiano, whose texts "announce on the title page that they are 'narrated by themselves,' the *History* is "a collection of texts" as opposed to a straightforward autobiography. Not only is Prince's story mediated by Strickland, the text is "bolstered" by an editorial supplement and appendices, an "apparatus" almost equal to the narrative in length that is "designed to validate Prince's 'testimony.'" Despite Pringle's insistence in the preface that every attempt was made to retain "Mary's exact expressions and peculiar phraseology," there are moments in the narrative when Prince's "voice seems less discernible than others," such as toward the end of the narrative where the "syntax and idiom convey her palpable outrage at the mistreatment to which she has been subjected." Prince's *History* is not a narrative of a female slave's experiences, "but a composite text that has been assembled by an editor who had a clear agenda in mind" (xiii). Moreover, the "supplementary material framing her narrative is clearly an attempt to establish the authenticity of her life story and the truth of the details she supplies" (xiv).

22. For further discussion of "melancholy" in eighteenth-century England, see: Derek Jarrett, "The Vale of Tears," in *England in the Age of Hogarth* (New Haven and London: Yale UP, 1992), 175–197.

23. In a postscript to the second edition, Pringle writes of Prince's ailing health and need for money: "Mary Prince has been afflicted with a disease in the eyes, which, it is feared, may terminate in total blindness . . . I mention the circumstance at present on purpose to induce the friends of humanity to promote more zealously the sale of this publication, with a view to provide a little fund for future benefit" (4)

24. When Prince took the witness stand in court to corroborate the reports of poor treatment and brutality included in the *History*, she was "more frank about her sexual relations." As Salih argues, Prince's courtroom evidence provides us with important details that were excluded from her *History*, and it also highlights the instability of this text, which has clearly been 'doctored' by zealous anti-slavery causes," so as not to offend the sensibilities of its readers (xxx).

25. In his introduction to Vol. 4 (*Verse*) of *Slavery, Abolition and Emancipation*, Alan Richardson explains that "anti-slavery poems frequently deploy sentiment to mask racial anxieties and to soften colonialist rhetoric, naively idealizing the enslaved or colonial subject at best and lapsing into outright

racism at worst." This is most likely due to the "limitations of anti-slavery discourse," which lacked the virtues of direct appeal and plain fact." However, the implication here is that even those who seemed to situate themselves on the abolitionist side of the debates promoted "false portrayals of Africans and of Afro-Caribbean slaves" by giving credence to "stereotyped characters and situations" (x).

26. Equiano does, however, acknowledge the rudiments of economics that condition his life. As Houston Baker has argued, Equiano recognizes that only the acquisition of property will enable him to alter his status as property. Moreover, his awareness that Britain will not waver in its lust for economic power informs his concluding depiction of the "commercial utopia" that will result when the slave trade is abolished and free commerce is established between Britain and Africa. See: *Blues, Ideology, and Afro-American Literature* (Chicago: U of Chicago P, 1984), 31–50.

27. In addition, by having Mungo freely mingle fact and fiction, Dabydeen could be alluding to Vincent Caretta's suggestion that Equiano exercised his literary agency by manipulating the facts of his autobiography, particularly his account of Africa if he was not actually born there. See: "Olaudah Equiano or Gustavus Vassa? New Light on an Eighteenth-century Question of Identity." *Slavery and Abolition* 210.3 (1999): 96–105; Introduction, *The Interesting Narrative and Other Writings* (London and New York, Penguin, 2003), x-xi. Srinivas Aravamudan similarly notes that, while Equiano's narrative may be "willfully falsified" (617), and thus "factish" (618), it is just such historical debates that enable us to recognize that Equiano exhibited both a political and literary agency with his narrative. See: "Equiano Lite," *Eighteenth-Century Studies* 34.4 (2001): 615–619.

28. Other evidence of Newton's transformation is his contribution to the Privy Council investigation as one of Clarkson's witnesses against the trade.

29. The "real" Thomas Thistlewood moved to Jamaica in 1750, where he lived as an estate owner until he died in 1786, and where he kept meticulous records of his daily life and observations. In his presentation of Thistlewood's diary, Douglas Hall quotes heavily from Thistlewood's comments on his "relationships (sexual and other) between individuals of all social strata, free and slave," because he found "these relationships more human, and therefore far more complicated, than our generally stereotyped views have allowed us to observe." He also reproduces "every account of punishments that seemed to go beyond even the understood excesses of the time" (xix-xx), which would seem to indicate that Thistlewood was a particularly brutal slave owner. But rather than vilify Thistlewood, Brian L. Moore writes in his introduction to the text that Thistlewood's "voracious libido," which "manifested itself in countless sexual encounters" with dependant female slaves, "raises new questions about sex and power in master-slave relations." He then asks: "Did Thistlewood rape these women or were they consenting,

if unequal, partners within the restricted parameters of a patriarchal slave system?" (vi). Moore seems to be suggesting that it is possible to view master-slave sexual relations as something other than exploitive and abusive.

30. Claude Prosper Jolyot de Crebillon *fils*, *The Sopha, A Moral Tale*, 2 vols. (1742), 32, 60–61; quoted in Dabydeen, *Hogarth's Blacks*, 79, and Uglow, *Hogarth: A Life and a World*, 384–385. Hogarth hints at this same subject in *Taste in High Life*, in which an aristocratic lady suggestively strokes the face of an exotically dressed black boy.

31. Gilman adds that "the "colonial mentality that sees 'natives' as needing control easily shifts that concern to the woman, in particular the prostitute caste. Because the need for control was a projection of inner fears, its articulation in visual images was in terms which were polar opposite to the European male" (107). The innate fear of the "Other's" difference and of losing control over the "Other" led to the development and representation of stereotypes as a means of ordering the world, and fueled such action as relegating human beings to the status of laboratory animals (during slavery and the Holocaust) and "dangerous" exotics (during apartheid in South Africa) (241).

32. Tasch notes that "by the time the score and words were originally published, the friendship between Didbin and Bickerstaff had increased to the point that Didbin named his son (born on 27 October 1768) Charles Isaac Mungo Didbin, in honor of the author and the part that had won him fame (*The Padlock* having opened on 3 October 1768)" (155). *The Padlock* was so well received that it was produced fifty-four times at Drury Lane during the 1768–1769 season, a total of one hundred and forty times at Drury Lane, and seventy times at Covent Garden.

33. Cox points out that the play is even cited by Clarkson as a moment in his *History of the Abolition of the Slave-Trade* (1808) because of an epilogue by a "worthy clergyman," "which was attached to it soon after it came out" and which according to Clarkson "procured a good deal of feeling for the unfortunate sufferers" (vol. 1, 79–82). According to Cox, this epilogue, also printed later in *The Bee* (6 February 1793), "suggests we turn from laughter to reject the enslavement of Mungo and his fellow Africans" (xv).

34. Mungo plans to donate his archive someday to the Abolition Committee and imagines that perhaps it will be named "'the Perseus Collection.'" He considers, and rejects, other names: "'the Mungo Collection'" is too common; the "'Noah Collection'" confuses the Jew with the "actual black me"; "the Barambangdodo Collection'" (based on what may have been the name of his African village) is "too comic"; and, while "'The Augustus,' or 'The Gustavus Collection'" are "splendid names," no "owner had "blessed" him with that name (like Equiano). He hopes the plaque next to the exhibit will read "'Donated to the London Library by Mr Perseus Esquire/Negro Gent/Man of Taste/Famed Antiquarian/Servant of Scholarship.'" These are

the words, which could be used to describe Sancho, by which he would like to be known and remembered, rather than by the words and stories printed in the papers. This is the "identity" that he would chose for himself.

NOTES TO CHAPTER FIVE

1. John Gabriel Stedman, *Stedman's Surinam: Life in an Eighteenth-Century Slave Society.* An Abridged, Modernized Edition of *Narrative of a Five Years Expedition against the Revolted Negroes of Surinam,* Eds. Richard Price and Sally Price (Baltimore: Johns Hopkins UP, 1992), 43. Hereafter cited parenthetically in the text by page except where noted.

2. According to Nancy Armstrong, when Richardson wrote his first novel, *Pamela, or Virtue Reward* (1740), he "tapped into the power of written testimony by turning a series of exemplary personal letters into a kind of captivity narrative. To adapt a form designed to deal with the perils of colonial experience for the situation in England proper, he simply translated the basis for the heroine's identity from nationality and religion into class and sexual conduct" (374).

3. George William was born in 1784, soon after they arrived in England, but was killed in 1803. He was a lieutenant in the British Navy. Sophia Charlotte married into the illustrious Cotton family, uniting the family with the East Indian Company. Adrian distinguished himself in the battle of Aliwal against the Sikhs in the Indian war of 1846, but died at sea in 1849. Maria Joanna became the wife of Captain Horace John Aylward of the Royal Artillery. John Cambridge, Captain of the 34ᵗʰ Light Infantry, East India Company, was born just before his father's death, and was killed in 1824 whilst storming the Burmese fort Rangoon. See Stanbury Thompson, xiii-ix.

4. Quoted in Price and Price, xiv; Stedman's handwritten manuscripts at the James Ford Bell Library at the University of Minnesota, 1786, p. 20.

5. Quoted in Price and Price, lxi; from *Analytical Review*, September 1796, 225–226.

6. Quoted in Price and Price, lxii: from *Critical Review*, January 1797, 53.

7. Gelien Matthews argues, conversely, in *Caribbean Slave Revolts and the British Abolitionist Movement*, that slave rebellions fueled the abolitionist campaign in England, and that the transatlantic dialectic between antislavery activities in England and slave insurrections in colonies eventually contributed to bringing about the end of slavery. In the early nineteenth century "abolitionists sympathized with, justified, and positively conceptualized and esteemed the slaves' overt resistance to enslavement" (11–12).

8. John Gabriel Stedman, *Narrative of an Expedition Against the Revolted Negroes of Surinam . . .* (1796), facsimile reprint with an introduction by R.A.H. van Lier (Holland: U of Mass. Press, 1971), xvii.

9. In the 1796 *Narrative*, editors inserted a critical phrase that changed Stedman's meaning, and brought his views into agreement with the popular,

anti-abolition view: " . . . I wish from the bottom of my heart, that my words could be submitted to the consideration of that respectable body the British parliament; and so far be regarded, as to prevent the fatal decision of a total abolition of slavery till 1800, or the beginning of the next century." See: Stedman, *Narrative of a Five Years' Expedition Against the Revolted Negroes of Surinam*, ed. R.A.J. van Lier (Holland: U of M Press, 1972),

10. Stedman, *The Journal of John Gabriel Stedman*, Ed. Stanbury Thompson (London: Mitre Press, 1962), 9. Hereafter cited parenthetically in the text by page except where noted.

11. In the *Journal*, Stedman writes: "I was exceedingly melancholy. My friend dead" (55).

12. In the *Journal*, after Cunninghame's death, MyLord becomes Stedman's "most trusty companion" (59).

13. In the *Journal*, Stedman writes: "I cried most bitterly, having lost a friend who doated [*sic*] upon me, a friend who never, during his whole lifetime, did so much as once disoblige me, who was my whole ambition, and I his only delight . . . I mourned *in the heart* for that dear father, where I shall continue to mourn till I shall be no more" (108).

14. In the *Narrative*, Stedman writes: "The first object that attracted my compassion while visiting on a neighboring estate was a truly beautiful *Samboe* girl of about eighteen, tied up with both arms to a tree, as naked as she came to the world, and lacerated in such a shocking condition by the whips of two Negro drivers that she was, from her neck to her ankles, literally dyed over with blood" (145).

15. In the *Narrative*, Stedman writes: "Having testified how much I was hurt by the cruelty of the above execution, and surprised by the intrepidity with which the Negroes bore their punishment, a decent-looking man stepped up to me. 'Sir (said he), you are but a newcomer from Europe and know very little about the African slaves, without which you would testify both less feeling and surprise. Not long ago (continued he) I saw a black man hanged alive by the ribs, between which an incision was first made with a knife, and then an iron hook clinched with a chain. In this manner he kept living three days, hanging with his head and feet downwards, and catching with his tongue the drops of water (it being the rainy season) that were flowing down his bloated breast, while the vultures were picking in the putrid wound. Notwithstanding all this, he never complained and even upbraided a Negro for crying while he was flogged below the gallows.'" Stedman adds a footnote to this last point: "All Negroes cry out for mercy while they are being flogged, in hopes of having thereby the lesser punishment—but never, no never, where no mitigation is expected" (51).

16. In their introduction to *Stedman's Surinam*, Price and Price explain that, while working Stedman's manuscripts, "it quickly became apparent that

Thompson's work confused as much as it elucidated. Examination of the original notebooks and papers that Thompson had used (which are now in the James Ford Bell Library at the University of Minnesota) revealed that, not only had he inserted his own commentary into that of Stedman without any way of distinguishing the two, but he had changed dates and spellings, misread and incorrectly transcribed a large number of words, translated Dutch words (and mistranslated Sranan words) into English, reordered words and even whole passages, rephrased column lists as prose, included passages that had been carefully crossed out by Stedman, and deleted other passages without apparent reason—all this without indicating in his publication where the alterations had been made" (xxvii). In preparing their new edition of Stedman, they have relied exclusively on those manuscript diary pages, rather than what they refer to as Thompson's "flawed book." Nevertheless, in her novel Gilroy quotes a passage directly from the *Journal* and fully cites Thompson's edition (147–148).

17. See: *The Journals of Captain James Cook* (Hakluyt Society), No. 34–37. Ed. J.C. Beaglehole, 1955; 1999.

18. In addition to slave rebellions, the French Revolution significantly influenced the political climate in England, dulling the clamor for abolition. According to Lynn Festa, abolition's "association with radical ideas of equality alarmed those eyeing the rising tide of violence in revolutionary France and the emergence of popular radicalism (English Jacobinism) in Britain" (202–203).

19. Like Gulliver, Roderick Random can be understood as the object of the author's criticism because he represents what Anna Neill refers to as a "world in which profit and status are acquired without any consideration for the suffering of one's fellow creatures" (133).

20. Joseph's punishment for resisting Mrs. Booby is to be relieved of his position as a footman. He draws some strength from his love of Fanny Goodwill, a virtuous servant living on the Booby's country estate, and sets out on the "road of life." Parson Adams and, eventually, Fanny, join Joseph on the road to London, and the three travelers embark on a series of adventures. For the most part, these adventures consist of comically absurd encounters with such distinctly un-virtuous figures as highwaymen, sexual predators, corrupt innkeepers and hypocritical clerics. Joseph, Adams, and Fanny deal with each situation courageously and honorably until the reader cannot help but—in addition to laugh at them—worry about and admire them. The novel ultimately becomes what Fielding claims in the Preface: a "comic romance." In the novel's final Book, Lady Booby resumes her futile efforts to seduce the handsome Joseph. Pamela soon arrives, newly married to Mr. Booby as a reward for maintaining her virtue, although she is so transformed by her new social station that she objects to the marriage of Joseph and

Fanny, proclaiming that Fanny's status as a servant would be embarrassing to the family. But everything is remarkably resolved when Joseph, Pamela, and Fanny's true, aristocratic parentage is discovered. As it turns out, Joseph and Pamela are *not* sister and brother. Instead, Joseph is the son of a gentleman who identifies him by the "strawberry" birthmark on his breast. At the end of the novel, Joseph marries his beloved Fanny and settles down to a quiet life in the country, refusing to "make his Appearance in *High-Life*" (269).

21. Tom's romantic escapades continue on the road when he prevents Ensign Northerton from raping Mrs. Waters, who then seduces her rescuer in gratitude at Upton Inn. While Tom is in bed with Mrs. Waters, Sophia arrives at the inn, but quickly departs in a fury when she hears that Tom is in bed with another woman. When Tom discovers Sophia's hand warmer in his bed, he sets off with Partridge for London. In London, Sophia stays with Lady Bellaston, with whom Tom has an affair hoping she can lead him to Sophia. However, when Tom and Sophia reconcile, Lady Bellaston becomes jealous and arranges for Lord Fellamar, who has fallen in love with Sophia, to kidnap and marry her rival. Tom successfully breaks off the affair by proposing marriage to Lady Bellaston, who thinks he is only after her money and refuses him. In the meantime, Squire Western finds and rescues Sophia just as she is about to be raped by Fellamar. When Tom finds himself in prison after having been drawn into a sword fight, he wallows in despair, fearing that he may have killed his opponent and, having learned that Mrs. Waters is actually Jenny Jones (the woman he thinks is his mother), thinking he committed incest. To make matters worse, he receives a letter from Sophia who, having learned about his affair with Lady Bellaston, tells him she never wants to see him again. But as with *Joseph Andrew*, everything is resolved in the end when Tom's true parentage is revealed. As it turns out, Tom is the son of Mrs. Bridget, Allworthy's sister, and thus he is Allworthy's nephew. Once Squire Western learns that Tom is Allworthy's legitimate heir, he gives his blessing for Tom and Sophia to be married.

22. Initially runaway slaves, known as maroons, established communities in the wilderness and threatened white settlers by stealing supplies and enticing more slaves to run away. In the 1770s, the maroons established their colonies in the jungles close to the plantations and began attacking white "masters" and their families much more frequently. For further reading, see: Richard Price, *Maroon Societies: Rebel Slave Communities in the Americas* (Baltimore: Johns Hopkins UP, 1996).

23. Price and Price explain that the war was "characterized by the colonial troops' criss-crossing, more or less blindly, vast expanses of treacherous forests and swamps, wit the maroons—through an efficient system of spies and lookouts—almost always remaining at least a step ahead, and often setting fatal ambushes for their pursuers" (xxiv).

24. According to Joe Snader, because a captivity narrative "recorded a Briton's subjugation at hands of a supposedly inferior culture, it created a sense of cultural imbalance, a violation of the imagined hierarchy that placed Western above non-Western cultures. But in the fact of its publication, a captivity narrative marked the restoration of this imbalance by implying both the happy ending of the captive's release and the possibility of knowing and recording the captive-taking culture." In some cases, the narratives developed this "implicit cultural victory at more explicit levels," celebrating the captive's ability to not only endure "whatever an alien culture could impose, but also to turn such impositions to advantage, whether of increased knowledge, economic benefit, colonial endeavor, or simply escape. Thus one of the genre's most basic strategies involves transforming the situation of captivity into a basis for heroism of resistance and reversal" (63).

25. The *Narrative* was translated into German (1797), French (1798), Dutch (1799), Swedish (1800), and Italian (1818).

26. In the entry for 22 February 1773, Stedman writes: "A negro woman offers me the use of her daughter, while here, for a certain sum. We don't agree about the price" (121). In the entry for 11 April 1773, he writes: "J——a, her mother, and Q——come to close a bargain with me. We put it off for reasons I gave them" (123). We also know that he began a sexual relationship with Joanna prior to when the formal arrangements of their "Surinam marriage" were finalized. In the entry for 23 April 1773, he writes: J——a comes to stay with me. I gave her presents to the value of about ten pounds sterling, and am perfectly happy." (123). In the entry for 9 June 1773, he writes: "I dine with Joanna, with whom I resolve to lie no more for certain good reasons. Give her a gold medal to remember me, which my father gave my mother the night that I was born" (127).

27. According to Price and Price, Stedman altered and embellished his relationship with Joanna in *A Narrative* to project "an image of his own conduct in the colony that now seemed appropriate, from the perspective of his life as a middle-class gentleman established with his wife and children in the English country side, and in preserving the memory of a woman whom he had indeed come to love" (xxxii).

28. In the *Narrative*, Stedman's Joanna declares: "'I am born a low, contemptible slave. To be your wife under the forms of Christianity must degrade you to all your relations and your friends, besides the expense of my purchase and education. But I have a soul, I hope, not inferior to the best European, and blush not to acknowledge that I have a regard for you who so much distinguishes me above the rest. Nay, that now independent of every other thought I shall pride myself (in the way of my ancestors) to be yours all and all, till fate shall part us or my conduct shall give you cause to spurn me from your presence'" (48).

29. According to Sharpe, while Gilroy "does not go so far as to suggest that Joanna was Stedman's lawful wife, she does make their Surinam-style marriage equal to a Christian one, rather than the exchange of sexual and domestic services for payment, which is what the term *concubinage* implies" (102).

30. But Joanna is a slave and therefore always in danger of being raped by any European who desires her. While Gilroy's Stedman claims that he wishes only to protect the virtuous Joanna from torture and abuse, his words are saturated with sexual desire and seem to suggest that he rapes her with his eyes: "I watched her with increasing desire and decided to be her friend, and to protect her as far as I could, for to agitate such a fine body with a whip, hot iron rods, or any other instrument of torture would be sacrilegious" (44). Here, Joanna is comparable to the heroine of Richardson's second novel, *Clarissa*, who is not nearly so fortunate as Pamela. Like *Pamela*, *Clarissa* is composed of the letters of an abducted woman who refuses courtship and marriage on any terms other than her own. However, unlike Pamela, the beautiful and virtuous Clarissa comes from a wealthy family. Desperate to avoid an arranged marriage to a heartless man, she is tricked into escaping with Lovelace, whom she also refuses to marry. Eventually, Lovelace can no longer control his escalating passion for Clarissa and he rapes her. The implication in associating Joanna with Clarissa is that, regardless of whether she willingly entered into an economic or emotional relationship with Stedman, she is still a victim of sexual exploitation. As Mary Louise Pratt explains, "there could be no consensual relations between white men and slave women when the women were not in a position to choose their partners or to refuse the sexual advances of their masters and overseers" (102).

31. According to Gwilliam, "sentiment cannot eliminate the fact of Stedman's departure from Surinam, however he rewrites it; while Johnny is freed, Joanna remains a slave in Surinam" (666–667).

NOTES TO THE EPILOGUE

1. In *Ghosts of Slavery*, Jenny Sharpe includes one of the few comprehensive discussion of Phillips's *Cambridge* in the same chapter as her discussion of Gilroy's *Stedman and Joanna*. Sharpe describes *Cambridge* as a "postmodern historical novel written in the anachronistic prose of late eighteenth- and early nineteenth-century travel diaries and slave narratives such as *Lady Nugent's Journal* (Cundall 1907) and *the Interesting Narrative of the Life of Olaudah Equiano* (1987 [1789])." Sharpe argues that although Gilroy and Philips's novels were published the same year, they make "very different interventions into antislavery discourse. While *Stedman and Joanna* acknowledges the contribution of black people (both in England and the Caribbean) to the idea of a universal humanity that led to the emancipation

of slaves, *Cambridge* returns to a slaveholding past to implicate Victorian England in the West Indian plantation system from which it disassociated itself. While Gilroy gives the character based on Joanna an agency that exceeds Stedman's narrative control, Phillips unsettles the reader's desire for an authenticating voice of black resistance. While Gilroy's novel reconfirms a humanist faith in the possibility for mutual compassion across the master-slave divide, Phillips's novel shows how even the most benign and sympathetic position does not transcend the unequal relations of power under slavery" (89). See also: pp. 105–119.

2. Aravamudan adds that the "various literary antecedents" that are reworked in Equiano's text, which can be broadly characterized as "bourgeois empiricism and royalist romance, history and fiction, discovery and projection—continue a dialectic in English colonialist literature from *Oroonoko* onward. 'Vassa,' 'Crusoe,' and 'Othello,' if thought of as more generalized literary principles rather than just characters, mediate for Equiano as myth, symbol and precursor" (252).

Bibliography

Addison, Joseph, Richard Steele, et. al. *The Tatler, The Spectator, The Guardian, The Rambler, The Adventurer* and *The Idler*. 24 vols. London: John Sharpe, 1803–1815.

Amuta, Chidi. "From Myth to Ideology: The Socio-political content of Soyinka's War Writings." *The Journal of Commonwealth Literature* 23 (Dec. 1988): 116–129.

Appiah, Kwame Anthony. "Language, Race, and the Legacies of the British Empire." *Black Experience in the Empire*. Eds. Philip D. Morgan and Sean Hawkins. Oxford: Oxford UP, 2004. 387–407.

Aravamudan, Srinivas, *Tropicopolitans: Colonialism and Agency, 1688–1804*. Durham: Duke UP, 1999.

———. "Equiano Lite." *Eighteenth-Century Studies* 34.4 (2001): 615–619.

Armitage, David. "Three Concepts of Atlantic History." *The British Atlantic World, 1500–1800*. Eds. David Armitage and Michael J. Braddick. London and New York: Palgrave Macmillan, 2002. 11–27.

Armstrong, Nancy. *How Novels Think: The Limits of Individualism from 1719–1900*. New York: Columbia UP, 2006.

———. "Captivity and cultural capital in the English novel." *Novel*. 31.3 (Summer 1998), 373–398.

Ashcroft, Bill, Gareth Griffiths and Helen Tiffin. *The Empire Writes Back: Theory and Practice in Postcolonial Literatures*. London and New York: Routledge, 1989.

Baer, William, ed. *Conversations with Derek Walcott*. Jackson: UP of Mississippi, 1996.

Behn, Aphra. *Oroonoko*. Ed. Joanna Lipking. New York and London: Norton, 1997

Azim, Firdous. *The Colonial Rise of the Novel*. New York and London: Routledge, 1993.

Bates, W. *Harlequin Mungo; Or, A Peep into the Tower, In Two Acts*. London: Printed by J. Skirven, 65, Ratcliff-Highway, for J. Griffith, 1788.

Bickerstaff, Isaac. *The Padlock* (1768). Reprinted in *Slavery, Abolition and Emancipation: Writings from the British Romantic Period*. Vol. 5, *Drama*. Ed. and Intro. Jeffrey N. Cox. London: Pickering & Chatto, 1999. 75–107.

———. *The Padlock* (1768). Reprinted in *The Plays of Isaac Bickerstaff*. Vol. 2. Ed. and Intro. Peter A. Tasch. New York and London: Garland Publishing, 1981.

Binder, Wolfgang. "Interview with David Dabydeen." *Journal of West Indian Literature* 3.2 (1989): 67–80. Reprinted in *The Art of David Dabydeen*. Ed. Kevin Grant. London: Peepal Tree, 1987. 159–176. 260–269.

Bindman, David. "'A Voluptuous Alliance Between African and Europe': Hogarth's Africans," in *The Other Hogarth: Aesthetics of Difference*. Eds. Bernadette Fort and Angela Rosenthal. Princeton and Oxford: Princeton UP, 2001.

———. *Hogarth and his Times: Serious Comedy*. Berkeley and Los Angeles: U of California P, 1997.

Bogel, Frederic V. *The Difference Satire Makes: Rhetoric and Reading from Jonson to Byron*. Ithaca: Cornell UP, 2001.

Boucé, Paul-Gabriel. Ed. and Introduction. *The Adventures of Roderick Random*. Oxford: Oxford UP, 1979.

Bradshaw, Roxanne. "Beryl Gilroy's 'Fact-fiction': Through the Lens of the 'Quiet Old Lady.'" *Callaloo* 25.2 (2000): 381–400.

Breiner, Laurence A. *An Introduction to West Indian Poetry*. Cambridge: Cambridge UP, 1998.

Breslin, Paul. *Nobody's Nation: Reading Derek Walcott*. Chicago: U of Chicago P, 2001.

Breslow, Stephen. "Derek Walcott: 1992 Nobel Laureate in Literature." *World Literature Today* 67 (1993): 267–271.

Brewer, John. *Pleasures of the Imagination: English Culture in the Eighteenth Century*. Chicago: U of Chicago P, 1997.

Broadbent, R.J. *A History of Pantomime*. New York: Citadel, 1965.

Brown, Homer. "Prologue: Why the Story of the Origin of the (English) Novel is an American Romance (If not the Great American Novel)." *Cultural Institutions of the Novel*. Eds. Deidre Lynch and William B. Warner. Durham and London: Duke UP, 1996. 11–43.

Brown, Kathleen. "Beyond the Great Debates: Gender and Race in Early America. *Reviews in American History*. 26.1 (1988): 96–123.

———. "Native Americans and early modern concepts of Race." *Empire and Others: British Encounters with Indigenous Peoples, 1600–1850*. Eds. Martin Daunton and Rick Halpern. Philadelphia: U of Pennsylvania P, 1999. 79–100.

Bromley, Roger. *Narratives for a New Belonging: Diasporic Cultural Fictions*. Edinburgh: Edenburgh UP, 2000.

Brysk, Alison. Introduction. *Globalization and Human Rights*. Berkeley, Los Angeles and London: U of California P, 2002.

Burnham, Michelle. "Between England and America: Captivity, Sympathy, and the Sentimental Novel. *Cultural Institutions of the Novel.* Eds. Deidre Lynch and William B. Warner. Durham and London: Duke UP, 1996. 47–72.

Caminero-Santangelo, Byron. *African Fiction and Joseph Conrad: Reading Postcolonial Intertextuality.* Albany: State U of New York P, 2005.

Carey Brycchan, "'The Hellish Means of Killing and Kidnapping': Ignatius Sancho and the Campaign against the Abominable Traffic for Slaves," in *Discourses of Slavery and Abolition: Britain and its Colonies, 1760–1838*, Eds. Brycchan Carey, Markman Ellis and Sara Salih. New York: Palgrave Macmillan, 2004.

Carretta, Vincent. "Olaudah Equiano or Gustavus Vassa? New Light on an Eighteenth-century Question of Identity." *Slavery and Abolition* 20.3 (1999): 96–105.

———. Introduction. *The Letters of the Late Ignatius Sancho, An African.* New York: Penguin, 1998. ix-xxxii.

———. Introduction. *The Interesting Narrative of the Life of Olaudah Equiano, or Gustavus Vassa, The African, Written by Himself.* New York and London: Penguin, 1995. ix-xxviii.

Carretta, Vincent and Philip Gould. Eds. and Intro. *Genius in Bondage: The Literature of the Early Black Atlantic.* Lexington: U of Kentucky P, 2001. 1–13.

Césaire, Aimé. *Discourse on Colonialism.* Trans. Joan Pinkham. New York: Monthly Review, 1972; 2000.

Coleman the Younger, George. *Inkle and Yarico: An Opera, in Three Acts* (1787). Reprinted in *English Trader, Indian Maid: Representing Gender, Race, and Slavery in the New World.* Ed. and Intro. Frank Felsenstein. Baltimore and London: Johns Hopkins UP, 1999. 167–233.

Coleridge, Samuel Taylor. *The Rime of the Ancient Mariner. In Seven Parts.* (1817). Reprinted in *Romanticism: An Anthology.* Ed. Duncan Wu. Oxford: Blackwell, 1994. 578–595.

Chalmers, Alan D. *Jonathan Swift & the burden of the future.* Newark: U of Delaware P; London: Associated UP, 1995.

Child, Lydia Maria, ed. 1838. *Narrative of Joanna: An Emancipated Slave of Surinam.* Boston, Isaac Knapp.

Coetzee. J.M. *Foe.* London and New York: Penguin, 1987.

Colley, Linda. *Britons: Forging the Nation 1707–1837.* New Haven and London: Yale UP, 1992.

———. *Captives: The story of Britain's pursuit of empire and how its soldiers and civilians were held captive by the dream of global supremacy, 1600–1850.* New York: Pantheon, 2002.

Collins, Patricia Hill. *Black Feminist Thought: Knowledge, Consciousness, and the Politics of Empowerment.* 2nd ed. New York and London: Routledge, 2000.

Cooppan, Vilashini. "World Literature and Global Theory: Comparative Literature for the New Millenium." *Symploke* 9.1–2 (2001): 15–43.

Cox, Jeffrey N. Introduction. *Slavery Abolition and Emancipation: Writings in the British Romantic Period*. Vol. 5, *Drama*. London: Pickering & Chatto, 1999. vii-xxxiii.

Craton, Michael. "The Planters' World in the British West Indies." *Strangers within the Realm: Cultural Margins of the First British Empire*. Ed. Bernard Bailyn and Philip D. Morgan. Chapel Hill and London: U of North Carolina P, 1991.

Creed. Kevin A. "The Pamphleteers Protestant Champion: Viewing Oliver Cromwell Through the Media of his Day." *Essays in History* 34 (1992): 1–12.

Dabydeen, David. *The Intended* (1991). London: Peepal Tree, 2005.

———. *A Harlot's Progress*. London: Vintage, 2000.

———."The role of Black people in William Hogarth's criticism of eighteenth-century English culture and society," in *Essays on the History of Blacks in Britain*, Eds. Jagdish S. Gundara and Ian Duffield. Aldershot: Avebury, 1992.

———. *Hogarth's Blacks: Images of Blacks in Eighteenth Century British Art*. Athens: U of Georgia P, 1987.

———. *Hogarth, Walpole and Commercial Britain*. London: Hansib, 1987.

———. *The Black Presence in English Literature*. Manchester: Manchester UP, 1987.

Daunton, Martin and Rick Halpern, eds. *Empire and Others: British Encounters with Indigenous Peoples, 1600–1850*. Philadelphia: U of Pennsylvania P, 1999.

Davis, Charles T. and Henry Louis Gates, Jr., eds. *The Slave's Narrative*. Oxford: Oxford UP, 1985.

Davis, David Brion. *Inhuman Bondage: The Rise and Fall of slavery in the New World*. Oxford: Oxford UP, 2006.

Davis, Jessica Milner. *Farce* (1978). New Brunswick, NJ: Transaction, 2003.

De Bois, W.E.B. "The Strivings of the Negro." *The Atlantic Monthly* 80 (1897): 194–198.

DePorte, Michael. "Hopeless Worlds: The Third Voyage" (1988). Reprinted in *Readings on Jonathan Swift: Gulliver's Travels*. Ed. Gary Wiudner. San Diego, Greenhaven, 2000. 141–146.

Defoe, Daniel. *Robinson Crusoe*. Ed. Michael Shinagel. London and New York: Norton, 1994.

—. *Defoe's Review*. Reproduced from the Original Editions. Introduction and Bibliographical Notes by Arthur Wellesley Secord. 22 vols. Published for the Facsimile Text Society. New York: Columbia UP, 1938.

de Mel, Neloufer. "Caliban or Crusoe? Straddling the Paradigms of 'Post-Colonial' Identity: Derek Walcott and Jean Arasanayagam." *Nationalism vs. Internationalism: (Inter)National Dimensions of Literatures in English*. Eds. Wolfgang Zach and K. Goodwin. Tubingen: G. Narr 1996. 133–143.

Dolezel Lubomir. *Heterocosmica: Fiction and Possible Worlds*. Baltimore: Johns Hopkins UP, 1998.

Downie, J.A. and Thomas Corns. *Telling People What to Think: Early Eighteenth-Century Periodicals from* The Review *to* The Rambler. London: Franc Cass, 1993.

Dove, Rita. "Either I'm Nobody, or I'm a Nation." *Bloom's Modern Critical Views: Derek Walcott.* Ed. and Intro. Harold Bloom. Philadelphia: Chelsea House Publishers, 2003. 53–78.

Dryden, Robert G. "John Gay's Polly: Unmasking Pirates and Fortune Hunters in the West Indies." *Eighteenth-Century Studies* 34.1 (2001).

Edwards, Paul and Polly Rewt. Introduction. *The Letters of Ignatius Sancho.* Edinburgh: Edinburgh UP, 1994.

Ellis, Markman. *The Politics of Sensibility: Race, Gender and Commerce in the Sentimental Novel.* Cambridge: Cambridge UP, 1996.

Equiano, Olaudah. *The Interesting Narrative of the Life of Olaudah Equiano, or Gustavus Vassa, The African, Written by Himself* (1789). Ed. Werner Sollors. New York and London: Norton, 2001.

Erskine-Hill, Howard. *Swift: Gulliver's Travels.* Cambridge: Cambridge UP. 1993.

Faber, Eli. *Jews, Slaves and the Slave Trade: Setting the Record Straight.* New York and London: New York, UP, 1998.

Fabricant, Carole. "Swift's Political Legacy: Re-membering the Past in Order to Imagine the Future. *Locating Swift: Essays from Dublin on the 250th Anniversary of the Death of Jonathan Swift, 1667–1745.* Eds. Aileen Douglas, Patrick Kelly and Campbell Ross. Portland: Four Courts, 1998. 180–200.

Fanon, Frantz. *Black Skin White Masks.* Trans. Charles Lam Markmann. New York: Grove, 1967.

———. *The Wretched of the Earth.* Trans. Constance Farrington. New York: Grove Press, 1963.

Fee, Margery. "Resistance and Complicity in David Dabydeen's *The Intended.*" *The Art of David Dabydeen.* Ed. Kevin Grant. London: Peepal Tree Press, 1997. 67–88.

Felsenstein, Frank. Ed. and Intro. *English Trader, Indian Maid: Representing Race, Gender and Slavery in the New World.* Baltimore: Johns Hopkins UP, 1999.

Festa, Lynn. *Sentimental Figures of Empire in Eighteenth-Century Britain and France.* Baltimore. Johns Hopkins UP, 2006.

Fielding, Henry. *Joseph Andrews, with Shamela and Related Writings.* Ed. Homer Goldberg. London and New York: W.W. Norton & Company, 1987.

———. *The History of Tom Jones, a Foundling.* Intro. Martin C. Battestin. Ed. Fredson Bowers. Middleton, Conn.: Wesleyan UP, 1975.

Flynn, Carol Houlihan. *The Body in Swift and Defoe.* Cambridge: Cambridge UP, 1990.

Foucault, Michel. *Discipline and Punish: The Birth of the Prison* (1975). Trans. Alan Sheridan. Excerpt reprinted in *Literary Theory: An Anthology.* Eds. Julie Rivkin and Michael Ryan. Oxford: Blackwell, 1998. New York: Penguin, 1977. 464–487.

Garrick, David. *Harlequin's Invasion* (1759). *The Plays of David Garrick.* Ed. Harry William Pedicord and Frederick Louis Bermann. 2 vols. Carbondale: Southern Illinois UP, 1980.

Gates, Jr., Henry Louis, "An Interview with Wole Soyinka" (1975). Reprinted in *Conversations with Wole Soyinka*. Ed. Biodun Jeyifo. Jackson: UP of Mississippi, 2001. 48–67.

————. "Being, the Will, and the Semantics of Death" (1981). *Perspectives on Wole Soyinka: Freedom and Complexity*. Ed. Biodun Jeyifo. Jackson: UP of Mississippi, 2001. 62–76.

Gilman, Sandar. *Difference and Pathology: Stereotypes of Sexuality, Race and Madness*. Ithaca and London: Cornell UP, 1985.

Gilroy, Beryl. "Waltzing Across Four and a Half Decades." *Voices of the Crossing: The Impact of Britain on Writers from Asia, the Caribbean and Africa*. Eds. Ferdinand Dennis and Naseem Khan. London: Mackays of Chatham, 2000. 29–38.

————. *Leaves in the Wind: Collected Writings*. Ed. Joan Anim-Addo. London: Mango, 1998.

————. *Inkle and Yarico: Being the narrative of Thomas Inkle concerning his shipwreck and long sojourn among the Caribs and his marriage to Yarico, a Carib woman*. London: Peepal, 1996.

————. *Stedman and Joanna: A Love in Bondage*. New York: Vantage, 1991.

————. *Boy-Sandwich*. Oxford: Heinemann, 1989.

————. *Frangipani House*. Oxford: Heinemann, 1986.

Gilroy, Paul. *The Black Atlantic: Modernity and Double Consciousness*. Cambridge, Mass: Harvard UP, 1993.

Glissant, Edouard. *Caribbean Discourse: Selected Essays*. Trans. and Ed. Michael Dash. Charlottesville: UP of Virginia, 1989.

Glover, Jonathan. *Humanity: A Moral History of the Twentieth Century*. New Haven and London: Yale UP, 2001.

Gorra, Michael. *After Empire: Scott, Naipaul, Rushdie*. Chicago. U of Chicago P, 1997.

Greenblatt, Stephen. *Marvelous Possessions: The Wonder of the New World*. Chicago: U of Chicago P, 1991.

Griffin, Dustin. *Satire: A Critical Reintroduction*. Lexington: UP of Kentucky, 1994.

Guilhamet, Leon. *Satire and the transformation of genre*. Philadelphia, U of Pennsylvania P, 1987.

Gurnah, Abdulrazak. "Imagining the Postcolonial Writer." *Essays and Studies 2000: Reading the 'New' Literatures in a Postcolonial Era*. Vol. 53. Ed. Susheila Nasta. Cambridge: D.S. Brewer, 2000.

Gwilliam, Tassie. "'Scenes of Horror,' Scenes of Sensibility: Sentimentality and Slavery in John Gabriel Stedman's *Narrative of a Five Years Expedition against the Revolted Negroes of Surinam*. *ELH*, 65.3 (1998), 653–673.

Habermas, Jürgen. *The Structural Transformation of the Public Sphere*. Trans. T. Burger and F. Lawrence. Cambridge, Mass. MIT UP, 1989.

Hall, Douglas. Introduction. *In Miserable Slavery: Thomas Thistlewood in Jamaica, 1750–86*. Barbados, Jamaica, Trinidad and Tobago: U of the West Indies P, 1989.

Hall, Stuart. "The Local and the Global: Globalization and Ethnicity." *Culture, Globalization and the World System: Contemporary Conditions for the Representation of Identity*. Ed. Anthony D. King. Minneapolis: U of Minnesota P, 1997. 19–40.

———. "Old and New Identities, Old and New Ethnicities." *Culture, Globalization and the World System: Contemporary Conditions for the Representation of Identity*. Ed. Anthony D. King. Minneapolis: U of Minnesota P, 1997. 41–68.

———. Introduction: *Questions of Cultural Identity*. Eds. Stuart Hall and Paul Du Gay. London: Sage, 1996. 1–17.

———. "Cultural Identity and Diaspora." *Colonial Discourse and Postcolonial Discourse: A Reader*. Eds. Patrick Williams and Laura Chrisman. Hemel Hempstead: Harvester Wheatsheaf, 1993. 392–403.

Hamner, Robert D. Introduction. *Critical Perspectives on Derek Walcott*. Washington, D.C.: Three Continents, 1993. 1–12.

Hardwick, Lorna. *Translating Words, Translating Cultures*. London, Duckworth, 2000.

Harris, Michael D. *Colored Pictures: Race & Visual Representation*. Chapel Hill and London: U of North Carolina P, 2003.

Harris, Wilson. *Palace of the Peacock*. London: Faber and Faber, 1960.

Hawes, Clement. "Singing the Imperial Blues: The Scriblerians after Wole Soyinka." *Questioning History: The Postmodern Turn to the Eighteenth Century*. Ed. Greg Clingham. London: Associated UP, 1998. 139–159.

———. "Three Times Round the Globe: Gulliver and Colonial Discourse." *Cultural Critique* (Spring 1991): 187–214.

Higgins, Ian. "Swift's Politics: A Preface to Gulliver's Travels." *Jonathan Swift: A Collection of Critical Essays*. Upper Saddle River: Prentice Hall, 1995. 178–196.

Hirsch, "The Art of Poetry." *Critical Perspectives on Derek Walcott*. Washington, D.C.: Three Continents, 1993.

Hogan, Patrick Colm. *Empire and Poetic Voice: Cognitive and Cultural Studies of Literary Tradition and Colonialism*. Albany: State U of New York P., 2004.

Hogarth, William. *The Works of William Hogarth*. 2 vols. London: Printed for R. Scholey, 46, Paternoster Row; by T. Davison, Lombard Street, Whitefriars, 1810.

Hochschild, Adam. *Bury the Chains: Prophets and Rebels in the Fight to Free an Empire's Slaves*. Boston and New York: Houghton Mifflin, 2005.

Hulme, Peter. *Colonial Encounters: Europe and the Native Caribbean: 1492–1797*. London and New York: Routledge, 1987.

Hulme, Peter and Neil. L. Whitehead. Intro. and Eds. *Wild Majesty: Encounters with Caribs from Columbus to the Present Day: An Anthology*. Oxford: Clarendon, 1992.

Hulme, Peter and William H. Sherman, eds. *'The Tempest' and its Travels*. London: Reaktion Books, 2000.

Hunter, J. Paul. "*Gulliver's Travels* and the later writings." *The Cambridge Companion to Jonathan Swift*. Ed. Christopher Fox. Cambridge: Cambridge UP, 2003. 216–239.

Innes, C.L. *A History of Black and Asian Writing in Britain, 1700–2000*. Cambridge: Cambridge UP, 2002.

Ismond, Patricia. *Abandoning Dead Metaphors: The Caribbean Phase of Derek Walcott's Poetry*. Kingston: U of the West Indies P, 2001.

Jacobs, Dan. *The Brutality of Nations*. New York: Paragon House, 1988.

James, Winston. "The Black Experience in Twentieth-Century Britain." *Black Experience and the Empire*. Eds. Philip D. Morgan and Sean Hawkins. Oxford: Oxford: UP, 2004. 347–386.

JanMohamed, Abdul R. "The Economy of Manichean Allegory" (1985). Reprinted in *The post-colonial studies reader*. Eds. Bill Ashcroft, Gareth Griffiths and Helen Tiffin. London and New York: Routledge, 1995. 18–23.

Jarrett, Derek. *England in the Age of Hogarth*. New Haven: Yale UP, 1992.

Jay, Paul. "Beyond Discipline? Globalization and the Future of English." *PMLA* 116.1 (2001): 32–47.

Jekyll, Joseph. *Life of Ignatius Sancho* (1782). Reprinted in *The Letters of Ignatius Sancho*. Eds. Paul Edwards and Polly Rewt. Edinburgh: Edinburgh UP. 1994. 22–29.

Jeyifo, Biodun. *Wole Soyinka*. Cambridge: Cambridge UP, 2004.

———. *Perspectives on Wole Soyinka: Freedom and Complexity*. Jackson: U Press of Mississippi, 2001.

Johae, Antony. "Wole Soyinka's `Gulliver': Swift Transposed." *Comparative Literature* 53.1 (2001): 27–39.

Johnson, Howard. "The Black Experience in the British Caribbean in the Twentieth Century." *Black Experience and the Empire*. Eds. Philip D. Morgan and Sean Hawkins. Oxford: Oxford: UP, 2004. 317–346.

King, Bruce. *Derek Walcott: A Caribbean Life*. Oxford: Oxford UP, 2000.

———. *Derek Walcott and West Indian Drama*. Oxford: Clarendon P, 1995.

King, Lloyd. "Derek Walcott: The Literary Humanist in the Caribbean." *Caribbean Quarterly* 16.4 (1970).

King, Reyahn. "Ignatius Sancho and Portraits of the Black Elite." *Ignatius Sancho: An African Man of Letters*. London: National Portrait Gallery Publications, 1997. 15–44.

Kitson, Peter. Introduction. *Slavery, Abolition and Emancipation: Writings in the British Romantic Period*, Vol. 2, *The Abolition Debate*. London: Pickering & Chatto, 1999. ix-xxv.

Kitson, Peter and Debbie Lee, eds. *Slavery, Abolition and Emancipation: Writings in the British Romantic Period*. London: Pickering & Chatto, 1999.

Knowles, Ronald. *Gulliver's Travel's: The Politics of Satire*. New York: Twayne Publishers; London: Prentice Hall International, 1996.

Lamming, George. *The Pleasures of Exile* (1960). Ann Arbor: U of Michigan Press, 1992.

Lee, Debbie. *Slavery & the Romantic Imagination*. Philadelphia: U of Pennsylvania P. 2002.

Long, Edward. *The History of Jamaica* (1774). 2 vols. Ed. and Intro. Howard Johnson. Quebec and Kingson: McGill-Queen's UP, 2003.

López, Alfred J. *Posts and Pasts: a theory of postcolonialism*. Albany: State U of New York P, 2001.

Lynch, Deidre and William B. Warner. "Introduction: The Transport of the Novel." *Cultural Institutions of the Novel*. Durham and London: Duke UP, 1996. 10.

Mackie, Erin. Ed. and Intro. *The Commerce of Everyday Life: Selections from* The Tatler *and* The Spectator. Boston and New York: Bedford/St. Martin's, 1998.

Maes-Jelinek, Hena. "Postcolonial Criticism at the Crossroads: Subjective Questionings of an Old-Timer," *Towards a Transcultural Future: Literature and Society in a `Post'-Colonial World. ASNEL Papers 9.1.* Eds. Geoffrey V. Davis, Peter H. Marsden, Bénédicte Ledent and Marc Delrez. Amsterdam and New York: Rodopi, 2004. 1–19.

Mannoni, Octave. *Prospero & Caliban: The Psychology of Colonization*. Trans. Pamela Powesland. Ann Arbor: U of Michigan P, 1990; 2001.

Marshall, P.J. Ed. and Intro. *The Oxford History of the British Empire: The Eighteenth Century*. Oxford: Oxford UP, 1998.

Marx. John. "Postcolonial literature and the Western literary canon." *The Cambridge Companion to Postcolonial Literary Studies*. Ed. Neil Lazarus. Cambridge: Cambridge UP, 2004. 83–96.

Matthews, Gelien. *Caribbean Slave Revolts and the British Abolitionist Movement*. Baton Rouge: Louisiana State UP, 2006.

Mayer III, David. *Harlequin in his Element: The English Pantomime, 1806–1836*. Cambridge, Mass: Harvard UP, 1969.

McMinn, Joseph. "Swift's life." *Cambridge Companion to Jonathan Swift*. Ed. Christopher Fox. Cambridge: Cambridge UP, 2003. 14–30.

McKeon, Michael. *The Origins of the English Novel: 1600–1740*. Baltimore: Johns Hopkins UP, 1987.

McVeagh, John. "*Robinson Crusoe's* Stage Début: The Sheridan Pantomime of 1781. *Journal of Popular Culture* 24.2 (1990): 137–152.

Memmi, Albert. *The Colonizer and the Colonized*. Trans. Howard Greenfield. Boston: Beacon, 1967; 1991.

Mezciems, Jenny. "The Unity of Swift's 'Voyage to Laputa': Structure as Meaning in Utopian Fiction," *Jonathan Swift: A Collection of Critical Essays*. Ed. Claude Rawson. Upper Saddle River: Prentice Hall, 1995. 241–263.

Moore, Catherine E. "Robinson Crusoe and Xury and Inkle and Yarico." *Modern Language Notes* 19.1 (1981): 24–29.

Morgan, Philip D. "Encounters between Brtish and `indigenous' peoples, c. 1500—c. 1800. *Empire and Others: British Encounters with Indigenous Peoples, 1600–1850*. Eds. Martin Daunton and Rick Halpern. Philadelphia: U of Pennsylvania P, 1999. 42–78.

————. "The Black Experience in the British Empire, 1680–1810." *Black Experience and the Empire*. Eds. Philip D. Morgan and Sean Hawkins. Oxford: Oxford UP, 2004. 86–110.

Morgan, Philip D. and Sean Hawkins. "Blacks and the British Empire: An Introduction." *Black Experience and the Empire*. Eds. Philip D. Morgan and Sean Hawkins. Oxford: Oxford UP, 2004. 1–34.

Moses, Michael Valdez. *The Novel & The Globalization of Culture*. Oxford: Oxford UP, 1995.

Msiska, Mpalive-Hangson. *Wole Soyinka*. Plymouth: Northcote House Publishers, Ltd., 1998.

Naipaul, V.S. *The Mimic Men*. New York: Vintage, 1985.

Neill, Anna. *British Discovery Literature and the Rise of Global Commerce*. New York: Palgrave, 2002.

Newson, Adele S. "World Literature in Review: Guyana." *World Literature Today* 71.1 (1993).

————. "World Literature in Review: Guyana." *World Literature Today* 67.1 (1993).

Newton, John. *Thoughts on the African Slave Trade* (1788). Reprinted in *Slavery, Abolition & Emancipation: Writings in the British Romantic Period*. Vol. 2, *The Abolition Debate*. Ed. Peter J. Kitson. Edinburgh: Edinburgh UP, 1999. 77–117.

Novak, Maximillian E. "Friday: or, the Power of Naming." *Augustan Subjects*. Ed. Albert J. Rivero. Newark: U of Delaware Press, 1997. 110–122.

Nussbaum, Felicity. Introduction. *The Global Eighteenth Century*. Baltimore: Johns Hopkins UP, 2003. 1–18.

Oakleaf, David. "Politics and History," *Cambridge Companion to Jonathan Swift*. Ed. Christopher Fox. Cambridge: Cambridge UP, 2003. 31–47.

O'Brien, John. *Harlequin Britain: Pantomime and Entertainment, 1690–1760*. Baltimore and London: Johns Hopkins UP, 2004.

Ogude, S.E. *Hogarth's Blacks. Research in African Literatures*. 18:2 (1987): 244–277.

————. "Facts into Fiction: Equiano's Narrative Reconsidered." *Research in African Literatures* 13 (Spring 1982): 31–43.

Ogunbiyi, Yemi. "A Study of Soyinka's *Opera Wonyosi*. *Nigeria Magazine* 128–129 (1979): 3–14.

Ojaide, Tanure. *The Poetry of Wole Soyinka*. Lagos, Malthouse, 1994.

————. "The Voice and Viewpoint of the Poet in Wole Soyinka's Four Archetypes." *Research on Wole Soyinka*. Eds. James Gibbs and Bernth Lindfors. Trenton: Africa World Press, 1993. 163–163–171.

Orwell, George. "Jonathan Swift, An Imaginary Interview." *George Orwell: The Lost Writings*. Ed. W.J. West. New York, Arbor House, 1985. 112–116.

————. "Politics vs. Literature: An Examination of *Gulliver's Travels*." *Discussions of Jonathan Swift*. Ed. and intro. John Traugott. Boston: D.C. Heath, 1962. 80–91.

Osundare, Niyi. "Wole Soyinka and the Atunda Ideal: A Reading of Soyinka's Poetry."1994. *Perspectives on Wole Soyinka: Freedom and Complexity*. Ed. Biodun Jeyifo. Jackson: UP of Mississippi, 2001. 187–200.

Parry, Benita. "The Postcolonial: Conceptual Category of Chimera? *The Yearbook of English Studies: The Politics of Postcolonial Criticism* 27 (1997): 3–21.

Patey, Douglas Lane. "Swift's Satire on 'Science' and the Structure of *Gulliver's Travels.*" *Jonathan Swift: A Collection of Critical Essays.* Upper Saddle River: Prentice Hall, 1996. 216–240.

Paulson, Ronald. *Book and Painting, Shakespeare, Milton and the Bible: Literary Texts and the Emergence of English Painting.* Knoxville: U of Tennessee P, 1982.

Phillips, Caryl. Forward, *Ignatius Sancho: An African Man of Letters.* London: National Portrait Gallery Publications, 1997.

———. *Cambridge.* London: Faber and Faber, 1991.

Pieterse, Ian Nederveen. *Globalization & Culture: Global Mélange.* Oxford: Rowman & Littlefield, 2004.

Plasa, Carl. *Textual Politics from Slavery to Postcolonialism: Race and Identification.* London: Macmillan, 2000.

Plasa, Carl and Betty J. Ring. *The Discourse of Slavery: Aphra Behn to Toni Morrison.* London and New York: Routledge, 1994.

Porter, Roy. *The Creation of the Modern World: The Untold Story of the British Enlightenment.* New York and London: Penguin, 2000.

Pratt, Mary Louise. *Imperial Eyes: Travel Writing and Transculturation.* London: Routledge, 1992.

Price, Richard and Sally Price, Eds. *Stedman's Surinam: Life in an Eighteenth-Century Slave Society.* Baltimore and London: Johns Hopkins UP, 1992.

Prince, Mary. *Mary Prince: The History of Mary Prince* (1831). Ed. Sarah Salih. London: Penguin, 2000.

Punter, David. *Postcolonial Imaginings: Fictions of a New World Order.* Edinburgh: Edinburgh UP, 2000.

Quayson, Ato. *Postcolonialism: Theory, Practice or Process?* Cambridge: Polity Press, 2000.

Retamar, Roberto Fernández. *Caliban and Other Essays.* Trans. Edward Baker. Minneapolis: U of Minnesota P, 1989.

Richards, David. *Masks of Difference: Cultural Representations in Literature, Anthropology and Art.* Cambridge: Cambridge UP, 1995.

Richardson, Alan. Introduction. *Slavery, Abolition and Emancipation: Writings in the British Romantic Period. Vol. 4, Verse.* London: Pickering & Chatto, 1999. ix–xxvi.

Richardson, David. "Through a Looking Glass: Olaudah Equiano and African Experiences of the British Atlantic Slave Trade." *Black Experience and the Empire.* Eds. Philip D. Morgan and Sean Hawkins. Oxford: Oxford UP: 2004. 58–85.

Richardson, Samuel. *Clarissa, or The History of a Young Lady.* Abridged by George Sherburn. Boston: Houghton Mifflin, 1962.

Roach, Joseph. *Cities of the Dead: Circum-Atlantic Performance.* New York: Columbia UP, 1996.

Rodino, Richard H. "'Splendide Mendax': Authors, Characters and Readers in *Gulliver's Travels*." 1991. *Jonathan Swift*. Ed. Nigel Wood. London and New York, Addison Wesley Longman, 1999. 44–69.

Rogers, Pat. *Eighteenth Century Encounters: Studies in Literature and Society in the Age of Walpole*. Sussex: Harvester, 1985.

———. "Gulliver's Glasses," *The Art of Jonathan Swift*. Ed. Clive T. Probyn. New York: Barnes & Noble, 1978. 179–188.

Rousseau, Jean-Jacques. *Émile*. Trans. Barbara Foxley. Intro. P.D. Jimack. London: J.M. Dent, 1993.

Rubenstein, Anne and Camilla Townsend. "Revolted Negroes and the Devilish Principle: William Blake and Conflicting Visions of Boni's Wars in Surinam, 1772–1796." *Blake, Politics, and History*. Eds. Jackie DiSalvo, G. A. Rosso, and Christopher Z. Hodson. New York and London: Garland Publishing, Inc. 1998. 273–298.

Sabor, Peter. *Hogarth's Blacks. The Yearbook of English Studies* 18 (1988): 288–289.

———. "Wole Soyinka and the Scriblerians," *World Literatures in English* 29.1 (1989), 42–52.

Said, Edward. *Culture and Imperialism*. New York: Vintage Books, 1994.

———. *The World, the Text and the Critic*. Cambridge: Harvard UP, 1983

———. *Orientalism*. New York: Vintage Books, 1978.

Salih, Sarah. Introduction. *Mary Prince: The History of Mary Prince*. London and New York: Penguin, 2000. vii-xl.

Samad, Daisal Rafeck. "Caribbean Dish on the PostColonial Table." Conference Paper. An International Conference Organized by The Postgraduate School of Critical Theory and Cultural Studies, University of Nottingham, and the British Council, Morocco. 12–14 April 2001.

Sancho, Ignatius. *The Letters of Ignatius Sancho*. Eds. Paul Edwards and Polly Rewt. Edinburgh, Edinburgh UP, 1994. 1–21.

Sandhu, Sukhdev. "Ignatius Sancho: An African Man of Letters." *Ignatius Sancho: An African Man of Letters*." London: National Portrait Gallery Publications, 1997. 45–74.

Sarvan, Charles P. *A Harlot's Progress. World Literature Today* 73.4 (1999): 795.

Secord, Arthur, Wellesley. Introduction. *Defoe's Review. Reproduced from the Original Editions*. 22 vols. Published for the Facsimile Text Society. New York: Columbia UP, 1938. xv-lv.

Scott, Sir Walter. "A Life of Swift." *The Works of Jonathan Swift, D.D. Dean of St. Patrick's, Dublin; Containing Additional Letters, Tracts, and Poems, not Hitherto Published; With Notes and A Life of the Author, By Sir Walter Scott, Bart*. 2nd ed. Vol. 1. Edinburgh: Printed for Archibald Constable and Co.; London: Hurst, Robinson, and Co., 1824.

Sedlak, Werner. "Wole Soyinka's Cultural Activism: His Representations of Detention in *The Detainee, Madmen and Specialists, Season of Anomy* and *The Man Died*." *No Condition is Permanent: Nigerian Writers, Democracy and the Struggle for Civil Society. Matatu: Journal for African Culture and Society*. Eds. Holger G. Ehling and Claus-Peter Holste-von Mutius. Amsterdam and New York: Rodopi, 2001. 41–54.

Sharpe, Jenny. *Ghosts of Slavery: A Literary Archaeology of Black Women's Lives*. Minneapolis and London: U of Minnesota P, 2003.

Shesgreen, Sean. *Engravings by Hogarth: 101 Prints*. New York: Dover, 1973.

Sheridan, Richard Brinsley. *Imitations and Dramatisations. A Short Account of the Situations and Incidents Exhibited in the Pantomime of Robinson Crusoe at the Theatre-Royal, Drury Lane.* [i.e. R.B.B. Sheridan's "Robinson Crusoe, or Harlequin Friday."] Anonymous editor. Taken from the Original. London: T. Becket, 1781.

———. *Sheridania ; Or, Anecdotes of the Life of Richard Brinsley Sheridan; His Table Talk, and Bon Mots.* Anonymous editor. London: Henry Colburn, New Burlington Street, 1826.

Smith, Andrew. Migrancy, hybridity, and postcolonial literary studies." *The Cambridge Companion to Postcolonial Literary Studies*. Ed. Neil Lazarus. Cambridge: Cambridge UP, 2004. 241–261.

Smollett, Tobias. *The Adventures of Roderick Random*. Ed. and Intro. Paul-Gabriel Boucé. Oxford: Oxford UP, 1999.

Snader, Joe. *Caught Between Worlds: British Captivity Narratives in Fact and Fiction*. Lexington: U of Kentucky Press, 2000.

Sollers, Werner. "Retellings: Mercenaries and Abolitionists." *Neither Black Nor White Yet Both: Thematic Explorations of Interracial Literature*. Harvard: Harvard UP, 1997. 188–219.

Soyinka, Wole. *The Open Soar of a Continent: A Personal Narrative of the Nigerian Crisis*. Oxford: Oxford UP, 1996.

———. *Art, Dialogue, and Outrage: Essays on Literature and Culture*. Ibadan, Nigeria: New Horn, 1988.

———. *The Man Died* (1972). New York: The Noonday Press, 1988.

———. "The fourth stage." Reprinted in *Myth, Literature and the African World*. Cambridge: Cambridge UP, 1976. 140–160.

———. *A Shuttle in the Crypt*. London: Rex Collings/Methuen, 1972.

Spacks, Patricia Meyer. *Novel Beginnings: Experiments in Eighteenth-Century English Fiction*. New Haven and London: Yale UP, 2006.

Speck. W.A. *The Literature and Society in Eighteenth-Century England 1680–1820: Ideology, Politics and Culture*. London and New York: Addison Wesley Longman, 1998.

Sussman, Charlotte. *Consuming Anxieties: Consumer Protest, Gender & British Slavery, 1713–1833*. Stanford: Stanford UP, 2000.

Stedman, John Gabriel. *Stedman's Surinam: Life in an Eighteenth-Century Slave Society*. An Abridged, Modernized Edition of *Narrative of a Five Years Expedition against the Revolted Negroes of Surinam*. Eds. and Intro. Richard Price and Sally Price. Baltimore and London: Johns Hopkins UP, 1992.

———. *Narrative of a Five Year's Expedition Against the Revolted Negroes* of Surinam. Ed. and Intro. R.A.J. van Lier. Amherst: U of Massachusetts P, 1971.

————. *The Journal of John Gabriel Stedman 1744–1797: Soldier and Author.* Ed. Stanhope Thompson. London: Mitre, 1962.

Stremlau, John J. *The International Politics of the Nigerian Civil War,* 1967–1970. Princeton: Princeton UP, 1977.

Swift, Jonathan. *Gulliver's Travels.* 1726. 1735. Ed. Paul Turner. Oxford: Oxford World Classics, 1998.

————. "The Drapiers Letters." *The Works of Jonathan Swift, DD. Dean of St. Patrick's Dublin; Containing Additional Letters, Tracts, and Poems; Not Hitherto Published; With Notes, and A Life of the Author, by Sir. Walter Scott, Bart.* 2nd ed. 19 vols. Edinburgh: Printed for Archibald Constable and Co.; London: Hurst, Robinson and Co., 1824. Vols. VI and VII.

————. "The Conduct of the Allies." *The Works of Jonathan Swift, D.D., Dean of St. Patrick's, Dublin; Containing Additional Letters, Tracts, and Poems; Not Hitherto Published; With Notes, and A Life of the Author, by Sir. Walter Scott, Bart.* 2nd ed. 19 vols. Edinburgh: Printed for Archibald Constable and Co.; London: Hurst, Robinson and Co., 1824. Vol. IV.

————. "Journal to Stella" and "The Examiner." *The Works of Jonathan Swft, D.D. Dean of St. Patrick's, Dublin, Containing Additional Letters, Tracts, and Poems; Not Hitherto Pubished; With Notes and A Life of the Author, by Sir. Walter Scott, Bart.* 2nd ed. 19 vols. Edinburgh: Printed for Archibald Constable and Co,; London: Hurst, Robinson and Co., 1824. Vol. III.

Sypher, Wylie. *Guinea's Captive Kings: British Anti-Slavery Literature of the Xviiith Century.* Chapel Hill: U of North Carolina P, 1942.

Tasch, Peter A. Introduction. *The Plays of Isaac Bickerstaff.* 2 vols. New York and London: Garland Publishing, 1981. ix-xxxii.

————. *The Dramatic Cobbler: The Life and Works of Isaac Bickerstaff.* Lewisburg: Bucknell UP, 1971.

Taylor, Patrick. "Myth and Reality in Caribbean Narrative: Derek Walcott's *Pantomime. Critical Perspectives on Derek Walcott.* Ed. Robert D. Hamner. Washington, D.C.: Three Continents, 1993. 292–299.

Thieme, John. *Derek Walcott.* Manchester: Manchester UP, 1999.

Tiffin, Helen. "Postcolonial Literature and Counter-Discourse." *The postcolonial studies reader.* Eds. Bill Ashcroft, Gareth Griffiths and Helen Tiffin. London and New York: Routledge, 1995. 95–98.

Tobin, Beth Fowkes. *Picturing Imperial Power: Colonial Subjects in Eighteenth-Century British Painting.* Durham and London: Duke UP, 1999.

Tournier, Michel. *Vendredi, ou les Limbes du Pasifique* (1967). Trans. Norman Denny. Baltimore: Johns Hopkins UP, 1969.

Turner, Paul. Introduction. *Gulliver's Travels.* 1726. 1735. Oxford: Oxford World Classics, 1998. ix-xxxviii.

Uglow, Jenny. *Hogarth: A Life and a World.* New York: Ferrar, Straus and Giroux, 1997.

Uzokwe, Alfred Obiora. *Surviving in Biafra: The Story of the Nigerian Civil War, Over two million died.* New York and London: Writers Advantage, 2003.

Varney, Andrew. *Eighteenth-Century Writers in their World: A Mighty Maze.* London: MacMillan, 1999; New York: St. Martin's, 1999.

Viswanathan, Gauri. *Masks of Conquest: Literary Study and British Rule in India.* New York: Columbia UP, 1989.

————. *Derek Walcott: Collected Poems 1948–1984.* New York: Farrar, Straus & Giroux, 1986.

————. Nobel Prize Lecture. 7 December 1982.

————. *Remembrance & Pantomime: Two Plays.* New York, Farrar, Straus and Giroux, 1980.

————. "The Caribbean: Culture or Mimicry?" (1974). *Critical Perspectives on Derek Walcott.* Ed. Robert Hamner. Washington, D.C.: Three Continents Press, 1993.

————. "The Figure of Crusoe" (1965). *Critical Perspectives on Derek Walcott.* Ed. Robert Hamner. Washington, D.C.: Three Continents Press, 1993. 33–40.

————. *The Castaway and Other Poems.* London: Cape, 1965.

Walder, Dennis. *Post-colonial Literatures in English: History Language Theory.* Oxford: Blackwell, 1998.

Wallace, Elizabeth Kowaleski. "The Untold Stories: Philippa Gregory's *A Respectable Trade* and David Dabydeen's *A Harlot's Progress, Novel: A Forum on Fiction* 33.2 (Spring 2000): 235–253.

Warner, Michael. "The Mass Public and the Mass Subject." *Habermas and the Public Sphere.* Ed. Craig Calhoun. Cambridge, Mass: MIT, 1992; 1997. 377–401.

Wilkinson, Jane. "Wole Soyinka." 1990. *Conversations with Wole Soyinka.* Ed. Biodun Jeyifo. Jackson: UP of Mississippi, 2001. 143–166.

Wilson, A. E. *Christmas Pantomime: The Story of an English Institution.* London: George Allen & Unwin, 1934.

Wilson, Kathleen. "The good, the bad, and the impotent: Imperialism and the politics of identity in Georgian England." *The Consumption of Culture 1600–1800: Image, Object, Text.* Eds. John Brewer and Ann Birmingham. London and New York: Routledge, 1995. 237–262.

————. *The Sense of the People: Politics, Culture and Imperialism in England, 1715–1785.* Cambridge: Cambridge UP, 1995; 1998.

Wolfthal, Diane. "Imaging the Self: Ritual and Representation in a Yiddish Book of Customs," in *Race-ing Art History: Critical Readings in Race and Art History.* Ed. Kymberly N. Pinder. New York and London: Routledge, 2002. 21–36.

Wood, Marcus. *Blind Memory: Visual Representations of Slavery in England and America 1780–1865.* New York: Routledge, 2000.

Wood, Nigel. Introduction. *Jonathan Swift.* London and New York: Longman, 1999. 1–25.

Wright, Derek. *Wole Soyinka Revisited.* New York: Twain Publishers, 1993.

Index